ST. JOHN'S SEMINARY COLLEGE LIBRARY
3 3613 00071 5509

D0520897

UNDERSTANDING JUDAISM

296
B736u

56905

296
B736u

56905

Borowitz
Understanding Judaism

DATE	ISSUED TO
APR 2 3 '86	
MAR 8 0 1987	

ST. JOHN'S SEMINARY
COLLEGE LIBRARY
CAMARILLO, CALIF.

EUGENE B. BOROWITZ

UNDERSTANDING JUDAISM

296
B736u

FROM THE LIBRARY OF:
NEW ST. ANDREWS COLLEGE
MOSCOW, ID 83843

56905

Union of American Hebrew Congregations
New York _____

ST. JOHN'S SEMINARY
COLLEGE LIBRARY
CAMARILLO, CALIF.

The author and publisher thank Rabbi Joachim Prinz
for permission to quote from one of a series of taped interviews.

Doubleday & Company, Inc. Excerpt from *The Diary of a Young Girl* by Anne
Frank. Copyright © 1952 by Otto H. Frank. Reprinted by permission of
Doubleday & Company, Inc.

Schocken Books Inc. From *Israel and the World: Essays in a Time of Crisis* by
Martin Buber. Copyright © 1948, 1963 by Schocken Books Inc. Copyright
renewed © 1975 by Schocken Books Inc. Reprinted by permission.

Library of Congress Cataloging in Publication Data

Borowitz, Eugene B.
Understanding Judaism

SUMMARY: Discusses the fundamental beliefs of
Judaism as summarized in the 1976 statement by the
Central Conference of American Rabbis.
1. Judaism.   2. Jewish religious education—
Text-books for young people.   [1. Judaism]
I. Title.
BM105.B66   296   78–31651
ISBN 0–8074–0027–0

© Copyright 1979 by the Union of American Hebrew Congregations
838 Fifth Avenue
New York, New York 10021

Manufactured in the United States of America

4   5   6   7   8   9   10

איחוד
ליהדות
מתקדמת
באמריקה

Published to
honor the memory of
I. H. and Anna Grancell

gift

Chautauqua Society

12-28-84

In esteem and affection, I dedicate this book to

Paul M. Steinberg

Dean of the New York School of
Hebrew Union College-Jewish Institute of Religion

in appreciation of his leadership which has been
instrumental in maintaining and enhancing
Reform Judaism's academic presence in the largest
Jewish city in the world.

Acknowledgments

THIS BOOK has benefited from the suggestions made by those who read it on behalf of the CCAR-UAHC Commission on Jewish Education and I therefore express my thanks to: Herbert Baumgard, Morton Bauman, Roland Gittelsohn, Jordan Pearlson, Steven Reuben, M. Robert Syme, and Bernard Zlotowitz. I am particularly grateful to Judy Rothstein for her detailed help with regard to matters of style and to Daniel B. Syme for conceiving and enthusiastically pursuing this project through its many complicated stages. It has been a special joy to me that this book has reunited me with my able colleague of many years ago, the Union's Director of Publications, Ralph Davis. And, in deep thankfulness, I add some words to R. Hiyya's private prayer,

יְהִי רָצוֹן מִלְפָנֶיךָ ה' אֱלֹהֵינוּ שֶׁתְּהֵא תוֹרָתְךָ אוּמָנוּתֵנוּ וְאַל יִדְוֶה לִבֵּנוּ וְאַל יָחְשְׁכוּ עֵינֵינוּ

"May it continue to be Your will, Adonai, our God, that Your Torah be our occupation so our hearts will not despair and our eyes never lose their hopeful luster."

Contents

Editor's Introduction   xi

Introduction: Will You Learn More by Listening or by Arguing?   xiii

Part One: WHAT IS THE RIGHT THING TO DO?
1. Why Is It So Difficult to Be Good?   4
2. Handling Temptations: Money, Sex, Drinking   13
3. Have Our Ethics Changed since Bible Times?   20
4. What Are Our Duties to Humanity?   30
5. Are Rituals Necessary?   37
6. Feelings versus Rules: The Case of Praying   43
7. Building a Jewish Life: Marriage and a Family   49
8. Why Don't Most Jews Do Very Much?   56

Part Two: THE JEWS AND THEIR DREAMS
1. How Did Judaism Start?   64
2. What Sort of Group Are the Jews?   71
3. Are We a Chosen People?   79
4. What Do We Expect in the Messianic Age?   86
5. What Does the State of Israel Mean to Jews?   95
6. Why Do Jews Have to Be Different?   103
7. Who Is a "Good Jew"?   111

Part Three: WHAT DO THE BIBLE AND TRADITION MEAN TO US?
with an Orthodox response by Rabbi J. David Bleich
and a Conservative response by Rabbi Seymour Siegel
Introduction   121
1. Did God Give the Bible?   123
2. How Does God Speak to People?   132
3. Why Are the Prophets Especially Important to Us?   139
4. How True Is the Bible?   146
5. How Has Judaism Changed since the Bible?   155
6. Must We Observe All the Commandments and Traditions?   163
7. Why Are There Three Branches of Judaism?   170

Part Four: ON BELIEVING IN GOD
1. Has God Changed since Bible Times?   180
2. How Can We Talk about God?   186

3. How Do We Know God Is Real?   193
4. What Do We Think God Is Like?   200
5. Why Does God Let Bad Things Happen?   207
6. What Happens after You Die?   216
7. Why Do We Have Different Religions?   224

In Parting: Do You Now Understand Judaism?   231

About the Photographs   233

Editor's Introduction

IN RECENT YEARS, the Jewish publications field has been flooded with volumes on the topic of basic Judaism. There has clearly been a renaissance of interest in Jewish study, and youths and adults alike have begun the exciting process of rediscovering and reclaiming their Jewish past and their Jewish identity.

Unfortunately, few if any of the newer books address themselves to younger readers. And fewer still reflect a liberal Jewish approach to fundamental Jewish concerns.

Understanding Judaism by Eugene B. Borowitz represents a genuinely unique effort—an elucidation of Judaism's basic teachings, created for young people, based on their questions, and written from the viewpoint of Reform Judaism. In his clear and succinct style, Rabbi Borowitz speaks to readers as the master teacher he is, crystallizing complex concepts through the use of examples common to everyday life. Drawing freely on biblical, midrashic, and talmudic sources, he renders Jewish learning accessible to the young, searching mind.

More than that, the author enables the student to compare and contrast Reform, Conservative, and Orthodox perspectives on a series of key issues. Basic Judaism and comparative Judaism, then, blend and interconnect to form a sense of Judaism's richness and diversity.

We hope that you—students, teachers, and parents—will utilize *Understanding Judaism* in your classrooms and your homes as a vehicle for the development of increased Jewish literacy, commitment, and identity. We are proud to offer it to you and grateful to Rabbi Borowitz for this new gift of his knowledge and wisdom to our people.

Rabbi Daniel B. Syme, *Director*
UAHC Department of Education

Introduction:

Will You Learn More by Listening or by Arguing?

THIS IS a book about the ideas of the Jewish religion. Jews have usually studied them in two different ways. One has been by listening respectfully to what scholars said about our basic teachings. That seemed sensible since there's so much to know about Judaism. Many books are important in our religion. The Bible and Talmud are both really like small libraries. Most Jews haven't studied Judaism in depth but the scholars have. So as they teach us about our tradition we get all the centuries of Jewish wisdom in a simple form.

This way of studying a religion, by listening to its sages, is found among all world religions. A few religions go a bit further and get their teachers to write statements of their faith. Then you must believe these statements or else you can't be part of their group—the dogmas and creeds of Christianity for example. What is unusual among the religions of the world is the other accepted Jewish way of studying beliefs, arguing over them. The case of Maimonides can teach us a great deal.

Our greatest philosopher wanted us all to be thinkers

Maimonides did most of his writing in the late 1100s C.E. (Common Era). Without doubt, he was the most important Jewish thinker of the Middle Ages. Jews from all over the world sent letters to him to get guidance on the right Jewish way to live. His books on Jewish law were used by almost all rabbis even when they sometimes disagreed with his decisions. He was also a philosopher and he was convinced that the most important thing in religion was thinking correctly. Knowing that most people couldn't understand philosophy, he simplified Judaism down to thirteen major beliefs (called "Thirteen Articles of Faith") which he put in simple language. He thought this was the least every Jew ought to understand and believe.

Many Jews were excited by what Maimonides had done. Now they felt that they had a good idea of what Judaism was all about. Once people started printing prayer books, a short version of Maimonides's "creed," as it is called, was often put after the **XIII** morning service. (You may know its next-to-last sentence from the Holocaust song, "*Ani Maamin,*" "I believe. . . .") Other Jews turned the list of thirteen beliefs into poems and some people set them to music. The best-known one is called *Yigdal* from its opening word, "Glorified [be God] . . .," and is included in the opening part of the morning service. (You will find it in *Gates of Prayer,* on pages 731–732.)

I have always found this turn of events quite interesting. Maimonides wanted to teach Jews philosophy. They ended up singing a song. There's quite a difference between the two. A philosophy is quite serious and tries to be exact, so we can think clearly. A song doesn't ask us to take its words too seriously. It is designed to make us feel more than to think. Maimonides wanted us to think as he did.

We were willing to listen to him respectfully but we wouldn't let even him tell us what we had to believe. We ended up letting him provide the words for one of our most important religious songs. That way we can keep in touch with what he said but we don't have to agree with him. More, the song is only a custom. You don't have to sing it. Maimonides was our greatest philosopher but even he couldn't ask Jews to stop thinking for themselves.

Maimonides is only one example of studying Judaism by arguing. Jewish thinkers in his day and since have disagreed with him. Joseph Albo said there were only three, not thirteen, basic Jewish beliefs. Hasdai Crescas said there were seven. One thinker said there should be twenty-six and quite a few others said you really couldn't make a list of what the basic beliefs of Judaism are. The argument went on for several hundred years. Since the Sanhedrin (the supreme Jewish court and legislature went out of existence when the Temple was destroyed in 70 c.e.), there was no one to settle the argument. Yet the debate itself, the thoughtful challenging of other people's ideas, and the need to give reasons for one's own position were highly educational. Intelligent arguing brought new ideas into our tradition and kept Judaism alive.

In recent times, the Reform Jews have been particularly interested in discussing ideas rather than merely accepting them. Being modern means learning to think for yourself and making up your own mind as to what you think is right. Reform Jews believed that Judaism could fit into the modern world very well. They were certain that if you explained Judaism to Jews in an up-to-date way they would see how true and valuable it was. Mostly we prefer to do our teaching by discussion. That is the way people can best test out ideas to see what they might mean to them personally. Besides, there are many topics on which modern Jews have different opin-
XIV ions. We do not agree on everything today and our clash of ideas is a

modern form of Jewish argument. Looking at the different, modern ways we might think about God or Torah, it becomes easier for us to figure out just where we personally stand. Much of this book, then, is devoted to explaining or starting Jewish study-arguments. Some I'll open up by giving you different modern ideas on a topic. Some you can carry on with me or yourself as you read. Others should arise in discussion with your teacher and classmates. Perhaps you can get your rabbi or family to talk over these questions with you.

Yet there have to be some limits even to Jewish arguing

But we can't argue about everything. Sometimes we are simply not in the mood for chasing ideas around and around. Then we'd just as soon know what reasonably trustworthy people have thought. Some questions, like what the Bible or Talmud says, are more a matter of knowing than giving someone's opinion. And there are some positions on which Reform Jews are pretty well agreed. On all such matters I'll try to give you the facts as fairly and as simply as I can. I may be wrong and, if you wish to correct my errors, please write me at the New York School of the Hebrew Union College-Jewish Institute of Religion, explaining what you think I should have said. Helping other people get their ideas straight is an important part of Jewish study.

When I quote from the Bible or later Jewish teachers, I try to make the material as understandable as possible. I do not quote it word for word or use the standard translations. I have used a lot of comments by Chasidic rabbis. They are easy to keep separate from those of the rabbis of the Talmud. (The Chasidic sages are generally called "Rebbes" and are identified by the small East-European towns they lived in.) The Rebbes say a lot to us because of their emphasis on each person's inner sense of religion. When I talk about Reform Judaism, I will not give my own opinion unless I say "I think" or other such words. Otherwise I shall be following what the Central Conference of American Rabbis said about our movement and its beliefs in its "Centenary Perspective" statement of 1976.

I have tried to answer the questions about our beliefs which research showed Reform Jewish teenagers were asking. I won't be disappointed if after reading this book you end up with many more questions than you had when you started. That will be in the spirit of Jewish argument if your new questions arise out of more mature belief. That's the mixture of knowing and searching which Judaism hopes you will carry on all your life. Thoughtful Jews have been doing this for centuries and we think you're old enough now to join the process. I hope you enjoy our discussions.

UNDERSTANDING
JUDAISM

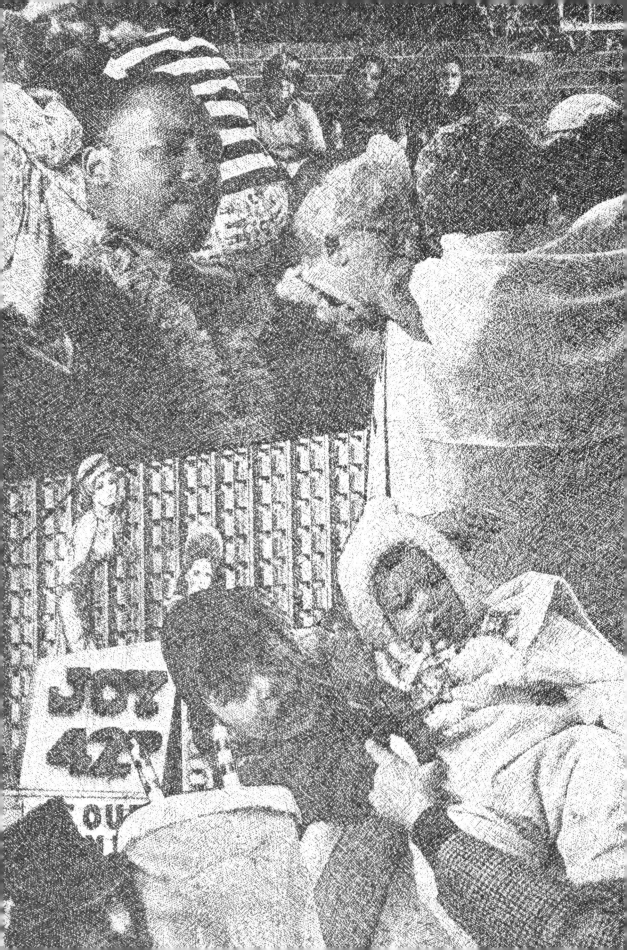

Part One
WHAT IS THE RIGHT THING TO DO?

1. Why Is It So Difficult to Be Good?
2. Handling Temptations: Money, Sex, Drinking
3. Have Our Ethics Changed since Bible Times?
4. What Are Our Duties to Humanity?
5. Are Rituals Necessary?
6. Feelings versus Rules: The Case of Praying
7. Building a Jewish Life: Marriage and a Family
8. Why Don't Most Jews Do Very Much?

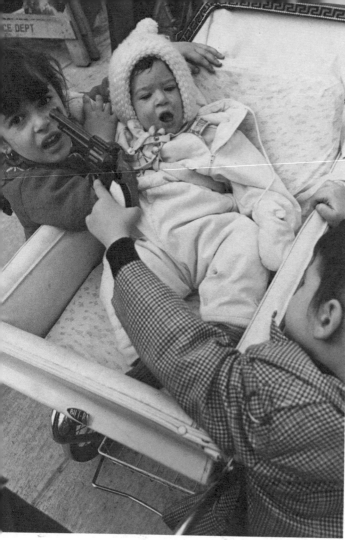

1
Why
Is It
So Difficult
to Be Good?

DOES this sound like you?

"Everyone keeps telling me to be good. My parents say, 'Do what's right.' My conscience nags me, 'Do this, don't do that.' My rabbi and teachers urge me, 'Follow the Torah, observe the commandments.' And I want to. There's something in me that likes to be good. Sometimes a strong feeling comes up inside me and says I should try to be perfect. Then I think of **4** giving up the money and cars and fame that everyone cares about and devoting my life to the poor or sick or aged that everyone forgets.

"That side of me is easy to live with. I like knowing I'm a

good person and have such high ideals. The trouble is that there's another side to me and I don't like it very much. When it comes out, I'm lazy or forgetful. I let things pile up in my room or don't remember that I was supposed to run the laundry. That doesn't sound so bad except that it happens over and over again. And if it's not my room or the laundry it's a hundred other things. Not only do my folks get angry with me but I get mad at myself. I've promised myself dozens of times I wouldn't let it happen to me again—but it does. That can make you feel pretty bad, almost as if you'll never learn any better.

"What's worse is the itch I get to do something I know is wrong. It gets so strong, often, that I give in. I watch TV when I should be studying. I eat the chocolate or potato chips I'm supposed to stay away from. Worse, I pick on my little brother until he cries. I talk back to my parents, steal from a store on Main Street, or go drinking with some kids. While I'm doing these things, they don't seem so bad. Afterward, I realize they're awful. I'm not only sorry I did them, I feel terrible about myself. I don't like being that kind of person. Sometimes I get the feeling that I must be one of the worst people in the world. It's almost as if there's no hope for me. It can really get me down."

Many teenagers feel this way. I thought it would be helpful, then, to open our discussions by talking about the problem of doing what's bad. Most of your Jewish education, I'm sure, has been about doing the good. By this time you know a lot about that and it will keep coming up in your other Jewish studies. Instead of adding to that, I'd like to introduce you to the Jewish explanation about why we do evil and the Jewish teaching of what we can do about it.

Two good reasons for starting with this topic

Teaching how to handle our bad side is a major part of Judaism. It's as important a part of the Torah as the commandments and ethics are. Our religion knows that despite our good intentions there's something about all of us that gets us to do what's bad. If we want people to do the good, we'd better do more than teach them rules and encourage them. That's why many Jewish teachers have tried to help us understand and control what makes us behave badly.

You're now old enough to appreciate this Jewish teaching. Little kids certainly know the difference between right and wrong and they have strong feelings about it. However, when you get to be a teenager these feelings are very much stronger—but since you are older you can also think about them more clearly. Learning how to live with your feelings, letting them help you become the kind of person you truly want to be, is one of your most important tasks now. Let's take a look, then, at what Judaism has to say about the bad side of people.

Three ideas with which we begin

It will help to get three things out of the way quickly.

First, according to Judaism, it's perfectly normal to feel that there are two sides to you, a good and a bad. Modern psychology agrees with this. Having different feelings doesn't make you abnormal. From Bible times on, people have done good and evil. The result has been that they've felt wonderful and terrible about themselves. Of course if you're always wildly happy or deeply depressed you may have an emotional problem that needs looking into, and perhaps you should have a talk with a counselor. Remember it's a Jewish commandment to get help when you think you're not as healthy as you ought to be.

Second, in the Jewish religion how you act is the most important thing. Some religions emphasize thinking. Buddhism says we need to understand a truth: all suffering comes from wanting things. Hinduism teaches that we need a clear idea that the world and things are really a sort of dream. Other religions make meditation central. Judaism is more outward-going and active than these faiths. We don't believe you should worry too much about having strange feelings or odd ideas. When we talk about good and bad we are talking about what you actually do, not what inner sensations you have.

Third, not every act is worth serious concern. Some people are proud of how much pizza they can eat, others get disgusted with themselves because they gained a pound and a half. Neither has very much to do with what sort of person you really are. Lying, cheating, stealing, being mean and inconsiderate, or loving and thoughtful, being unkind to people and to animals or fair and generous to others; these and the things your parents and synagogue most care about are the right things by which to judge yourself. Sorting out the foolish from the worthy standards is another important task you'll be working at for many years.

The key idea: because we are free
we are responsible

The root of Jewish teaching about human beings is that God "made" us free. (The quotation marks signal the special use of a word. We'll discuss talking about God in Part Four, Chapter 2.) Animals, like turtles or monkeys, aren't free to make up their minds about what to do. They follow their natural instincts or what they have learned. People also have instincts and they, too, develop habits. But, particularly when they are mature, they are also free to stop before doing an act and choose what they will do. Think of what happens when one of your friends dares you to prove how grown up you are by doing some shoplifting. You are free to say "yes" or "no." It's up to you whether you will steal or not steal. Of course, people are not free to do absolutely everything they might want to do. There are limits on all of us—for example, how we were brought up, how we feel, what rewards or penalties are involved, and what our goals are. It is remarkable to what extent we can do what we choose to do right now.

Because we are free, we are responsible for our acts in a way that horses and chimpanzees aren't. They pretty much can't help doing what they do. Mostly we can. Therefore we are responsible for what we do as no other animal is. That's why we feel so good when we've learned a new musical piece, finished a school project, or helped out at the home for the aged. It's also why we feel so bad when we've broken something and lied about it or when we've told a secret we'd sworn to keep. Being responsible for our acts brings us our glory and our guilt. No wonder we keep wanting to blame other people for the evil we do. The Bible has Adam say, when God accuses him of eating from the forbidden tree, "That woman you gave me, she made me eat from it" (Gen. 3:12). Judaism knows there are many influences on us. Despite them, it insists that we are free and so, responsible. The book of Ben Sirach (translated into Greek about 132 B.C.E.) sums up the Jewish view this way, "Don't say 'God made me do evil' for God doesn't want people to be evil. . . . If you want to, you can keep the commandments. Besides, it's simple sense to do what God wants. Life and death are in front of you. You'll get what you choose."

The rabbis' theory of the struggle inside us

In the Talmud the rabbis worked out an imaginative theory to explain why people so often use their freedom to do evil. Looking back, we can call it their sort of psychology. Since this was long before modern science, they didn't experiment in laboratories. They based their notions on their personal experiences and their experiences with others. Today's psychologists talk about what moves us to do things in terms of chemicals, nerves, drives, learning, and such. Besides your inner makeup, you are influenced by where and how you grow up. People are quite complicated. Studying psychology is very helpful in getting to understand yourself and other people. Still the old "talmudic psychology" can be valuable to us. The rabbis' folksy way of putting things often makes it easy to get their point. And what they say, though it has an old-fashioned flavor, still seems very wise.

The rabbis said that all human beings are directed by two urges inside them. One (as you would guess) is the *Yetzer Hatov,* the urge-to-do-good, or, more simply, the Good Urge. The other is the *Yetzer Hara,* the urge-to-do-evil, or the Evil Urge. And, the rabbis say, they are almost always fighting with one another. Imagine yourself standing before a dish of delicious candy before dinner. If you're like me, you'll feel the fight at once. "Take some." "Don't." "It won't hurt you." "It'll kill your appetite." "Just one piece." "Yeah. And then you'll want just one more." On and on and on.

The good urge is always being challenged

8

Almost all the rabbis of the Talmud thought the Evil Urge in us was much stronger than our Good Urge. That's why, despite good intentions, education, family, synagogue, and the rest, we commit so many sins. One opinion said the Evil Urge started with you at birth but the Good Urge didn't get its power until you were thirteen. (The teachers in the Talmud expected a *Bar Mitzvah* to be able to follow the commandments.) All agreed that the Evil Urge was always ready to attack us. You could defeat it for a moment but it would come back again. You may be educated, famous, respected, or old. It makes no difference. The Evil Urge will try to get you to sin. It never gets tired. It never slows down. No matter who you are or what you have achieved, all your life you will have to struggle against it. And the Evil Urge is very clever. It has all sorts of ways of getting you to do evil. It can make the bad seem good. As one rabbi put it, after you commit a sin a few times it seems like something you're permitted to do. Or the Evil Urge will suggest that, since God will surely forgive you for it, there's no good reason not to sin. And if you try to be too good and holy, the Evil Urge will still trap you. As Yehiel Mikhal, the Chasidic Rebbe of Zlotchov, commented about two hundred years ago, "One of the favorite tricks of the Evil Urge is to tell people that they really ought to be perfect. When they find they can't be, they give in to the Evil Urge altogether."

The rabbis balance our good against our evil

This description almost sounds as if the rabbis thought people were evil beings—but that can't be right.

When you think of the rabbis' idea of the Evil Urge, try to keep in mind all the positive things they also believed about people. We are created in God's "image"; we know something about God; we have been given God's Torah; we are free and can do God's commands. For Judaism, no creature on earth is as wonderful as a human being. The Book of Psalms says, "God, you made us just a little less than what You yourself are." The rabbis took all this very seriously. In addition, I'm convinced that just because they thought people were so extraordinary they figured the Evil Urge must be so strong. That is, they knew human beings are great—in theory. In practice, the rabbis were deeply disappointed in the way we behave. Why are we so bad when we should be so good?

Because, said the rabbis, the Evil Urge is so powerful. If we are to become the good people we were created to be we must spend our whole lives battling with the Evil Urge.

There are two major ways of meeting this human problem

Christianity and Judaism have one of their biggest differences here. The two agree that evil is a terrible thing. They disagree over what this says about people. Many Christian groups have taught that there's something about just being human which makes you guilty before God. (Older views said that Adam's sin in the Garden of Eden—the "original sin"—was passed down to all people. Modern views say it's just something built into human nature.) Since you're guilty before God, there's nothing you personally can do to make this up to God. Out of love, God sends the Christ to change things. By his life and particularly by his suffering, he clears up our sin before God. Now for the first time, says Christianity, you can find a way to do the good.

The Jews disagree. We recognize that people do a great deal of evil. That's not because they are evil but because they use their freedom badly and let the Evil Urge win that battle. But our doing evil doesn't ever take away our freedom to stop acting badly and to start doing the good. This important Jewish idea was expressed in one of the opening stories of the Torah. When Cain complains at being punished for killing Abel, the Torah has God say something that makes us see a picture in our minds: "Sin is like a wild animal. It hides at your door and waits for you to come out so it can bite you. [The Evil Urge wants to "get" us.] But you can rule over it!" (Gen. 4:7). The Evil Urge is powerful—but human beings can fight it and, very often, win out.

Because Judaism believes you never lose your power to do good, our religion doesn't think you ever need a Christ to help you. If you're ready to straighten things out with God after acting badly, do so. You still have your Good Urge; you only need to follow it. If you do, we believe, God will certainly "accept" you. The prophet Ezekiel, hundreds of years before Jesus, taught us what God really "wants" of people: "I don't want sinners to have to be punished and die. I'd much rather that they turned away from the evil they are doing and live" (Ez. 18:32).

God can be compared to sensible parents. No matter how many foolish things you've done they'll overlook them if you'll change and start behaving decently.

The rabbis' teaching about starting over again

Judaism called this changing *teshuvah,* literally "turning around." The normal English word is "repentance." The rabbis suggested four steps for repentance: (1) Learn to feel sorry for doing bad, and, if you don't overdo such a feeling, it will lead you to want to do good. (2) Try, as best you can, to make up for the evil you have done. (3) Tell God what you've done and how you now feel about it. This will help you realize how bad you were and help remind you how important it is to do good. (4) Promise God, as sincerely as you can, that you will make a new start and try to do better. If you do that, our tradition teaches, God will forgive you for what you have done. (Isn't that what we'd expect from parents or someone we're close to?) One rabbi imagined it this way: in heaven, the gates of *prayer* are sometimes open and sometimes shut—we don't always get what we ask for. But the gates of *repentance* are always open.

Judaism is quite different, here, from Christianity. You can do what needs to be done. You don't need a Christ or a priest or a special ceremony. You don't need to wait for Yom Kippur. Like doing good, repentance must be a daily part of a Jew's life. (Yom Kippur is for the people of Israel, as a group, to gather before God and ask for forgiveness.)

One rabbi said that, though God gave us the Evil Urge to fight with, God also gave us the Torah by which we might win out over it. I think he meant that, in a way, the whole Jewish religion is a plan to strengthen your Good Urge. You can think of it like training for a competition in a sport. Study and services, blessings and rituals, law and teachings, traditions and customs, family and community, our Jewish memories and messianic hopes, all help keep us in condition to defeat the Evil Urge. If we are better Jews, the Evil Urge will have less power over us—it's that simple.

Modern times have made things easier for the Evil Urge

I think it's harder for people to stay good today than it was some generations back. People once lived very close to their families and mostly did what their families said. In addition, communities had clear standards of what was forbidden. Today we are urged to get out into the world. We discover that people do all sorts of things. What you don't hear about at school you're likely to see on television or in the movies. We are freer to try things and so the Evil Urge can get at us in ways it couldn't have used when your parents were your age.

Much of our new freedom is very good. Men can be nurses and women, engineers. But when we use our freedom to steal or to take drugs, we harm ourselves and our society. Freedom shouldn't mean there are no limits to what we can do. The good is seen not only in the things we do. It is also made plain by what we refuse to do. Usually, it is easier to say what we shouldn't do rather than what we should do. For this reason, there are more negative than positive commandments in Judaism. Some people insist that it is right to try everything. But that doesn't mean that everything is permitted. If everything were permitted, then nothing could be called bad. For freedom truly to be good, it must have some limits—the bad must be defined.

Life isn't easy, for the Evil Urge is always struggling with us. We need all the help we can get so that it doesn't overwhelm us. Good friends are very important in this battle. So you should think about the sort of influence your friends have on you. Your parents—for all that you want to make your own decisions and whatever their shortcomings—are still your best guides to what's good. And you have your Judaism to teach you about life and to strengthen you in your struggle to be a good person.

Change a few words and this prayer of a rabbi of nearly two thousand years ago says what we often feel:

> Ruler of the universe, You know that we truly want to do what You have asked of us. What keeps us from doing it is the Evil Urge and the many harsh things the Roman government asks of us. May it be Your will, O God, to save us from the trouble that comes from inside us and from outside us. Then, with a full heart, we will do all the commandments that You have given us.

2 Handling Temptations: Money, Sex, Drinking

LIFE could be a lot simpler. For example, if candy tasted bad we wouldn't have any problem with it. However, the Evil Urge, being very smart, tempts us with things that are good to get us to do bad. To get good grades we start to cheat, to become popular we tell lies, to save time for our hobby we stop being helpful around the house. There was nothing evil about what we wanted. Only we got to wanting it so much, we didn't care what we did to get it. When you're little it may be ice cream or attention you want. When you get older it may be fame or money or other things you desire. Temptation is all around us during our lives. How we respond to it shows what sort of person we are.

Judaism has a special way of dealing with temptation. It's one of the most important things our religion has to teach you. It won't make temptation go away or be easy to overcome. The Evil Urge is too sneaky for that. But it can help you understand what is going on in your life and strengthen you in your effort to do the good. Let me discuss three things that often tempt people to do evil: money, sex, and drinking. (I'll talk about drugs when I talk about alcohol.)

Judaism does not teach that money, sex, and drinking are always bad

Jews have always thought it was better to have money than to be poor. That seems a natural choice. When you are able to buy nice clothes, have a fancy hi-fi set or movie camera, give lovely parties, and go to all sorts of interesting places, people think you are special. A Yiddish proverb says: When you've got money to spend, everyone thinks you're smart, good looking, and you even sing very nicely. Maybe Jews have thought being poor was so undesirable because they've been poor so often in their history. Having money makes it possible for families to live decently. Often, during the times when Jews were persecuted, money saved Jewish communities. People thought twice about throwing the Jews out of their towns for Jewish businesses created jobs and paid taxes. Besides, the well-to-do Jews could often bribe officials to leave them alone.

Everyone wants money because it seems like it can get us everything we desire. But some people get to wanting it so much they forget what's right. They'll lie, steal, even murder. Most of us don't go that far. We just cheat a little here and kind of bend the rules there. We say, "Everyone does it." We make dishonesty part of our lives and that's how the world starts falling apart.

Sex and drinking, like money, are also quite pleasant. It's nice to have somebody hold you, kiss you. It's one of the great human joys. A little beer or wine, once your body gets used to handling it, can make you feel very warm and friendly. Then the temptation starts. We want someone to be close to us, so we'll do almost anything to please that person. Then soon we're untrue to ourselves or to our friends. We like what a drink does to us, so we take one more and then another. Soon we're sick or drunk or acting foolish.

Is the danger so great we should stay away from things that tempt us?

Any of these desires can get out of our control, but alcohol and drugs are the worst because one gets addicted to them. Drugs become the most important thing in an addict's life. When addicts don't get drugs they don't have their "high." They also hurt terribly from withdrawal. That's why we say addicts are "hooked" and why hard drugs are so dreadful—once you get started, you're caught. Alcoholics are also addicts. They are "drink addicts." Even though they eventually make themselves sick by drinking, they too are "hooked" and alcohol becomes the most important thing in their lives.

Most of us aren't addicted to our temptations, but if we allow it to happen the Evil Urge can run our lives. Money may become so important we neglect our family and friends. Sex may be our chief interest and we may chase after our pleasure instead of truly caring for a loved person. Drinking may turn out to be the only way to get our work done and to face the real world. Soon we stop caring about what we really want to be and what decent people think of us. What began as a great joy ends as a deep tragedy.

According to some religions, temptations like money, sex, and alcohol are too powerful for us. They teach that human beings are too weak to handle them. People who follow these religions think it would be best if we gave up money, marriage, and alcohol. And if most people can't, at least the specially holy people should. Americans see such teachings in various Christian groups, but one can find this idea in many religions around the world.

Some Jews, during the first century of the Common Era, had a similar idea. Philo, the Jewish philosopher who lived in Alexandria then, tells us about the Essenes. They refused to live in cities because they feared the temptations there. They were against saving money or buying much land. They did only the farming and natural crafts that were needed to keep them alive. From other accounts we gather that they gave up family life but maintained their community by getting new people to join them. Many scholars have connected the people who wrote the Dead Sea Scrolls with the Essenes. Whoever they were, they also felt that they could be holy only by living in the wilderness.

Judaism teaches us neither to give in nor to run away from temptation

Almost all later Judaism took another direction. The rabbis of the Talmud scolded people who took on special hardships to please God more. Specifically, the Torah has rules for people who want to be specially holy to God for a period of time. They are called Nazirites. Such people must not drink wine or cut their hair while they are Nazirites. (Samson was a Nazirite, so when his hair was cut his vow to serve God was broken.) When their period of time as Nazirites was over, these people had to bring special sacrifices to the Temple. Among these, the rabbis noted, was a sin-offering. Rabbi Elazar Hakapar then argued: "These people who deny themselves a little wine are called sinners. How much more reason do we have then for calling Jews sinners for denying themselves all sorts of other things!" Another talmudic comment puts it this way: "Doesn't the Torah prohibit enough things? Why do you have to add more prohibitions?"

Judaism's attitude to temptation is summed up in a quite unexpected statement of the rabbis: Even the Evil Urge has some good to it. The great teacher Samuel said that if it weren't for the Evil Urge most people wouldn't build homes, take wives, have children, or start businesses. Let's face a truth about ourselves: many of us do good things for bad reasons. If we only did things when we were absolutely certain we were being saintly, we wouldn't do many of the good things we do. We need to try to keep the good in us in control, not insist on being perfectly pure. Besides, saying "absolutely no" to things that we have an itch for only makes us want them more. Jews think it's not human to deny yourself the pleasures of money, sex, and drinking just because they can easily get out of hand. The rabbis were too practical for that. They were willing to say that, even if we had the wrong reasons to start doing what the Torah calls on us to do, what was good in our acts would some day lead us to do them for the right reasons.

Know how dangerous your desires can be and use them in the right way

The first step in handling temptation is to admit how strong and clever our Evil Urge is. All the more reason then why we must learn to fight with it. As Ben Zoma said, "Who is a true hero? One who can control the Evil Urge." One way to do that, the rabbis teach, is to do some—but not too much—of any one thing which is dangerous. A side comment in a talmudic tractate says that there are eight things of which a little is good but a lot is bad: travel, sex, money, work, alcohol, sleep, spiced drinks, and medicine.

Another way one keeps from difficulty is putting the tempting things to a good use. We expect Jews to work hard and try to earn enough so their families will live decently. Yet even if you have a small income you must share it with the poor. The more money you have, the more we expect you to give to charity. *Tzedakah* is a brake on wanting too much money for yourself. We would like all Jews to marry. Then their desire for sex can increase their love and create a family. When you love someone so much that you want to spend your whole life with that person, then you have found the right partner in sex, too. And your love will not only make you happy, it will keep the Jewish people and its messianic dream alive.

A drink can be good; drunkenness is disgusting

The Jewish attitude toward drinking deserves special attention. Alcohol is part of Jewish religious life. Some people might insist on having grape juice at Kiddush each Shabbat, but most Jews celebrate with wine. Because of its alcohol it has a special effect on us. As the Book of Psalms says: "Wine makes peoples' hearts jolly" (Psalms 104:15). So we use it at every major celebration. Eastern-European Jews had a nice custom—whenever somebody could afford to bring a little whiskey to the daily morning service, people would stay for a few minutes afterward to share it.

With all that alcohol in our tradition, you'd think Jews would be among the worst drunks in the world. Wrong. Until recent years, Jews had the least number of problem drinkers of any group. The reasons seem clear. We didn't prohibit drinking but rather taught people to drink moderately. We connected our drinking with our families, our people, and our God—the things we cared about most. Our drinking was part of our being good. Drinking too much couldn't be good. It makes people do foolish or wild things. They start acting more like animals than like people. Getting drunk is ugly.

You can tell our attitude from our rule that we are supposed to say a blessing to God before we touch our wine. (Even little children know that.) There's also a blessing for beer or whiskey or any other alcoholic drink. "We bless you Adonai our God, Ruler of the universe, by whose word all things (including this drink) came to be." You can't kill the Evil Urge, but the next time you want to know whether you should be drinking I suggest you try saying the proper blessing to yourself. If you can say it honestly to God, the chances are your Good Urge is still in control.

Let wine be your Jewish guide to meeting temptation

Drinking gives us a clear example of how Jews should handle temptations. We do some but not too much. When in doubt, we ask what the Torah teaches, what our community thinks, and what we believe God wants of us. Drugs are so strong that it's hard to have any control over even a little of them. That's why they are such a difficult problem. That's particularly true of young people who are still learning to control their normal emotions. Let's say for the moment that there are some drugs that won't make you an addict or harm you physically. There's a big argument over this and it's important not to get taken in by someone who may want to get you started on drugs. Our families and religion don't have years of experience to help us keep their use reasonably safe. Look what's happened to our controls over our drinking. As Jews have begun practicing their Judaism less and have adopted secular drinking styles more, the number of Jewish alcoholics and problem drinkers has increased. Despite all our Jewish experience and teaching, alcohol is becoming a problem in our community. How many more lives will be wrecked and families broken up if we get involved with drugs? Please remember this talmudic statement: Sin starts out as slender as a hair, becomes as thick as a cart rope, and soon has you tied up with hawsers as thick as those by which a ship is held to a dock.

Money, sex, liquor shouldn't be ignored, but neither should they be worshiped. They and all the other things that tempt us have a place in our lives when they help us serve God as part of the Jewish people.

3 Have Our Ethics Changed since Bible Times?

THE MINUTE you talk about women you realize that our sense of what is good seems to have changed over the years. Not so long ago, single women, even those with good jobs, couldn't get bank loans; married women always had to have their husbands sign for them. And also not so long ago, everyone expected women to be nurses, teachers, or secretaries. Some few "pushy" ones may have become doctors or school principals, but almost none was ever allowed to become a superintendent of schools or to run a business. If you had suggested then that those practices were bad, people would

20

WHAT IS THE
RIGHT THING
TO DO?

have been shocked. They were only trying to do what was "best" for women. Females are so delicate, it was said, that they shouldn't undertake great burdens of education or management. Creatures with such a fine spirit should be shielded from the ugly and harsh facts of the business or political world. From this point of view, one did good for women by protecting them.

I find there are lots of people today, young and old, women as well as men, who still think that way. Yet it's clear to many others that this attitude toward women is bad. It never gives them a chance to say what *they* think is good for them. It doesn't permit them to see what their abilities are and to develop them in the real world. Reform Judaism has tried to remedy this attitude in our religion. It has pioneered for women's rights—though, typically enough, it has taken us a long time to put our theory into action. (Would your congregation have a woman as its rabbi? If you had two rabbis, would a qualified woman be the senior rabbi and have a man as assistant rabbi?)

All people want to know how the good can change and still be good

I think the question of women's rights in society or in Judaism is important. A lot has been written about both topics and I hope you and your friends, perhaps in class, will want to talk about them. But I want to move on to a more general question teenagers ask. If our sense of good and bad can change, how do we know that what's good today is really good? Maybe tomorrow we'll think it's bad. Besides our attitude toward women, we've changed in many other areas. We think students have rights at school and that there are limits to what teachers can do. We think employers should care about whether factory conditions make workers sick and not just about how much profit they can make. We think people shouldn't pollute the environment or use public property any way they please. If our ideas about what's good and bad change, how can they be true?

From these examples you can see that this is not just a Jewish problem. When we discuss questions of ethics, there is much overlap between our Jewish teaching and that of our neighbors. Christians, worshiping the same God as we do and having a similar sense of what it means to be human, have a similar sense of what is good. I think that is one reason the Jews have felt so much at home in the United States and Canada. For all that, I want to talk about this general ethical question—change in ethics—from the standpoint of the Jewish tradition. That is where most Jews get their special sense of ethics. I also think that we have some special Jewish problems in this area which deserve mention.

Only what is dead stops changing

Right off I want to explain a concept you will meet again and again in this book because it is one of the great ideas of Reform Judaism: the truth "changes"—or, more precisely, what we know keeps growing and developing. Anything that's alive has to change in this way. If anyone of us had the same ideas today that we had three years ago, we'd all be pretty worried about one another. As we mature, we hope our ideas become deeper and wiser. The same is true in Judaism. Our religion has "changed." That doesn't mean we now worship idols or have decided that people are best off living like hermits in caves. We haven't changed to something the opposite of what we were. We've changed by growing. Judaism, because it is alive, has become deeper and wiser as a result of all our experiences. We've been "growing up." Our present ideas continue what we've always believed, but in a new and better way.

This process of religious growth goes far back in Judaism. I want to present two examples. (I'm sure one example would do but the first is so alien to contemporary minds, I thought you might have some fun with it—particularly since teenagers and their parents often are at odds.) The second is a much-discussed law in the Bible that you ought to know about.

22 The son who refuses to accept discipline

WHAT IS THE RIGHT THING TO DO? Here is the example I thought would be "fun" for you, the Torah's mind-shaking law about a disrespectful son:

If someone has a stubborn and rebellious son who won't listen to what his father and mother say though they punish him, let them take him to the elders of the city (at the city gate). Let them then declare, "This son of ours is stubborn and rebellious. He doesn't listen to what we tell him. He's always stuffing himself with food and always getting drunk." Then the men of the city should throw stones at him until he's dead. That will get rid of this evil in the community. Moreover, other Jewish sons will hear about it and be afraid to act the same way (Deut. 21:18–21).

This law does give the child some protection: The parents can't just kill him. They must bring him to court. The Bible gives no instance of this law ever being carried out. But the law is there and, as a questioning liberal Jew, I believe we are entitled to guess where it came from. (Chapters 1 and 2 of Part Three explain our Reform Jewish attitude toward the Bible.) Studies of ancient societies show that many of them gave parents life-and-death power over their children. I'd guess that the earliest Jews also gave parents this right. Thus we have this law. But, as they came to know and understand the God of the Torah, Jews realized it was evil for parents to kill their children, no matter how angry they got with them. This religious growth reaches a climax in the Torah story in which God forbids killing one's child even, supposedly, for God's sake (Gen. 22). Abraham thinks he's obeying God by sacrificing his dearest "possession," his son Isaac. Abraham is stopped from doing so and God "says" that Jewish parents are never to kill their children for God's sake, as some nearby tribes did. The Torah law about the rebellious son is not yet at that level.

By the time of the Talmud, the change was so great that the rabbis could say: "There never has been a 'stubborn and rebellious son' of the sort the Torah describes and there never will be. The law was put into the Torah only for purposes of study and discussion for which there is great reward."

That is my first example of how Jewish ethics changed before modern times. (Isn't it a consolation to know that no matter how angry with you your parents sometimes become, there's a 4,000-year-old tradition which taught them to control their impulses?)

The Torah law of "an eye for an eye"

My other example has to do with the Torah's rule of justice, the so-called *lex talionis,* the law of equal punishment. It comes up three times (Exod. 21:23–25, Lev. 24:19–20, Deut. 19:21), always in connection with damage actually done or attempted. It says the punishment should equal the crime. This is the formula: "life for life, eye for eye, tooth for tooth, hand for hand, foot for foot, burning for burning, wound for wound, stripe for stripe."

To a modern person it sounds horrible. It would make the punisher almost as wicked as the evildoer. Let's try to imagine what this law meant in Bible times.

In order to do this, I suggest that we think for a minute of what we mean when we say we want "to get even" with others. We're saying that we want to get back at them for something they have done to us. Only we generally don't want it to be just "even," that is, to do to them exactly what they did to us. We get "even" by making them suffer more than we did. This is called revenge. Here is an old boast by a biblical figure named Lamech (Gen. 4:23):

> I've killed people for wounding me,
> Tough young men for bruising me.
> Cain used to get even by doing 7 times
>   worse than what was done to him.
> I'm not satisfied until I've done
>   77 times.

That is certainly an exaggeration, but it reminds us that people then too were anxious to take revenge. In such a world, "life for life, eye for eye, tooth for tooth" was a great advance. It puts justice, equal punishment, in the place of revenge.

There is no case of the use of this law in the Bible. In the Talmud the rule is interpreted in this new way—pay money to

make up for the damage. The worse the damage, the more

you should pay. The court will figure the amount according to the rule, "An eye's worth for an eye, a tooth's worth for a tooth. . . ."

What stays the same and what changes in our ethics?

There you are. As early as the times of the Bible and the Talmud our Jewish sense of good and bad was growing. Reform Judaism insists that it must continue to develop and change. But does nothing stay the same? Is everything about our ethics becoming different?

To answer these questions I must ask you to keep four things separate: (1) our deepest beliefs, (2) our basic ideas, (3) our ethical rules and teachings, and (4) the present-day challenges to our sense of what is right. They are all closely connected, but they don't all change at the same rate. Our deepest beliefs in Judaism haven't changed very much over the years. We still think God is one and cares that we should do what's good. Our ideas about our beliefs have changed somewhat more and the rules that we have for living by our beliefs have changed even more. Naturally, whenever Jews have come into a new and challenging situation, a major change has been called for. Modern times have raised lots of questions about how Jews should live, so we have made many changes in how we believe Jews today should try to do what's good. I want to say something more about each of these, but I'll only be able to give you some key ideas about some complicated matters.

The faith we have will give rise to ideas about ethics

Our deepest beliefs about God and human beings have a great influence on how we feel we should act. This is so personal a matter that these beliefs are, unfortunately, very hard to put into words. What more can you say after you've said that, though there are lots of things in the world, the deepest reality in it—God—is one. We Jews may have talked about God's oneness differently over the years, calling God, The King or The Power or The Idea. Yet, Jews today feel that what we're saying about God is only a more adult, full form of what earlier Jews believed. You will read more about this as this book goes on. (Chapters 1 and 2 of Part Four talk about God and change.)

This deep sense of God and people has given rise to definite

Jewish ideas about what is good. Like our beliefs, these basic ideas of our ethics seem not to have changed much over the years. Scholars argue over just what they are and how we should define them. Many agree that probably the most basic idea in Jewish ethics is that all people are created in God's "image." (Many people use the Bible's symbol-word "image," but it's difficult to explain. To me, it suggests that people, as distinct from all other animals, are especially like God.) This means all human beings, all of them, are precious. This notion is quite revolutionary. Compare it to the attitudes, say, that athletes or the rich or Blacks or Hindus are disgusting or deserve special privileges. The Talmud is quite clear about the equal power and worth of all human beings. Akiba and Ben Azzai differed over which was the most basic statement in the Torah. Akiba said it was the rule to love your neighbor as you love yourself (Lev. 19:18). Ben Azzai said that even more fundamental was the idea found in the verse, "When God created people, in God's own image did God make them" (Gen. 5:1). Whichever teacher you follow, your Jewish sense of what is good will be shaped by the basic idea that to God all humans are precious and equal.

And, briefly, there are a few more basic ideas of Jewish ethics to mention.

The importance of action:

> As valuable as study is, doing is more important.

The strong emphasis on the worth of life:

> The Torah was given to live by, not to cause your death. Therefore, in a real emergency you may break any of its rules except those against idol-worship, sexual sins, and murder.

The duty never to lose hope:

> Until the edge of the sword actually hits your neck, don't give up.

Everyone, not just Jews, has an ethical sense. In the Talmud, Rabbi Johanan is reported as saying you could even learn it from animals:

> Had the Torah not been given to us, we could have learned cleanliness from cats [who wash themselves];

honesty from ants [who work hard]; sexual decency from doves [who seem shy]; and proper behavior between husband and wife from chickens [who seem to talk to each other]. (See also Part Two, Chapter 3.)

All these basic ideas of Jewish ethics still seem true.

Most rules are written
for a definite time and place

Our problems become more complicated when we put our deepest beliefs and our basic ideas into specific ethical rules or teachings. Some of them, though written down thousands of years ago, still make sense. That's one reason for knowing and studying the Jewish tradition. Some rules and teachings which made sense in other times and places no longer seem to express our sense of what is good. In such instances as in the case of women, Reform Judaism will insist that the old rules be changed in terms of what we have learned over the centuries. Let's study examples of both sorts of rules.

Many of the Torah's laws still make sense. When Reb Shmelke became the Chasidic Rebbe of Nikolsburg, the people requested that he give them some new rules to follow. Shmelke said he'd first like to get to know the community. After they bothered him a great deal, he finally wrote down his special directions for them: the Ten Commandments. I'd say that's still the best place to start our ethics (though, technically, the first four are not "ethics" but religious rules). Leviticus, Chapter 19, is another example of rules that are still true today. It talks about not oppressing one's neighbor, not keeping a day worker's pay until the next day, not gossiping, not hating people (even yourself), not taking vengeance, not bearing a grudge, and protesting when there's a great wrong. Apparently the Evil Urge works today very much the same way as it did in Torah times.

Not every law in our tradition still seems right

I believe that the ethical rules of the Torah which most seem to need change these days are the ones about women. Compared to the laws of other peoples, Jewish law treats women very well. Compared to our modern sense of God's image in all people, regardless of sex, the laws are not as ethical as they might be. Women should be allowed to serve as witnesses, give divorces, be counted in a *minyan,* and serve as rabbis. That is so clear ethically that Reform Jews have broken with the Talmud and the rest of the Jewish community on these matters. In this and other such areas, what we discovered about being good made the traditional laws wrong for us.

Figuring out which Jewish traditions should still be an ethical standard for us causes great argument in the Jewish community. Would it be right to take away the intravenous feeding of a patient who doctors say is soon likely to die? Should someone who is healthy be allowed an operation to stop an unwanted pregnancy? Should we be discouraged from having our faces lifted to keep us from looking older? Modern Jewish scholars are working on dozens of such questions. Keeping up with their answers is important and is one reason why you should be part of a synagogue and its adult education program.

A new life for Jews has brought many challenges

The biggest changes in Jewish ethics came with the ideas of modern times. One of these was democracy, with its notion that everyone is a person and has rights. Put so simply, it sounds very much like the old, basic idea of all people being precious. Yet, until recent times, most people thought equality meant only for their group or their kind of person. In practice, Americans didn't extend it to Blacks or Chicanos or Orientals. They certainly didn't extend it to women. For many groups, Jews were not entitled to equality. Once we stop asking, "Are you my equal?" and start asking, "Are you a person?" then all the old barriers fall. Regardless of your skin, your religion, your country of origin, your ideology, you are still a person. That means I need to treat you as someone who

28 has rights. The struggle for minority rights, for women's

WHAT IS THE RIGHT THING TO DO? rights, for the rights of any person who has been deprived of rights, is rooted in this powerful ethical idea. I think you can see why it appeals so much to modern Jews.

But the idea of treating us like persons also raises a new problem for Jewish ethics. Among the most precious rights individuals have is the right to make up their own minds. In ethics, we say that people shouldn't be forced to go against their consciences. But, if all human beings should do what they personally think is right, it will be difficult to have any rules. How, then, can we have a society? We Jews are especially touched by this problem because our tradition stresses the importance of creating a good community. Besides, we have traditionally taught our people to be ethical by getting them to follow ethical rules. If we make being a person one of our basic Jewish ideas, how can we ask all Jews to follow the same ethical rules? We are still arguing over that.

Should you then not make any ethical decisions until we settle all the questions we have raised in this chapter? After all, ten years from now we may know better. Of course, ten years after that we would be wiser. But with such reasoning you will never decide anything. You'll wait around forever. Moreover, the ethical questions will not hold back until we find answers to them. They come up every day. To refuse to answer them as best we can now is to deny our special human capacity to be ethical. True, we cannot know everything about what we ought to do. Yet we know a great deal. Out of our deepest beliefs and our basic ethical ideas, seeking the guidance of our tradition, we can gain that sort of powerful ethical sense for which Jews have been noted. Perhaps we do not pay enough attention to the last of Hillel's three ethical questions: If I don't stand up for myself, who will stand up for me? But if I am only interested in myself, what good am I? And if not now, when?

4 What Are Our Duties to Humanity?

"ARE the French in the eyes of the Jews their brethren or their enemies? In either case, what duties does Jewish law prescribe for the Jews toward the French who are not of their faith?"

These are two of the dozen questions Napoleon asked the leaders of the French Jewish community as part of the change in France giving the Jews equal rights. The date was 1806, almost thirty years after a revolution which talked about "Liberty, Equality, Fraternity."

To us, Napoleon's questions sound stupid and insulting. That's because we know that Judaism stresses doing good to

WHAT IS THE
RIGHT THING
TO DO?

all people and working for a better society. In Napoleon's time that certainly wasn't clear to non-Jews—and the fact that they were so uninformed was mostly their fault. After 315 c.e. when Christianity became the official religion of the Roman Empire, the Jews were forced to live under special restrictions. Moslems, after their religion began in the early 600s, did much the same to the Jews. So, for many centuries, Jews were kept out of general society and had almost no part in running its affairs. France was one of the first modern countries where your religion was a private matter. Yet people like Napoleon were so used to Jews being outsiders they thought it was a Jewish choice. They overlooked the fact that they had kept us segregated. We wanted to continue our separate religion, but that didn't mean Judaism had no concern for other people. We simply didn't have a reason to think about our duties to general society during most of Jewish history. In the 1800s when Jews began to get freedom, Judaism's sense of general ethics was quickly spelled out. This was another of the great, early accomplishments of Reform Judaism.

The Talmud's attitude toward humanity

The French Jewish leaders answered Napoleon directly: Judaism teaches that the French non-Jew is a "brother" and not an enemy. They knew this from the Bible. It teaches that all people are descended from Adam and Eve. Hence they are basically one family. The rabbis of the Talmud took this very seriously. The book of the Mishnah about the Sanhedrin, discussing court cases where the sentence might be death, reminds us how precious all life is: God began humankind with but a single person "for the sake of peace among people." As a result, no one can ever come along and say, "My father is greater than your father." The Talmud reports this saying of the teachers of Yavneh: "I am a creation of God and other people are creations of God. My work is in the city while their may be in the country. I rise early to go to my work and they rise early to go to their work. As they can't do my work very well, so I can't do what they do very well. When you are tempted to say that you do more and they do less, remember what we have been taught—It doesn't make any difference how much you do as long as you direct your heart to God." I'd guess the early teachers were thinking mostly about their own Jewish community, but what they say reaches much further.

No matter how different Jews felt from idol-worshipers, no matter how they were discriminated against by Christians and Moslems, this sense of the unity of humankind stayed with them. I like the way it comes out in the East-European folk saying: Hating a person is like hating God.

Caring for humanity is a part of the Torah's commandments

A concern for non-Jews was also an official part of Jewish law. The rabbis taught that Gentiles had seven commandments to follow, while the Jews had 613. (See Part Two, Chapter 3.) This means that Jews and non-Jews share certain laws: no stealing, no murder, no sexual sins, proper justice for all people. Josephus, who was a general in the Jewish rebellion against Rome that ended in 70 C.E., wrote about this. He was probably trying to make a good impression on his non-Jewish readers. Still, he describes our Jewish teaching pretty well. "Our laws tell us to do many things for all people. We must give fire, water, and food to anyone who needs them. We give them proper directions. We don't let a corpse go unburied. We are supposed to treat even our enemies with decency. We don't set fire to their country or chop down their fruit trees. We don't loot those killed in battle and we must not ill-treat captives, particularly women. Our law is so concerned with our being gentle and humane that it even has rules about how we are to treat our animals. . . ."

The Talmud has a nice title for Jewish duties to non-Jews. It calls them laws "for the sake of peace." In a city of both Jews and non-Jews, the Jewish charity collectors take contributions from both groups, feed the poor of both, visit the sick of both, bury the dead of both, comfort the mourners in both groups, and restore the lost goods of people in both groups, all for the sake of peace. All later Jewish law about our general duties to non-Jews builds on that passage.

Two major themes
of proper Jewish behavior

We can take this a step further. Jews are supposed to act in such a way as to bring credit to their God. This means that, if an act is not specifically required by the law, Jews should do it for God's sake.

The rabbis call it *"kiddush hashem,"* making God's name holy among people. They tell with pride the story of Shimon ben Shetah who sold an animal to a non-Jew. The new owner then discovered a precious jewel hidden on the beast. He took the jewel back to Shimon who refused to accept it since he had meant to sell the animal and its gear. The buyer then exclaimed, "Blessed be the God of Shimon ben Shetah." That's what we mean by acting so God's name is made holy among people.

Unfortunately, we often do the opposite. We behave badly. That, say the rabbis, is like making God's name foul to people. They call this *"chilul hashem"* and consider it a terrible sin. When Jews are not fair in their dealings with non-Jews, the Talmud notes, that is a *chilul hashem.*

The feeling that every Jewish act says something about God was always to be found among Jews, even though it was difficult in some periods for Jews not to hate those who destroyed them. Yaakov Yitzchak, the Chasidic Rebbe of Pzhysha, may have meant only Jews in his comment on this talmudic statement, but his idea goes much beyond that: the Talmud says that the stork has the lovely name *chasidah* (literally, "the loving one") because it cares so much for its mate and children. But then, asked Yaakov Yitzchak, why is it not a *kosher* bird, one that Jews may eat? Alas, he answered, a stork only gives love to its own.

And on the lighter side, there is this clever Yiddish proverb: Love your neighbor—even when he plays the trombone.

When Jews were made citizens
they made plain their general ethics

Democracy made it possible for the Jews to take up these traditional teachings and develop them into a major part of modern Judaism. Having been segregated for so long, Jews were thrilled to participate in society. If democracy could really be made to work, if, regardless of religion or skin color or background, people had equal rights and opportunities, then the Jews would at last be safe. If any people could be denied equality or made inferior, the next victims might be us. Because we had suffered so much from discrimination we know how bad it is and we fought to end it in America. In a way, the discrimination we suffered was a modern version of our slavery in Egypt. (The Torah commands us to be kind to strangers because, having been strangers in Egypt, we know what it feels like to be a stranger.) Many people remained afraid of democracy. They said, "We can't change things. There's always been injustice and there will always be injustice." We know better. Society has changed its attitudes toward Jews. Our lives prove that social change can bring greater justice. We made that experience an important part of our modern Jewish ethics.

The prophets taught us much about our duties to society. We applied to our democracies what they said about creating the good Jewish community. Amos, for example, sounds like he is speaking to us about problems we face today:

> You make justice have a bitter taste. You throw righteousness into the dirt. . . . You hate people who try to correct things in the court. You despise people who speak the truth. You squeeze everything you can out of the poor; you take away their last grain of wheat. . . . You punish the innocent. You take bribes. You pay no attention when needy people come to court. It is such an evil time that people who are careful keep quite quiet. Seek good not evil if you really want to live. Then Adonai, the God of hosts, will be with you, which is what you say you want. Hate evil. Love good. Establish justice in your courts. . . . [God says], "I hate, I despise your festivals. I will take no pleasure in your solemn services. I will not accept the burnt-offerings and meal-offerings you bring me or peace-offerings of your best cattle. Take away from Me the noise of your songs and let Me not hear you play on your psalteries. Rather, let justice pour down like water and let righteousness become a mighty stream." (Amos 5:7–24).

34

The prophets didn't hesitate to attack the rulers of the society for their corruption. Isaiah said they were as bad as the rulers of Sodom were and that the Jews were doing as much evil as the people of Gomorrah (Isa. 1:10). Jeremiah called the priests and prophets hypocrites and said that the Temple in Jerusalem wouldn't protect the Jews from being punished for doing so much evil. The prophets regularly defended the poor and the powerless against the rich, the important, and the famous. Some problems haven't changed much since the days of the prophets. With our cities so big, institutions so impersonal, government so full of red tape, business so concerned with profit, the little people suffer. Democracy doesn't work very well for the old, the poor, the handicapped, and even many ordinary folk. Unhappy and bitter people often take out their anger on minority groups. So Jews believe that for the sake of society—and for their own sakes—it should be an important religious duty to make life better for everyone.

The Holocaust has taught us the importance of ethical action

In recent years Jews have had a special reason for taking a stand for what's right: the world kept quiet when the Nazis began the Holocaust. The words of Lev. 19:16–17 now carry a special force.

> Don't stand there and do nothing when your brother's blood is being spilled. I am *Adonai!* Don't hate your brother in your heart. You must protest your neighbor's doing evil and not become a sinner yourself by being silent when he sins.

That's always been a difficult set of commands to carry out. But listen to the words of Joachim Prinz and you can feel how important they are to us.

> When I was the rabbi of the Jewish community in Berlin under Hitler's regime, I learned many things. The most important thing that I learned under those tragic circumstances was that bigotry and hatred are not the most urgent problems. The most urgent, the most disgraceful, the most shameful, and the most tragic problem is silence.

That, too, has become part of modern Jewish ethics.

Trying to make society better is very difficult. Even after almost two hundred years of effort, Jews still don't have full equality in our society. Many other minorities are worse off, some suffering very much indeed. Changing our society, our world, will take more than a few months or years. We will have to keep at it all our lives. And when we lose important battles for the good, we must be strong enough not to despair. We can get some courage from knowing that the Jewish people will carry on until our dream of a perfect time becomes real on earth.

I must call to your attention a new problem which has recently arisen in Jewish ethics. Once it seemed as if everything that was good for the Jews would be good for democracy and the other way around as well. Now it's not always so clear. When we start bussing to integrate schools or have government-sponsored integration of neighborhoods, that would seem to build greater democracy. Yet it might also break up neighborhoods that Jews struggled to create. Such issues are very complicated, and it's not easy to figure out the right thing to do. That's why people get so excited over these issues—but trying to think as clearly as possible would be far more helpful. Though our social duties aren't always clear today, much of the time we know what we ought to do. Concerned as we are about all human beings, believing that Jews are safest in the truest democracy, we have a deep religious responsibility to work for a just and caring society.

5
Are
Rituals
Necessary?

WOULDN'T it be sad if, when your birthday came this year, nothing special happened? If people like us, they should say "Happy Birthday" when they see us, or send us a birthday card, or give us a gift. Better yet, we'd like a party, even if we have to give it for ourselves. We'd certainly want a birthday cake with candles. Someone will light them in another room, the lights will be turned down, and the cake brought in. Everyone will be quiet while we make a silent wish and try to blow out the candles with one breath. Then everyone will cheer, the candles will be taken out of the cake, we'll cut the first slice, and then the cake will be cut for everyone to eat.

In some ways you can say this is all quite silly. Maybe we don't like cake or are on a diet. It's a waste to burn a bunch of candles just for a minute and then throw them out. We don't believe that wishes work and certainly not by the magic of blowing out all the candles with one breath. So why go through this cake rigmarole?

Some grouches may disagree, but most people think birthday cakes are fun. Little children get terribly excited over it. Bigger ones still want it. And adults get a tickle out of it when a birthday cake appears for them too—even if it's only a cupcake with one candle in it! Even knowing in advance gets us excited before we see the cake. We've had birthday cakes ever since we were little. It's a tradition. Every time we get a new one, it's like reliving all the old parties and the presents and the fun. Besides, the celebration brings us closer to our family and friends. Celebrating by ourselves wouldn't be as much fun. And all this works because it's connected with something very important: us. You could make a big fuss each year when the first new ears of sweet corn arrive but it wouldn't mean as much to you as your birthday.

Having a birthday cake is a ritual. You may have thought all rituals were religious. Not so. We use the word *ritual* for any act which tries to show something special is happening. It is done at a special time, with special things, in a special way. That's how human beings mark an important moment.

Groups like to show
that some times are very important to them

This is also true of groups. A few years back the United States celebrated its two-hundredth birthday. July Fourth hadn't been too exciting in the years before 1976 because people were disturbed by our economic and political troubles. But you couldn't overlook a bicentennial and it was too important for just one day's celebration. There were events going on all year—TV historical spots, the re-creation of Revolutionary War battles, and such. Independence Day celebration in 1976

38 was quite special. Mostly there were things to do that were

fun—parades, outdoor concerts, fireworks. One event seemed to have little to do with the country's birthday, but it gave us a special thrill. A great many of the tall sailing ships that are still in use came into the New York harbor. They sailed up the Hudson River, turned around, and sailed back to the ocean. There's nothing especially American about that. But even on television there was something about those majestic old-fashioned ships moving through the harbor that gave us a great lift. No parade of ocean liners or aircraft carriers could have moved us as much.

There were also serious events on Bicentennial Day: readings from the Declaration of Independence, exhibitions of Colonial Period clothes and pictures and documents, speeches about the meaning of the day. The founding of the United States has meant too much to us and to all humanity for us just to get together for a good time.

The Jewish people celebrate as all peoples and religions do

All this helps explain why we have rituals in Judaism. Human beings like to celebrate and to mark important events with special ceremonies. No society has lived without some sort of rituals. There are many of them and we learn about them as we grow up in our society. When a time comes for us to celebrate we take our rituals from our group—like having a party, presents, cake. Sometimes we create new things to do that seem right for a special occasion—the tall sailing ships. On rare occasions, a new idea becomes part of a people's celebration—like collecting for UNICEF on Halloween. Tradition is an important part of celebration. In fact, ancient objects sometimes say more to us than anything new could— like a *shofar* and not a trumpet on Rosh Hashanah; a handwritten Torah scroll and not a printed one to read from.

In Judaism we celebrate three main themes: our lives, our people's history, and how close we feel to God. All three are part of our lighting a menorah or saying the *motzi* before we eat.

Judaism urges us to mark the great events in our lives. We shouldn't let them slip by without rejoicing with our people and God. Weddings are probably the grandest example. What really counts is that two people love each other and will do their best to live happily together. All they must do, then, is promise that to each other. When you see how much money and what silly things some people do to make their weddings outstanding, doing it by yourselves seems sensible . . . but not for long. For one thing, happiness grows when you share it. It's also a little selfish to deprive family and friends, who have cared so much about you, of the joy of celebrating with you. Since you're part of the Jewish community, they, too, should be involved if only by having at least ten people present, a *minyan*—the smallest number that stands for the whole people of Israel.

Our tradition has special ways of marrying people. So, we have an exchange of promises, to show we mean it. Traditionally, the groom signed a contract. He also had to give the bride a gift worth at least a penny. By this act, he showed that he would share his wealth with her. Of course, custom says you give a ring and you know how strong a custom that's become! Most of the ceremony, however, is made up of our saying seven blessings thanking God who made this marriage possible, asking God's help for the couple and for our people Israel.

Some rituals fall out of favor
while others get to be widely done

Rituals can gain or lose popularity. For centuries it was the Jewish custom to have the groom break a glass at the end of the wedding ceremony. Then all the guests would yell, "*Mazal Tov*," "Good Luck." The early Reform Jews did away with the glass-breaking. To them, it seemed like a crude and vulgar way to end a beautiful ceremony. Besides, there seemed to be no good reason for it. Traditionally, two reasons had usually been given. One, at happy moments we should remember that there will also be sad ones. Two, it was important to remember that the Temple in Jerusalem was still destroyed. Reform Jews didn't want the Temple rebuilt so that Jews could go back to offering God goats and sheep and other sacrifices. And the sermon, for example, seemed a better way to remind people that life is bitter as well as sweet. So they stopped breaking a glass, but many Reform Jews still practice the custom today. They say they want to do it because it's an old Jewish tradition and they like the idea of it.

Emotions do play an important part in deciding what rituals you want to follow. Many of us have grown up with so

40

few rituals in our lives that I think it takes an effort for us to relax and enjoy them. When it comes to celebrating, I find many people have been deprived. May I encourage you to get a good feel for a ritual before you make up your mind about it? Do it long enough to be comfortable with it. Then judge if it's right for you. I also believe you ought to keep your community in mind. How have Jews celebrated this in the past and what are other Jews doing today? Sometimes wanting to feel part of the Jewish people when you celebrate is enough reason to keep a ritual—our group has its special events just as we do in our personal lives.

Without the Jewish people and its traditions, you and your family would probably be quite different from what you are. The more you care about being a Jew, the more you'll want to celebrate its special events in its special ways. The most obvious example is probably the Passover Seder. Each spring we remember that we escaped from being slaves in Egypt. We've never stopped thanking God for that. You could be grateful without putting a lamb bone and a burnt egg on your Passover symbol plate. They're only a reminder of Temple sacrifices we don't believe in. But they're so much a part of the Seder that Reform Jews never gave them up. As to the rest of the Seder, I don't need to tell you how much fun it can be. Family and friends and wine and foods and songs. It's a whole evening of rituals we've known and loved since we were young children.

Let's try a harder question. How strict will you be, avoiding bread and cake all Passover week? If you're a bread addict and you care deeply about being part of the Jewish people, you'll want to carry some *matzah* with you when you eat out. That's not fun, as the Seder is, but it's important in Jewish tradition and to many Jews today. So, though we might not personally care about being strict about *matzah,* we might carry some with us to eat during Passover for our people and our tradition's sake.

Rituals: sort of poems
made with acts instead of words

There's one more reason we follow rituals: to express or refresh our closeness to God. It's not easy to be certain of our belief in God. It's harder still to get and stay close to God. We all have many things to do, for ourselves, our families, our schools, even for the Jewish community. All those good things seem to leave us no time to remember God.

Yet nothing could be more important than trying, from time to time, to feel what God wants of us. At special events, we do think of God. We recite the *Shehecheyanu* blessing ("Who has kept us alive and sustained us and brought us to this day"). For a moment, we feel grateful. But what about every day? Isn't waking up each morning a special event in your life? Isn't finishing another day in some decency quite an accomplishment? Each day, and all day long, Jewish tradition says, we have reasons to say blessings: for being able to stand up, for seeing that our body is still working when we go to the toilet, for having food to eat, for the good news or the bad news that comes to us. You can do that without *Baruch Atah Adonai* and so forth—but it's not just the Hebrew we forget. We mostly don't think of God and we ignore our being Jewish. The result is that we start becoming, like so many other people these days, less human than we ought to be.

Often, when we want to draw near to God, words don't seem good enough. That's why we like the silent prayer at services. Nothing gets between us and God. But people also need to express what they feel, and acts go far beyond words. We light candles, lift the wine cup, look at the *mezuzah*, carry the Torah, and sense something more than we can say.

Ritual goes a step beyond poetry. In a poem, we put words together in a special way to say more than we can with plain prose. Often it's about an important feeling and you can understand why we have many religious poems (the Psalms are the most famous). But the feeling can go so deep, no words seem grand enough for it. We may then want to cry or yell or jump up and down. A ritual is an act by which religions help you express such deep feelings about God, yourself, and the Jewish people. Maybe it will help to think about rituals this way—they are religious "poems" we write with acts rather than with words.

Everyone needs some rituals. Jews who love their people and God will want many rituals in their lives. Some they will **42** create for themselves. They will take over many more from their people. When they follow them they will enrich their lives with traditions that go back centuries and which tie them to other Jews and to God.

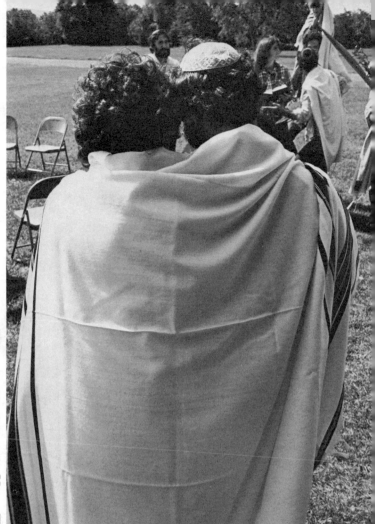

6
Feelings versus Rules: The Case of Praying

IN SOME WAYS Mother's Day is nice. We love our mothers but most of the time don't bother to show it. They are so busy doing things for us or trying to get us to do things that we can end up rushing around or fighting with each other. Taking one day to show our mothers how important they are to us is a good idea.

Only Mother's Day can be a nuisance. You don't "have to" get her a present but if you don't you'd better have a great substitute ready. Since that's easier to say than do, you're stuck with getting her something. Then you wind up with the same old things—perfume or a scarf. Or maybe you're supposed to make dinner, only you'd rather be out taking a bike ride. Since everyone is supposed to be especially friendly on Mother's Day, what happens if you're not in the mood to be lovey-dovey? Maybe we shouldn't try forcing ourselves to do something we're really not in the mood for.

Why do we have to celebrate it anyway? Everyone knows that Mother's Day was invented by business to get us to buy cards and flowers and presents. Unlike National Pickle Week, it caught on and most Americans observe Mother's Day. It's an idea which doesn't always express what we feel, but when next May comes we'll probably observe Mother's Day. I think it is a good example of a problem which bothers us in many areas of our lives.

Should we do things only when we feel like it or because a rule says so? If we wait for the right feeling, things may not get done. If we only follow rules, we'll do things we don't mean.

Rules and feelings don't often work in harmony

The problem is complicated. I love my country, so most of the time when the flag goes by I stand at attention. I have great respect for older people, but sometimes when they come into a room I think I'd rather not be bothered. Yet it also happens that, though I don't feel like it, when I follow the rule and go over to them, I get the feeling that this was the right thing to do. Sometimes doing can bring on feeling. That is one important argument for having rules of what we should do. But it doesn't always work. Think of how bored you've felt as you recited the pledge of allegiance or sat politely as older people talked for what seemed like hours. Sometimes following the rules can give us very unpleasant feelings.

There you are. We ought to do something regularly about things we care about—hence we have rules. But people's feelings don't follow clocks or calendars—hence we often **44** hate rules. Human nature being what it is, there's no good

way around that problem. Learning to balance regular duty with what you feel you want to do now is one of the main tasks in becoming mature.

Feelings are basic to Jewish life,
yet we emphasize following rules

All that is doubly true in religion. It's a Jewish sin to be a hypocrite, someone who does one thing but really means another. A hypocrite is a double sinner. You lie to people and you act as if you can fool God and yourself. Judaism calls on us to be sincere, to "love *Adonai* your God with all your heart, with all your soul, and with all your might." Yet, if pushed to a decision, the Jewish tradition believes more in following the rules than our feelings. Reform Judaism, though it stresses personal freedom, leans more toward doing one's duty than in following one's inclinations. Let's explore this question by studying a tough question: When should we pray? (I hope you'll get some answers to *why* we should pray—another difficult question—in Part Four of this book which talks about God. Here, we're interested only in rules versus feelings. When to pray is the example we're using.)

In some religions what's done at the altar at services has its effect without any involvement by you. Not so in Judaism. The Talmud calls prayer "worship done with the heart." Maimonides gave these instructions for praying: "Prayer without devotion is no prayer at all. . . . So, before starting to pray, a person ought to stop everything for a little while in order to get into a prayerful mood. Then one should pray quietly and with feeling, not like somebody who carries a burden and finally drops it, quite relieved. Even after prayer, one ought to sit quietly for a few minutes and only then go on one's way." Once, when Menachem Mendel, the Chasidic Rebbe of Rymanov, came into the synagogue, on Rosh Hashanah, seeing the many people, he called out to them: "You're a fine crowd of Jews but I can't carry you all on my back. Every one of you must do your own work here!" (How'd you like your rabbi to start the High Holy Day services with that announcement?)

The talmudic approach
to our feelings when we pray

The rabbis of the Talmud call doing an act with proper, inner feelings *kavanah*. They would like us to do all our duties with *kavanah*, but they know this isn't practical. Much of the time we can't bring the proper feelings or *kavanah* to what we're doing. Should we then do nothing until we get *kavanah?* Knowing human nature, the rabbis didn't think so. How much charity would we give, how many sick people would we visit, how often would we study, if we always waited for the right mood? The rabbis encourage us to get *kavanah* but they rarely require it. Rather, they insist that we follow the rules of the Torah. They hope that doing good deeds will, itself, bring on *kavanah.*

One reason for the rabbis' attitude is that many Jewish duties are done by a community, not by just one person alone. Take praying, for example. If it was something you did only on your own, maybe it could be left to your mood (there is such a private prayer in our tradition). However, the main form of Jewish prayer takes place in a community. We gather to remember and renew our people's closeness to God. Mendel, the Chasidic Rebbe of Kotzk, used ideas going back to the Talmud when he taught:

> When a man prays, even if he does so all alone in his house, he ought to unite his heart with the whole people of Israel. In every true Jewish service it is really the community that is praying.

Both things are true: individuals make up the community and one is a Jew by being part of the Jewish people.

There are advantages to doing things with others. One is simple—it's much harder to be selfish when you're with other people. Learning to say and mean the "we," "us," and "our" which are so much a part of Jewish prayers is a great way to stop being self-centered. Then, too, we sometimes "catch" *kavanah* from other people. Pinchas, the Chasidic Rebbe of Koretz, said:

> When a man is singing but cannot lift his soul with his song and another comes who can sing with spirit, then the first will also be able to sing with his soul. Such is the secret bond between the spirits of people.

46 Rules are the way to get to heights we did not know were there

WHAT IS THE
RIGHT THING
TO DO? The rabbis made rules about what prayers we should say to help us learn to pray at a proper level. The Baal Shem Tov,

the founder of the Chasidic movement, put it simply:

> When a man has only an ordinary closeness to God it's best for him to follow the *siddur,* the prayer book, closely. When he reads what is written there and tries to bring as much *kavanah* to it as he can, he'll achieve a much higher level than he could on his own.

Uri, the Chasidic Rebbe of Strelisk, even though he thought people had to find their own ways to God, taught that there were limits to creativity. When King David was in the mood to pray, *he* could write a psalm. *We* can't, Uri noted. But we *can* recite what David wrote. Maybe we can rise to the heights of his prayer.

The rabbis knew that their rule to pray the service three times every day might make the prayers boring. They, therefore, made rules which introduced certain changes into the service. Some things stay pretty much the same. We're glad to be alive and thankful for all God does for us. God is greater than the greatest thing we can imagine and we'll keep trying to keep that feeling fresh so we can serve God properly. (All those praises in the service aren't for God's benefit but for ours. They are there to give us a hint of God's greatness. They are like stretching exercises which help us reach out further and further to God. Generally, we don't like the praises because we want to talk about what *we* want. We come to services to see what we can get God to do for us. We know what we want. Services should also help us understand who God is and what God wants of us.) We are proud to be Jews and we promise to keep the Jewish tradition alive. We hope God will help us speed the day when all people will live in love and peace.

Some things in the service change. There are rules about which words shift from service to service. The music is different from weekday to Shabbat and different again for holy days. New prayers come in for special occasions and others are dropped out. We study the Torah at some services but not at all of them. You're supposed to put your own ideas into the prayer words as you say them. And in the silent prayer, a high point of the service, you are encouraged to pray on your own. All that is part of the Jewish tradition's rules for praying. We try to have rules which make things personal.

Reform Judaism found new ways to meet the modern mood

Reform Jews felt that modern times demanded even more changes in our services. This was the main reason for starting the movement. Every twenty-five years or so we've created a new prayer book. This enables us to put into our prayers the themes that move our generation. Our newest Reform prayer book, *Gates of Prayer,* has many more different services than any previous Reform prayer book—ten for Shabbat evening alone. Yet this hasn't provided enough opportunity for some people to gain *kavanah.* Some Reform Jews, particularly teenagers, have found it useful to create their own services when they meet to pray. They are often deeply appealing because they express what we feel and do so in our language and with our sort of music. That makes them exciting. But praying needs to be a regular part of our lives. God is worth more attention than one or two Friday nights a month. That's the difficulty which these creative services highlight. Nobody can be very creative Shabbat after Shabbat and certainly not year after year. After you've attended ten or twenty creative services, most of them sound pretty much the same. Try using one several times, you'll find it is rarely satisfying. It's not fresh enough to be interesting. It's not old enough to be tradition. To our surprise it turns out that we like having some familiar things in our services. Certain prayers begin to "speak" to us. We get so fond of some tunes we're a little irritated when new ones are put in (until we learn them).

There's our problem. We like things to be new and exciting; we also want them to be old and rich with memories. We care mostly about ourselves and our needs; we also don't want to be selfish, so we're glad we're part of the Jewish people and its old relationship with God. We don't want to be hypocrites just following rules; we also know that if we didn't have rules to follow we wouldn't be as good as we are or do good things regularly.

There's no easy solution to the problem of rules versus feelings. Traditional Judaism puts the emphasis on rules, though it thinks feelings are very important. Reform Judaism tries to make more room for your feelings, but it still stresses doing your Jewish duty. That sets a good balance between my need to have rules and my desire to think for myself.

48

7 Building a Jewish Life: Marriage and a Family

TEVYE, the dairyman of *Fiddler on the Roof,* didn't worry about what he should do with his life. He lived in Anatevka because his parents had lived there or in a *shtetl* like it nearby. He was a dairyman most likely because his father had been one before him. Golda had a marriage arranged for her and she was lucky. Her husband was a decent person. She had children and spent her life caring for her family because that was what Jewish women in Eastern Europe did. She and Tevye were Jewish in the way their parents had been, who, in turn, had done what their parents did before them. Tevye and Golda had a problem but it wasn't how to build a Jewish life. It was how to make a living.

Things had already begun to change for Tevye's daughters. The oldest was like her parents: showing a bit of initiative, she married a man she loved but one who still lived in the old style. The second daughter married a revolutionary and went off to Siberia to live with him. For them, socialism took the place of Judaism. The third daughter married a non-Jew and broke with her parents' way of life. In the century since then, Jews have moved their homes and changed their lives radically.

Few Jews today even live in the same countries in which their great-grandparents were born—still fewer in the same cities. How we shall live a Jewish life is for us more a matter of choice than an established practice.

Two things make our situation more difficult than that of the Jews who, generations back, moved to Babylon or Spain or Poland. First, most modern Jews have stopped believing that God is responsible for all our Jewish laws and customs. They mostly believe—a Reform Jewish idea—that people are as much responsible for them as God is. (See Part Three, Chapters 2 and 5.) This is the reason we feel we have a right to change. This also raises the question of how much we should change. Second, the society into which Jews came, particularly in the United States and Canada, was itself open to new ways of living. It encouraged people to create styles that fit in with democracy. That gives us the question of how much to go along with our neighbors.

We are free to choose much of what we will be as people and as Jews

Growing up today means making a lot of choices. Unlike Tevye and Golda, you don't have to be just like your parents. There are many possibilities in our exciting, if difficult, world. Making your many decisions over the next few years will be one of the most important and somewhat frightening things you will be doing.

That also holds true for your life as a Jew. There's much
you'll want to take over from your family and community style. There's also a lot you'll want to change. Almost all people want a better Jewish education for their children.

Many people wish they had grown up with a richer sense of Jewish ceremony or that their community had been more involved in fighting social injustice. Then, too, America keeps changing and I'm sure you will be reacting to that. Where will you live as an adult? You may wind up in a town where Jewish life is so poor that you'll have to become a leader to make it better.

How do you go about building a Jewish life today? That's too difficult to answer in a few pages. We'd have to discuss all sorts of Jewish duties—such as study, prayer, ritual, ethics, charity, synagogue, community life. Here, let's take just one answer to our question: create a Jewish family. I think it's a good example of how to build a Jewish life. There are many modern questions about it, yet it's important to being a Jew.

We won't spend any time on the first two steps in the process. You need to care about being a Jew and you need to understand the problems we face. Most of this book is about both of them. Now what do we do with our lives?

What does Judaism teach about families?

The next step is to ask: What does Jewish tradition recommend? In our example, the family, it is quite positive. In telling about Adam, the Torah has God saying, "It isn't good for a person to be alone." The story, then, says that just as Adam discovered that he and Eve made a pair so people ought to grow up, leave their parents' home, and get married. (The rabbis of the Talmud playfully interpreted this to mean that God performed Adam's and Eve's marriage ceremony.) In Bible times, fathers arranged their children's marriages. Love, as the *Song of Songs* shows us, was pretty much the same then as now. "Let him kiss me with the kisses of his mouth; for your love is better than wine" (1:2). (The good wife described in Proverbs 31:10–31 sounds like quite a liberated woman to me.)

The rabbis of the Talmud teased bachelors, calling a bachelor only half a man. Some said that a man who has no wife lives without blessing, joy, help, good, peace, and without a defense against sexual temptation—in short, he has no real life. Yet the rabbis knew that not every marriage works out well. Rabbi Yochanan once said, exaggerating to make his point, that it's as hard to arrange a good marriage as it was for God to divide the Sea of Reeds. Jewish law allows for divorce. The rabbis didn't like it—almost no one does. It's sad because two people who came close to finding great happiness have now lost it. And now their children don't have both parents living with them. Still, we are only human. Maybe we made a mistake when we got married. Maybe we changed as we got older and became bad for each other and our children. Whatever the reason, Judaism agrees that divorce is sometimes desirable, particularly if it lets us go on to another marriage and again start building a happy Jewish family.

Of course you don't have to be married to be a Jew. You're still part of a Jewish family, and in a way the Jewish community is your family. The rabbis admit that there are some good reasons why a person might not want to get married. Wanting to devote yourself to the study of the Torah is one. And there were always some people for whom no marriage could be arranged. Single or married, rich or poor, young or old, in a village or a big city, there is always a way to build a Jewish life.

The Jewish concern for children goes back to our earliest days

The Bible and the Talmud recommend marriage because they consider children a great blessing. Bringing up children and teaching them the Torah's ways seemed one of the greatest privileges of being human. It was also a way of keeping the Jewish people alive until the Messiah came. The rabbis thought children were so important that they had a rule: After ten years of marriage with no children, a couple should be divorced. But they also thought that love was so important they hardly ever enforced it.

Jewish family life has a strong sense of children's duties to their parents. One of the Ten Commandments calls for honoring them; another law in the Torah speaks of having proper respect for them. The rabbis considered these responsibilities so serious they compared them to what we must do for God. If you are poor, they excuse you from giving money to the Temple, God's house. But, no matter how poor you are, you must support your parents even if you must go begging from door to door. Incidentally, people who stay single always keep this part of Jewish family life. They still have their relationships with their parents, their brothers and sisters, their other relatives—the unmarried also have Jewish families.

Most important, the Jewish family has a certain mood. It's hard to describe because people's personalities influence it. Still, you can feel it, that subtle mix of duty and respect, of love and being oneself, that Jews admire. I'm not suggesting that "in the good old days" everyone was a saint and no one ever had a fight. Jews know the difference between trying to be good and having to be perfect. (See Part III, Chapter 6.) People are people. I'm saying that if you try to live by our tradition and are part of a good Jewish community you're likely to create a special mood in your family. Listen to what a medieval Jewish father wrote to his son:

> Let your home be a place where quiet and happiness dwell. Instead of harsh words, let a spirit of love, friendship, modesty, gentleness, and respect rule. Don't limit that attitude to your home, but take it with you from there into your dealings in the greater world.

That's not easy to work out day by day, even when people really love one another. Still it shows that what we're seeking in a Jewish family hasn't basically changed in centuries.

The next step is to ask
what we can learn from modern society

Our tradition will teach you much about life. So will the modern world. Many of its good ideas will also raise new problems. I'll mention a few of these for you to think about, and for you, your teachers, and your friends to discuss in detail. Modern culture has taught us to value what makes us individuals. We therefore want to make decisions for ourselves. We don't want an arranged marriage. We want one which comes from love. That's obviously a good idea. But now that we don't have matchmakers how should the Jewish community help people who don't fall in love or who want to be married but can't find someone to marry?

Since we are individuals maybe many of us would be better off staying single or getting divorced. Not everyone can adjust to marriage. The new emphasis on being "true to yourself" has made it harder to stay married these days than it used to be. Years ago, people got married and stayed married, simply because that was what they were supposed to do. Today we have a choice. What complicates it is that, since people marry for love, they expect their spouses to make them happy. But that's difficult, for people living with one another must make demands on each other. If you want only to be loved, if you don't want to take on the responsibilities for the other person that come with love, you can't have a good marriage. Many people today aren't good at marriage, not because they are individuals, but because they are selfish.

People more easily accept the need for a divorce today. In some ways that's right. A bad marriage can't create a good Jewish family. But some people get married as if they were buying a car. They give it a try for a while. Then, when they're dissatisfied, they move on to another model. People are too important to be treated that way. Marriage needs to be a serious matter, though divorce ought to be available when a marriage really can't work.

Another problem comes from the wonderful educational or career possibilities we have. People wait to marry until they receive their degrees or have some years on a job. This is particularly valuable for young women. It frees them from feeling that if they're not married in their twenties their lives are over and it allows them to establish whatever business or professional lives they wish. In our society, unfortunately, the older you are, the harder it is to meet people to marry. If the Jewish community still cares about marriage, how do we help such people? And the divorced? And the widowed?

Are children so important?
54 What rights do family members have?

It has been suggested that some married couples shouldn't have children. Some people aren't suited to raising families and, too, there's a real problem of world population growth. I don't know anyone who takes Judaism seriously who accepts those arguments. It's not the people who are worried about being bad parents who harm children. They know enough to seek help. It's the parents who think they're great—when they're not—who are the real problem. Having children means we'll finally have to face our own problems as adults—that's another reason Judaism wants us to have children. Maybe they'll force us to do something about our immaturity, if only to help our children to be better adults than we are. The argument about world population is even less convincing. For the last forty or fifty years, Jews in the United States and Canada have had so few children that we have had zero population growth. With fewer Jews getting married these days, we need more children just to keep up our population. And since one-third of our people were killed in the Holocaust, perhaps all Jewish families should have at least one extra child to bring our population back up to what it was in the 1940s.

Finally, if everyone is an individual, what about people's rights in the modern Jewish family? Wives may want an outside job or the sharing of family duties or an equal part in making family decisions (money is usually the big problem). Children don't want to be told what they must do merely because they're young or depend on their parents' money. It's a good idea for everyone to have rights but just how do you work that out? Our grandparents didn't know too much about women's or children's rights, and today's family is only beginning to meet this challenge. We have a lot to learn before we create a family style with a good, modern mixture of rights and duties.

Building a modern Jewish life is complex. Not everything that is fashionable today is good, even as not everything in our tradition makes sense to us. Still, the steps we should take are clear: we need to know what we believe as Jews, to identify our modern problems, to explore what our tradition teaches us, and to listen to what the modern world is saying to us. Putting these four things together and creating a way of life from them is more than one person can do. That is one task in which our rabbis and the Jewish community can be of great help to us.

8 Why Don't Most Jews Do Very Much?

SUPPOSE your school has a clean-up day. All classes are called off so people can come and work at the building to make things look better. Everyone is excited. Student government organizes committees and working teams. The art classes do posters and banners. The English classes write news stories and poems. Music and science, the band and the orchestra, all start whipping up enthusiasm. If there are five hundred students in your school how many would you expect to show up? Four hundred? Less? What if only one hundred people showed up? Seventy-five? If only fifty people showed up to wash and paint and rake and plant, I imagine you'd have pretty mixed feelings by the end of the day. It's great to

WHAT IS THE
RIGHT THING
TO DO?

accomplish something important. It's also pretty disgusting that most people won't do one day's work to make their school more beautiful. Where were all those people who talk about community spirit and ecology when the sponges and buckets were being given out?

That's the way it goes in every sort of group. Even when people vote for a certain project, only a minority shows up to work for it. The harder the job, the less the glamour, the longer it takes, the smaller the number that get involved. We can do some things to change this, but mostly we have to face this brutal fact: Most people won't do much—even of what they say they believe should be done. Then why should you be the sucker, doing all the work so they can enjoy it? Even worse, people who did little or nothing are likely to get the credit for getting it done. It's enough to make you swear you'll never get involved in such a project again.

Yet if all the hard workers quit doing things, nothing worthwhile would be accomplished. If you really care about something you've got to work on it, even if other people won't. What if the rebels against Great Britain had quit trying to found the United States? What if black people had given up fighting for their civil rights? What if the Jews of the Soviet Union had thought their efforts to get out of Russia would fail because they were such a tiny minority? Some of the greatest things in history were done by minorities who cared so much they wouldn't give up. I'd agree that if what you were trying to do was nice but not critical—for instance collecting wild flowers to plant in your park—it's better to give up if others won't help. But if it's a noble and lasting ideal—like making democracy work for everyone or working for the Messianic Age—then I hope you will never stop working for it no matter how few other people are there to help.

Jews know how important a minority can be

Being a Jew and creating a worthy Jewish community are some of the grandest ideals human beings have ever thought of. That's one reason there are still people who, after thousands of years, are still working at them. But many Jews don't care about Jewish ideals and it wouldn't be fair not to

57

talk about them. Why don't more Jews do what the Jewish religion asks of them?

Generally ours is not a religious age, and the Jewish people has special reasons for believing and doing relatively little. However we mustn't exaggerate our difficulties. Most of Jewish history shows a struggle between the Jews who were trying to live up to the Torah and those who weren't. The Bible has many stories of Jewish sinfulness, of which the most shocking is the worship of the Golden Calf. The Torah tells the sad tale this way: The Jews at Mt. Sinai, hearing God's own voice give them commandments, were so frightened that they asked Moses to go up Mt. Sinai and have God speak to him alone. When Moses stayed away for a few weeks, they got Aaron to make them an idol—the Golden Calf—to worship. Reading the story, as it is told in the Torah, leaves you with the feeling that people couldn't be more ungrateful and disobedient.

The rabbis of the Talmud often talked about the Golden Calf when they tried to understand why Jews in their day didn't follow the Torah. Much of what they said applies to us. Many people just don't care very much about God or the Torah, certainly not enough to make a sincere effort at being good Jews. People are somewhat selfish and lazy, and it's a bother having to do our Jewish duties. That gives the Evil Urge plenty of room to work. Sometimes the uncaring Jews are a small minority in the community, who don't influence the rest. Then the community—as in Eastern Europe—seems reasonably observant. But it also works the other way around. Most Jews care a little bit but they tend to follow their leaders. If the leaders are the people who don't do much religiously, then the whole community seems unobservant. Fortunately, there's always been a minority of those who did care very deeply—prophets, rabbis, or simply pious Jews—who kept us true to our people's old agreement with God. (See Part Two, Chapter 3, where this is explained.)

58 Coming into the modern world, Jews have not given their energies to Judaism

WHAT IS THE
RIGHT THING
TO DO? In modern times, the Jews who don't care much have pretty well dominated Jewish life. Perhaps that was because all the

things which kept Jews loyal became weaker: they believed less in God and Torah, cared less about the Jewish community, and found the effort it took to be Jewish too much for the reward it gave. By contrast the general society seemed highly exciting. Business and government, community affairs and social activities, these were where they built their lives. Golf and tennis, clothes and appearance, these count in the "real" world. Jewish things—study and blessings, rituals and maybe even ethics—seem small and local compared to the great world of modern culture.

Jews have thrown themselves into every aspect of Western society with extraordinary energy. What they have accomplished as a result of this has been incredible for a group so tiny. The leadership of Jews in industry, culture, and general human betterment is limited mainly by the quiet restrictions there still are against them. We have good reason to be proud of that record. But it has also cost us a great deal. Taking the world so seriously, many Jews turned their backs on Jewish tradition. Some complained about it, saying it was old-fashioned and outdated, that it put barriers between people where it should be building bridges. Some were simply too busy for it. Some wanted to run away from their people.

There are still some such Jews around. They are easily seen among adults. They're the Jews who have energy for every troubled group in America or Africa but none for other Jews. They are always busy learning some new craft, like weaving or Chinese low-fat cooking, but they never have time to study about Judaism. They love going to other people's celebrations, midnight Mass or a Zen tea ceremony, but they are bored by Jewish festivals and rituals. There's something odd about such Jews. Underneath it all, I'd guess they don't like the fact that they're Jewish. That's more than just a shame. It's pretty sad. They're denying an important part of themselves and missing the satisfaction which comes from keeping this old, great Jewish people alive and well.

Fortunately most Jews aren't like that. They are rather proud of being Jewish. Other Americans talk about their Polish or Irish heritage and Jews easily discuss Jewish foods and expressions and activities. They enjoy having their non-Jewish neighbors join their fun at a Seder or at a wedding celebration. For all our complaining, many of us get certain pleasures out of Jewish life (one of which is complaining about it). We say services are boring, but every once in a while we like being there—hearing the old words, singing the familiar songs, and being with our community. Our fund-raising affairs take too much of our time and keep asking us for too much money, but we also like being part of an involved, caring Jewish community. And, if we have built ritual and prayer into our Jewish life at home, we find them the background of everything we do.

I think that's how many Jews feel today. Being Jewish is of some importance to them so there are some Jewish things they want to do and enjoy doing regularly. Compared to how most American Jews felt twenty years ago, we've made great progress.

But compared to the Jewish ideal, things are pretty bad. You know how little many Jews care or do or know. You've seen them most of your life. That's what exists. More important is what you think you ought to do about it. You can join those who are fed up with being Jewish and want to run away from it. You can become part of the majority of Jews who care a little and do something about being a Jew. That's not bad, for at least your heritage will be a part of your life. But that won't change things.

The rise of a new minority in our Jewish community

There is one other possibility. There is a minority in our Jewish community today—as there has always been—which truly cares about Judaism and is making a strong effort to live it in a modern way. The rise of this minority of concerned Jews is the most exciting thing about Jewish life these days. They are people of every age group who have discovered that being a Jew is much more important to them than they once thought. They now want to know what it truly means to be a modern Jew. More important, they are asking how they can make their Jewishness a part of their lives. They try new ways of celebrating Shabbat; they meet with friends for

celebration or study; they learn to pray or even meditate in a mystic Jewish style. They search, as liberal Jews always have, for the right way to combine Jewish tradition with the modern world. This concerned minority feels that, after working so hard for so long at being modern, we now need to adjust our balance and to be more Jewish.

I don't know if this minority will ever be large enough to influence the rest of the Jewish community. Maybe some of their observances are only fads. Still there have been such devoted Jews in every generation. They are the ones who, particularly in difficult times, have kept our people alive and true to their heritage.

Is this the kind of Jew you want to be?

I hope you will want to be part of that minority. We need every serious Jew we can find. But you're probably going to have to do it pretty much on your own. Your friends are likely to find it a little odd that you're interested in Jewish things. The world won't give you any rewards. People respect sincere religion but consider it somewhat peculiar. You may not even get much encouragement from Jewish organizations in your community. Most of them are geared to members who don't want to do too much. Your rabbi will probably be of some help—but a rabbi isn't the usual American Jew. Chances are, to be a deeply caring Jew today, you'll have to start on your own way, based on your own deep feelings. It can be lonely. It can leave you feeling like quite a minority indeed. Yet, if you care deeply enough and refuse to give up trying to be a good, modern Jew, you'll soon see how much Judaism can give you. You'll also find some few other Jews who care as you do. That is the beginning of a true Jewish community. Everything we care about in Jewish life starts with such Jews. I hope you will be one of them all your life.

Part Two
THE JEWS
AND THEIR
DREAMS

1. How Did Judaism Start?
2. What Sort of Group Are the Jews?
3. Are We a Chosen People?
4. What Do We Expect in the Messianic Age?
5. What Does the State of Israel Mean to Jews?
6. Why Do Jews Have to Be Different?
7. Who Is a "Good Jew"?

1 How Did Judaism Start?

A TEASER: Why is it true to say that Judaism started only about 150 years ago?

An objection: That sounds false. Abraham and Moses, Elijah and Jeremiah, Johanan ben Zakkai and Akiba, Maimonides and the Baal Shem Tov lived many centuries ago. Surely they believed in and taught Judaism.

The solution: The statement is true; but, like so many comments that get people excited, it is only half-true. The whole truth is that the word "Judaism" became widely used only in the early 1800s. You won't find it in the great Jewish books written before then.

That should make clear what our real questions probably

64

**THE JEWS AND
THEIR DREAMS**

are: How did the Jewish religion get started? And, related to it, where did the Jews come from? We'll spend this chapter talking about those questions. But I began with my teaser because I also want to say something about how the Jewish religion came to be called Juda-ism—the "ism" of the Jews.

The earliest archeological find which mentions the Jews comes long after they must have gotten started. It is on a stone with the victory hymn of Merneptah, an Egyptian pharaoh. Scholars date him about 1225 B.C.E. In the course of boasting about Merneptah's victories the poem says, "Israel is laid waste. His people no longer exists." Since, according to this poem, Israel was "destroyed" as early as 1225 B.C.E., it had to have existed for a long while before. That's as far back as modern history can definitely trace the Jews. (In an odd way, this Egyptian poem tells you something about Jewish history from its earliest centuries. People were always trying to wipe out the Jews. But the Jews live on.)

The traditional version
of how our religion got started

The Bible says our tradition began with Abraham. God came to him and asked him to serve God in special ways. In turn, God promised to make Abraham's family and descendants a mighty nation, to give them a land, and to protect them. (Abraham's story is good reading—Genesis, Chapters 12-23.) However, people forget that the Bible doesn't start with Abraham. He only appears many years after the world was created. To understand him and the Jews as the writers of the Bible did, you need to remember what went on before him.

The first two people God created (and put in the Garden of Eden) broke God's command to them. Those who came later weren't much better. God, wanting good people, brought a flood that destroyed everyone but Noah and his family. Despite this, the people who came later also defied God and, when they built the Tower at Babel, God had to act again.

Imagine, as best you can, God's problem as the Bible stories express it. God wants people to be good. But God made people free, not like other animals who follow their instincts. If you're free to do good, you're free to do evil. People often use their freedom to disobey God—for instance Cain, the murderer, or the wicked citizens of Sodom and Gomorrah. That is God's "problem": How to let people be free but get them to follow God's laws. Since another flood wouldn't change things, God tried a new approach. God started a people that will be especially loyal and obedient. Through this people everyone will get to know about God and finally come to serve God. That's how our religion began, says the Bible. God started it. Abraham didn't think it up while playing in his father's idol store—that's a story of the rabbis. We enjoy the story because modern people prefer talking about what *we* do rather than what *God* does. But as long as people believed the Bible was God's book (see Part Three, Chapter 1), their answer to the origin of the Jews was that God did it. Abraham is honored because he had the genius to know it was God "talking" and to do what God "said." (On such words, see Part Three, Chapter 2.)

The liberal approach
grows out of what we know of history

Liberal Jews aren't satisfied with "God did it." We want to know what part people played in what happened. We know more about how people act than how God does things, so we feel more certain explaining things first by what people probably did and, only then, saying where God came into it. Starting from what we know about human nature and history how did Judaism get started?

From the Bible and archeology we'd guess that the origin of the Jews—more properly, the Hebrews—goes back to about 2000 B.C.E. The stories of Abraham, Isaac, and Jacob, though they probably got mixed up as they were told over the centuries, fit into what we know of the ancient Near East. The Hebrews were one of the peoples of that area.

They apparently didn't become a full nation until after their experience in Egypt. The ancient records of Egypt tell a lot about its history, but they say nothing about Hebrew slavery, plagues, or the exodus of a great people from Egypt. Some scholars suggest that only some of the Hebrews were in Egypt, particularly the tribes connected with Joseph, the tribes of Ephraim and Menasseh. The exodus of such a small group wouldn't bother the Egyptians. Yet it might have had so great a religious impact on all the other Hebrews, it grew into the story of the founding of the whole nation.

We know even less about what "really" happened at Mt. Sinai. (That's where the Bible says our religion truly began. There, God "gave" the Torah and the Hebrew people agreed to serve God in a specially close way.) From what we know of other peoples it's not difficult to imagine what took place. A group of people who had been through a great event—leaving Egypt—believed that God had helped them become free. So they dedicated themselves as a people to serve God. Much of what we're told in the Torah sounds reasonable, even if it doesn't make the early Hebrews look very good — the Golden Calf story and all those arguments with Moses. We have no sources outside the Bible by which to check any of this. We just have to try to figure out from what we know of history what probably happened and how people thousands of years ago would have understood and told about it.

There is one interesting bit of data that we don't quite know what to do with. A number of documents of the 1400s and 1300s B.C.E. from this area mention a group called the Habiru. Some scholars say that this is the same word as *Hebrew*—which it certainly looks like in English—though other scholars disagree. Since the group is in a number of places about the time of the Exodus, one theory says the Habiru are the originators of the Hebrews. Many scholars disagree. Their reasons? The Habiru aren't a family-based group with their own language. They are a certain class of workers, particularly hired warriors. That's far from what the Bible tells us about the early Hebrews. I think the Habiru theory still needs a lot more proof to be convincing.

How did the unique religion of the Jews begin?

Now let's turn to the start of the Jewish religion and how it developed ideas about God and people which were radically different from those of their neighbors. Some years back it seemed sensible to say that ideas evolved the way plants and animals did. Maybe religion just naturally grew from the primitive to the more advanced, from many gods to few gods to one God. It sounds logical, but when we study the history of religions we find that it simply didn't work that way. Besides, if evolving to one God was so natural, why did only the Hebrews do it? And why—for centuries—did everyone else continue worshiping idols? In fact, in the few other places in the world where something like the belief in one God does appear, it comes as a sudden break with the past and not out of gradual growth and change.

Another suggestion fascinated many people (including Sigmund Freud who wrote a book about it). Perhaps Moses got the idea of one God from the unusual religion of the Egyptian Pharaoh Amenhotep IV, also known as Ikhnaton. Most scholars today reject the idea. We can't easily connect Moses with this pharaoh whose religion died with him. Then, too, there's quite a difference between Ikhnaton's worship of only the sun-disc—his one god—and Moses' sense of God. Besides, if Moses had gotten his idea from Ikhnaton's worship of the sun-disc, it still wouldn't really answer our question. For, if the answer was reasonable, we'd then want to know where Ikhnaton got *his* revolutionary religion.

Is it modern to speak of religious geniuses?

There was a small scholarly fuss a few years back when one of the great scholars of Near-Eastern literature, E. A. Speiser, wrote a commentary on the Book of Genesis. Though he was a historian, Speiser felt that, when all was said and done, historical reasons couldn't really explain where someone like Abraham came from. Speiser figured that Abraham was simply one of those geniuses who comes along every once in a while in human history and changes things. He also felt that when it comes to such unusual people we have to admit that we don't know why they come up with ideas no one else has. Some scholars, however, felt that this was a bit too "religious" for the way modern people ought to study history.

I don't know how we can settle that question, but I don't see why there couldn't have been geniuses then even as there are today. Of course, I think God "spoke" to people then as God does today (see Part Three, Chapter 2). I can even imagine a little of what it must have been like for someone who grew up as an idol-worshiper to suddenly get a sense that God was really one and not many. Maybe you can too. But we shouldn't

68

THE JEWS AND
THEIR DREAMS

just concentrate on how a genius like Abraham got his great ideas. There's something else very important to starting a religion: people to carry on the founder's beliefs. In our religion, we give a lot of credit to the many Jews who came after Abraham. Once in a while they slipped into worshiping idols but, unlike what happened elsewhere when geniuses may have taught about one God, the whole Jewish people stayed faithful to God. It's a bit of an exaggeration, but I think the Jewish people should get almost as much credit as Abraham does for starting our religion. *He* may have gotten the idea but *they* kept it alive.

That's about as much as we can say now about the beginning of the Jewish people and its faith. Perhaps new discoveries of ancient writings will one day give us a better idea of what happened. When they do, liberal Jews feel they'll only help us appreciate our religion more. We know Judaism makes sense. So if we have to change our ideas about how it started that won't bother us. Liberal Jews are free to change their ideas as their knowledge grows. That's one of the joys of our approach to Judaism.

The curious way the Torah became an "ism"

Now let me say something about the word *"Judaism."* It came into common use in the early 1800s when Jews were gaining their freedom in various countries in Western Europe. These nations only allowed religions like Catholicism and Protestantism to exist as separate groups. So the Jews said they, too, were a "religion." In that period, too, religions were often called "isms." My dictionary defines an "ism" as meaning "a distinctive doctrine, cause, theory, or system." Good examples of that usage are communism and fascism. They are theories of politics that people follow. So when you call a religion an "ism" you can easily give the impression that it's mainly a system of ideas. Mostly religions are not systems of ideas—here are two examples. Moslems object to the term "Mohammedanism" because they say they do not have a doctrine, an "ism," thought up by Mohammed. He was a prophet, inspired by God to bring people to the proper worship of God. They call their religion "Islam" which means "full religious obedience to God." So, too, Hinduism is less a religious theory than many families of religion which are found in India.

Being a Jew is a lot more than believing in an "ism." To us, life is more important than ideas. In our tradition, doing things with other members of our people has meant more than what one did in one's head privately. A feeling for God, a concern for other Jews, a delight in our tradition, an insistence on being a fine person and a good Jew are not really an "ism." To say we believe in Judaism is sometimes used as an excuse to turn our rich, folk religious heritage into a few ideas or a mere philosophy. Our tradition has many more sides to it than that. When people ask me my religion, I'd be happier if I could say "I follow the Torah in a modern way." Since most people would find that answer strange, I'll go on using the word "Judaism." But I wanted you to know how the word got started and why I'm looking for a better term for our tradition. I want to talk about this in another way in the next chapter.

2 What Sort of Group Are the Jews?

FACT: Many Jews say they don't believe in Judaism and don't belong to any religious institution. Fact: The State of Israel calls itself a "Jewish state" but it's not a religious state (run by its rabbis) and the majority of its people say they are not religious. Fact: Jews have lots of things that we don't normally associate with a religion—for example, foods, jokes, even languages (Yiddish and Ladino as well as Hebrew).

I guess that's why people keep asking what sort of group the Jews are. The obvious answer—a religious group— somehow doesn't explain all the facts. Let's spend this chapter exploring some of the terms we might use to describe the Jews and why none of them is quite right.

The Bible isn't much help here. It has no word for "religion" and many of its books—about kingdoms and wars, politics and society—don't seem "religious." When the Bible does talk about the Jews it treats them like the other "nations" of the Near East: the Moabites, the Edomites, the Amalekites, and so forth. These people all had their own language, a land, a history, and thus a sense that they were a distinctive group. They also usually had their own sort of religion. Sometimes (the Jews included), they had their own king; sometimes they were part of someone else's country. (In the 400s B.C.E., the Jews were part of the Persian Empire.) Of course, even in the Bible the Jews were different. They were trying to serve the one God of all the universe. The problem of Jews being like other groups and yet different from them goes back that far.

The earliest attempts to explain who the Jews are

In Roman times, with large numbers of Jews living among non-Jews, we get the first efforts by Jews to explain their group to other people. About the year 40 C.E. the Jewish philosopher Philo, who lived in the large Jewish section of Alexandria, Egypt, went to Rome. He was trying to get the emperor to stop the local anti-Semites who kept rioting and harming the Jews. Philo wrote a book about that and in the course of it talks about the Jews. He calls Jerusalem his "native city" (I guess he means his "Rome") and talks of the "colonies" which it has sent all over the civilized world. Philo speaks in what we call "national" terms. To him, the Jews are part of a city-nation, like the Rome-ans are. Roman law regularly calls them "Judeans," people from the province of Judea. (So in German they are "Juden," pronounced "Yuden," from which comes the name of the language, Yiddish. In English, the "d" dropped out of "Jude" leaving our word "Jew.")

Philo is proud of the unique beliefs his nation has, but in his day it wouldn't have made sense to talk about Jews as a "religion." Another Jewish writer, about forty years later, was Josephus. He received a Roman pension for going over to the Roman side during the Jewish rebellion which ended in the destruction of the Temple. Living on a small estate north of Rome, he wrote books explaining the history of the Jews to Roman readers. What he stresses most about the Jewish "nation" is that their laws unite them the world over. Without any ruler to force them to obey these rules, Jews everywhere follow the same law. In Roman days, nation and religion were so closely united that you didn't need to speak much about your special practices once you mentioned where you were from.

The problems with saying
we are a national group

Yet if the Jews are a nation why didn't they die out when they lost their state and, in due course, when almost all of them left their country? They had even stopped speaking Hebrew and started using Aramaic, a cousin language, long before that. They then gave up Aramaic for the languages of the peoples among whom they came to live. All Jews no longer had a common state or land or language. They were, you would think, no longer a nation but a religious group. Yet they kept their "national" side alive. Hebrew was their language of prayer and scholarship. They prayed each day for a return to Jerusalem and the Land of Israel. Even the religious calendar was "national." If you live in a northern city it may not yet be springtime in your area when Passover comes, but it is in the Land of Israel. (Can you imagine what it's like on the other side of the Equator, say, in Australia or Brazil, to have Passover come out in the fall?) The peoples among whom Jews lived also kept them separate. For many centuries, Jews had their own courts, collected taxes themselves for the government, and from 1500 c.e. on lived apart in ghettos or in *Shtetls.*

When Jews got to be citizens
they called their way of life religion

You probably recall that, early in the nineteenth century, Jews in Western Europe began to get full rights. Some countries decided to be "secular," that is, they now would not be officially Christian. Thus, Jews could, for the first time, be citizens. They could keep separate as a religion if they wished to as long as they were loyal to their country. Now, after hundreds of years of hatred and separation, these countries asked the Jews a major question: Are you a "nation" of your own or are you a religious group? Napoleon, remember, even called a Great Sanhedrin of French Jews together to give him an official answer to that question. The Sanhedrin replied: The Torah's "political laws no longer apply" when the Jews don't live in the Land of Israel and have their own king. In France, only the "religious" laws are in effect. That has been the main answer of Jews in free and democratic countries ever since: The Jews are a religious group.

The French Sanhedrin met in 1807, before the Reform movement began. But the idea that Jews are not a nation and are only a religious group has been closely associated with Reform Judaism. I imagine that is because Reform Jews were the first to give up many of the old "national" Jewish practices. You can see this plainly in the first great American statement about Reform Judaism, the Pittsburgh Platform of 1885. It says that many of the laws of the Torah were meant for the Land of Israel and modern Jews should only observe those laws which are still spiritually uplifting.

"Religion" seemed a splendid word to use to describe what tied the Jews together. Was not the Bible the great Jewish book? Had not a midrash said, "A Jew is not an alien anywhere, for wherever he goes his God goes with him"? Did not Saadiah Gaon, the medieval Jewish philosopher, call the Torah our portable homeland? Has anything been more central to Jewish history over the ages than God and the way of life which our people "received" from God?

Are we perhaps a race?

To say Judaism is a religion ignores too much of Jewish life. It makes the Jews just another church group. That's wrong, we know, but just what the Jews are, then, still needs to be made clear. Early in our century, science seemed to solve this problem—and instead made a horrible blunder. Scientists suggested that what makes a group of people have a different way of life from other groups is their race. There was something in people's biology, their very life stuff, that produced their separate life styles. Race could be defined, as in skin colors or head shapes. Excited by the new findings and not having many other ideas about groups to work with, people began to apply the word "race" to all sorts of groups, like the Jews (only one group among several known as Semites) and fair, blue-eyed Germans (mislabeled "Aryans" by Adolf Hitler). At first it seemed harmless enough. But anti-Semites seized on it. They said Jews were a race and an inferior one. They were a biological menace to decent people so the world needed to get rid of them. Under Hitler that idea gained power. The result was the Holocaust. Since then the idea of a Jewish "race" has seemed utterly repugnant.

Don't be surprised, then, if books of fifty or seventy-five years ago call our people a race or speak of Jewish "blood." It once seemed a good, scientific explanation of what made the Jews a special group. Few ever dreamed it would turn into an excuse for mass murder. Now it is clear there never was any sound evidence to show that the Jews were a race and the idea is rejected by social scientists.

Perhaps we are really more a nation than a religion

Another idea of that period is helpful in explaining what sort of group Jews are. It is Zionism, the belief that the Jews are essentially a "nation." The Zionists felt that as long as Jews thought of themselves only as a religion they wouldn't organize, worldwide, to change the harsh conditions under which many Jews lived. In a country run by Jews they'd create a decent life for themselves. This would also ease the situation for Jews in trouble elsewhere who could always go to a Jewish country if they wanted to. Besides, there was much in Jewish life that had always been "national." But the national aspect of Jewish life had grown smaller once Jews left their country and became mostly a religious group. If Jews went back to their homeland they could take up all the other elements of being a Jewish nation, including, for those who wanted it, living the Jewish religion in its original home.

The theory of Zionism was too demanding for most Jews. From 1900 to 1930 hundreds of thousands of Jews came to the United States, but only tens of thousands went to Palestine, as it was called before the State of Israel. During the Holocaust, the Western countries refused to take in many Jews. Even after World War II, when the Western world knew about Hitler's mass destruction, it did little better. It was then that Jews immigrated to Palestine in large numbers, eventually leading to the establishment of the State of Israel. Can we then say that the old Zionist theory has been proved, that the Jews really are a nation?

How the national and the religious sides of being a Jew are intermixed

North American Jews do not think so. A nation is largely a political group and our ties to the State of Israel aren't political. Our political loyalty goes to the United States or Canada, not to the State of Israel. Equally important, we think of ourselves, our history, and our tradition as mainly religious.

Though the Israelis say they are only a political group, even they can't get rid of the religious side of the Jews. The Bible is their great national book and its real hero is God, not the Jews. Their calendar is the religious one, so they take Rosh Hashanah and Yom Kippur very seriously though there's nothing national about them.

Even their courts can't separate Jewish nationality and religion. Here are two famous court cases: the first dealt with a Jew who had converted to Christianity and asked to immigrate to the State of Israel under the law which says all Jews have this right. If being a Jew is a matter of "nationality," despite his Christian belief, he thought he had the right to immigrate. The Israeli court turned him down on the grounds that most Jews consider conversion to another religion as leaving the Jewish community. The second case had to do with the Israeli law in which all people are registered by nation and religion, thus providing for Israeli citizens who are Christian or Moslem. An Israeli Jew who said he was an atheist wanted his child registered as a Jew by nationality but without any religion. The court turned him down, too, apparently because if you are part of the Jewish people then you are part of the Jewish religion unless you convert to another one.

Trying to define
the special mixture we call the Jews

Probably the only good way of understanding the Jews is to say that we are a mixture of a religious and a national group. Fortunately there is a good term today that says much of this: ethnic group. To say you are part of an ethnic group—for instance, Italian, Irish, Chinese, or Black—means that you have some special cultural background, generally related to the country your family comes from. You can still be a good American or Canadian while enjoying your ethnic roots. The chances are that other people will enjoy eating some of your special foods and having fun at some of your group's celebrations. If you called your group a "nation," people would think you weren't really a citizen of that other country. (All of which is a little funny because "ethnic" comes from the Greek work "ethnos" which means nation.) Then why don't we simply call the Jews an ethnic group? We don't because that term doesn't show the importance of religion to the Jews. The Jews have a religion which is theirs alone. If there are no Jews, there is no Judaism.

Let's compare the Jews and the Armenians in order to see what I mean by this. The Jews and the Armenians both come from the Near East; many Armenians have left their homeland yet are loyal to their people; much of Armenian culture centers around their religion; the Armenians have been viciously persecuted by the Turks and went through a holocaust of their own about sixty years ago. The Armenians are Christians, of their own sort, to be sure, but not the only Christians in the world. Their way of being Christian is part of their ethnic life—but Christianity and being an Armenian aren't as connected as are Judaism and being a Jew.

Ethnic and religious:
one word won't do for the Jews

We are, it turns out, an odd mixture of religion and ethnic group. Think how people become Jews. In most cases it is through birth. That's hardly a religious act but it's normal for an ethnic group. To be Scottish, you don't have to "believe" in Scotland, you just have to be born into a Scottish family. But no matter where you were born you can convert to Judaism and you do that because, after studying it, you believe in Judaism. That's obviously religious and not ethnic. (Incidentally, a convert is as much a Jew as any born Jew. This bothers some Jews but Jewish law is absolutely clear on this. Any Jew who complains about converts does so not out of Jewish tradition but out of plain prejudice.) The children of a convert are born Jewish. That's a religious-ethnic mix, I guess, and that's what we are.

Another thing you might think about is a good name for our sort of people. If there were many such groups in the world we'd have a name for them. But there aren't, so we have to make do with words like "religion" or "ethnic group" which are almost, but not quite, right. I've tried to think up a good name but all I've come up with is "relethnic" or "ethnigious" groups. Do you have any good ideas about this?

3 Are We a Chosen People?

SUPPOSE you are honored with an *aliyah*. You go up (the meaning of *aliyah*) to the *bimah*, the raised platform from which the Torah scroll is read. Then you say the same blessing that's been said for 2,000 years, "Blessed are You, Lord, our God, Ruler of the universe, who chose us from among all peoples and gave us the Torah. Blessed are You, Lord, who gives Torah."

Read with the wrong intonation, that could sound as if Jews thought everyone else was inferior: "Chose US from among all peoples." But if read rather humbly, the blessing could mean: How wonderful that of all the peoples in the world ours created the Bible. Which of those two moods is right is the problem for the Jewish ideas of "the chosen people."

Being chosen generally means getting a prize. What the Jews got, as the blessing makes clear, is the Torah. That's not very much like being picked to be Miss America or winning a lottery. Instead of receiving something enjoyable, the Jews received a book of laws and advice. It wasn't for their pleasure. It gave them new responsibilities. So the Torah is hardly the kind of gift that most people really want. In an imaginative story in the Talmud, the rabbis tell how God couldn't find anyone to take the Torah. Nobody wanted to follow its rules. The story is somewhat prejudiced against the Romans and other nations but it certainly shows what the rabbis thought the Jews were chosen for: to do commandments.

Our tradition taught
God's love for everyone

God's "choosing" the Jews to get the Torah doesn't mean God is not interested in other people. The Bible and Talmud are clear: you don't have to be a Jew in order to know God. (That's why sending out missionaries has never been important to Judaism, even though we accept people who want to become Jews.) The key here is the "agreement" God made with Noah after the flood. Chapters 8 and 9 of Genesis put it this way: God "promised" that there would be no more floods to destroy the earth, that after it rained there would be a rainbow in the sky as a reminder the promise was being kept, and God gave Noah permission to stop being a vegetarian (like Adam) and to eat meat. God also gave Noah some commands, one of which is connected with his meat-eating. Noah shouldn't eat "meat with its life in it, which is the blood in it." (See Part Three, Chapter 4, where I discuss how "true" such stories are.)

This might be pretty dull except that Noah, like Adam, stands for all humanity. The Bible is saying that all human beings, not just the Jews, have a kind of "Torah." They have their own connection with God. One rabbinic statement makes the idea perfectly plain: "Righteous people among the

Gentiles have a full share in the life of the world-to-come."
That is still Jewish teaching today.

The rabbis of the Talmud had a sort of mathematical way of describing the religious difference between non-Jews and Jews. They figured the children of Noah (humanity) had seven commandments as part of God's agreement or covenant with Noah. How they found them in the Genesis story isn't clear but they generally agreed on these: (1) respect for God, (2) no idol-worship, (3) no murder, (4) no stealing, (5) no sexual sins, (6) setting up good courts, and (7) not eating meat cut from a living animal. But the rabbis said the Torah gave Jews 613 basic commandments. (Rabbi Simlai used this number and, although we don't know where he got it from, it's been used ever since.) So being chosen meant that the Jews had 606 more rules to follow—and, of course, all the hundreds of laws that grew out of the basic ones.

Being chosen doesn't mean superiority or suffering

Two more points are important. One is that being "chosen" didn't make the Jews feel they were superior to other peoples. That would be a sin at any time, since God "made" and "loves" everyone. It's especially horrible today because the Nazis said the Germans were a superior race and used that as an excuse to kill Jews and other groups. Nothing in the Jewish religion should ever sound like something Hitler said. The second point is that being chosen gave the Jews more duties. When they didn't perform their duties they would be punished. That's one of the chief lessons of the prophets. Being "chosen" by God doesn't mean freedom to do evil. Amos, the first prophet to write a book said, "Hear this word which the Lord spoke against you, O Children of Israel. . . . You only have I known of all the families of the earth. Therefore I will punish you for your sins" (Amos 3:2).

That leads us to the other problem: Jewish suffering. The Jews have had more trouble than most other peoples in history. It almost seems as if we were chosen to suffer. A Yiddish saying makes a bitter joke about it: "You chose us from among all peoples? So why did you have to pick on us?" The real problem here is the difference between the Jewish and the Christian attitudes toward suffering. In classic Christianity Jesus shows his obedience to God and his love for humanity by letting himself be crucified. Jesus, hanging on the cross (the crucifix), becomes a major symbol for such Christians. Suffering becomes an important way of serving God. Jews don't see suffering as an especially good way to serve God. Judaism doesn't encourage people to be hermits or not to marry or to beat themselves in order to be more holy. Besides, there's enough pain in most people's lives—they don't have to go looking for more. Of course, when suffering cannot be avoided, we bear it as bravely as we can and try to learn from it. Often we can see God "teaching" us something. (Sometimes, as in the case of the Holocaust, we can't come up with much of an answer. See Part Four, Chapter 5.) Mostly, though, our suffering has taught us how important it is for people to do good and to see how often they do evil. One other thing we know. We Jews weren't chosen to give other people an excuse to abuse us. We are Jews to remind them and everyone that there is a God and we should all be doing good.

With today's respect for all people, chosenness is a difficult idea

Modern Jews often are troubled by the idea of the chosen people. They think it says too much about God and has too little respect for non-Jews.

"Choosing" seems to make God "do" more than we can easily understand. Usually when we say God "does" something we are talking about what we feel inside ourselves. That's how we explain God "speaking" to us or "forgiving" us. God's "choosing" seems to point, not to our feeling for God, but to an act God did. That's difficult for many people to believe. God's "choosing the Jews" is even more disturbing. It says that God set up the difference between Jews and other people by giving us the Torah. It wasn't because of anything special about the Jews or what we did. (Remember, the story about Abraham breaking the idols is from the rabbis. Some of them also seem to have thought that choosing makes God appear to be unfair.) God should love everyone and not have a particular people as His favorite. This is one reason some modern Jews want to have a new idea of chosenness.

When the Bible and the Talmud were written, if you weren't a Jew you were an idol-worshiper. The Jews were the only people around who believed in God and, of course, they felt different from their neighbors. That is certainly not true today. In the United States and Canada, most Jews find themselves very much like their non-Jewish neighbors. And despite strange languages and customs in other parts of the world, we now know that people everywhere are basically alike. This makes it even more difficult for us to say that God made us different from all other people by choosing us to get the Torah.

Five modern ways
of looking at the Jews being chosen

With such strong arguments against the Jews being the chosen people, it won't surprise you to hear that we have several different modern ways of thinking about our people and God. Here are five viewpoints about chosenness our thinkers suggested:

Some people say we must *give up the idea* because it's too undemocratic. As long as people say God set them aside from others, there will be religious hatred. Instead, we should accept today's moral ideal that all people are equal. Besides, Jews don't need to say God "chose us" in order to say how good it is to be a Jew. We can love our people and enjoy its special ways without having to say God commanded them. We can say our people "chooses" to live by the highest standards, for every people ought to do that.

Some say that *all peoples are "chosen"* and make some contribution to humankind. If we knew more about peoples other than those of Europe we'd soon see how special they all are. Even in the history we know, the Greeks teach beauty, the Romans teach government, and the Hebrews teach religion. Why some peoples should make more important contributions than others we don't know. But that's natural and one can see it in every field of activity, just as one person can make a more important contribution than another.

Some people with this view want to make certain we don't forget how extraordinary the record of the Jews is. We've survived despite great persecution. We've gone on making major contributions to civilization. Given freedom and opportunity, we've greatly enriched modern culture . . . just think of all our writers, painters, musicians, and professors. And no group in the world comes close to our record of producing Nobel Prize winners. We are certainly an exceptional and extraordinary people.

Some feel the previous views leave God out of human experience altogether. If God is real we should consider how people came to find God, or, more precisely, *how they came to "choose" to accept and follow God.* As life moved from the animal to the truly human, creatures appeared that became capable of personal, conscious feeling for God. Mostly that feeling was expressed by idolatry or in nature worship. On rare occasions it became a major religion with a well-developed sense of God. But only in one case did a whole people choose to base its *ethnic* life on its consciousness of the one, commanding God. The people of Israel was this "choosing people." To the extent that God is "behind" what happens in history, we may also say that God "chose" the Jews. Since the Jews and God have been linked so closely for centuries, even though other peoples have come to know God, the Jews will always be special in human history.

Some Jews feel
that God sometimes is especially close

Some take that a step further and try to say something about what God "did." Compare it to your experience with those you love. When you feel especially close to people it's probably half because you know that they feel good being with you. They don't even have to talk. There's something about taking a walk together, or going to a ball game, or working on a project, that gives you the sense they feel that way. But you can't force that feeling to come just because you want to feel loved. Even with a best friend or a parent, you can't make every time special. Sometimes that great sense of being together is there, but both of you have to be ready for it. Something like that happens with God. People not only have to be there for God but God has to "be there" for them. In that sense, God "does" something and that's what God "chooses" means. At Sinai and again and again in Bible and later times, *God has "been there,"* not always, but often, *when our people searched for God.*

And some say we just ought to admit that we *can't understand everything God does.* We just have to accept some things. People are important, but God is "in charge" of history. Other peoples today may be beginning to know and serve God but that does not change the 4,000 years in which the Jews, alone, had the Torah and were loyal to God through the Torah. And, until the Messiah comes, God needs a people dedicated to God—above all and for all times. That is what we mean when we say we are God's "chosen" people.

Now you have learned about five ways we modern Jews use to talk about our "chosenness." I hope they will help you think about what it will mean to you when next you say, "Who chose us from among all peoples and gave us the Torah."

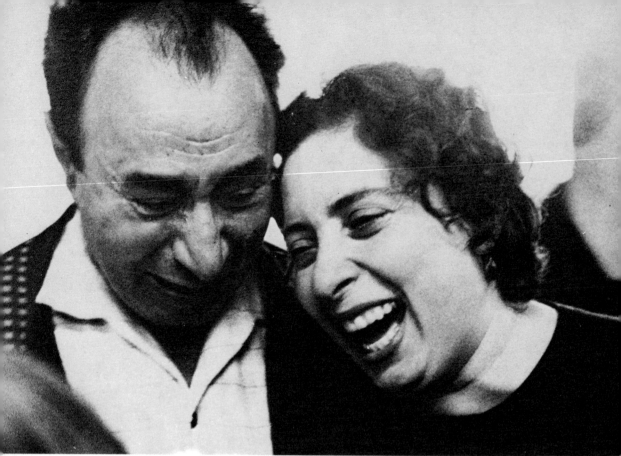

4 What Do We Expect in the Messianic Age?

HAVE you ever wanted something to be perfect, a birthday party, a picnic, a vacation? Most of the time it doesn't quite work out as you hoped. Even if it was good, it could have been better. If it was bad you are doubly disappointed because you expected so much; even what was nice didn't seem like much. Once in a while, though, things do work out just right and we say, "It was perfect." It's a great feeling. No wonder we all wish it happened more often.

Wouldn't it be wonderful if everything were perfect for everybody all the time? I'd say that was the heart of the

Jewish hope for the coming of the Messianic Age. Though this is one of the ideas people most connect with Judaism, we don't know too much about how it started. However, we do know it begins in the Bible. There have been many claims by Christians over what the Bible really says (so many in fact that one can imagine a Messiah talked about in places where the author probably didn't have one in mind), but the Bible does say two sorts of things that are combined in later Judaism's understanding of the Messiah. One has to do with the perfect king, the other with the perfect world. (That's sort of the "national" and "religious" sides of Judaism we talked about in Chapter 2.)

The Messiah as the best possible ruler

Before democratic republics, "government" meant "kings." Therefore, to have a perfect society, there would have to be a perfect king. To the later Bible authors, King David, for all his sins, seemed the best example of a ruler's doing what God wanted, and the hope for a perfect king became linked with him: the king would come from David's family. (The rabbis later called him simply, "the son of David.")

Here is part of Isaiah 11 which speaks of this idea:

> A sprout will grow out of the trunk of Jesse [David's father]
> And a twig will shoot up from his roots.
> The spirit of the Lord will fill him,
> The spirit of wisdom and understanding,
> The spirit of wisdom and might,
> The spirit of knowledge and of belief in the Lord. . . .
> With righteousness he will judge the poor
> And decide fairly for the little people of the land. . . .
> The wolf will get along with the lamb
> And the leopard lie down with the young goat. . . .
> No one will hurt people or destroy things
> In all My holy mountain
> For the earth shall be as full of knowledge of the Lord
> As the sea is full of water.

(There are lovely plant, animal, and water symbols in that passage; see Part Four, Chapter 2, on symbol-words.)

In this sort of prophecy the great, coming king is described but, typically, not called a Messiah. The Hebrew word *mashiach* (which became in English "messiah") simply means touched with oil, the ceremony by which priests and kings and others got their official status. By the time of the Talmud, the favorite name for the expected king was *Mashiach,* the one specially anointed (touched with oil). (As you'd expect for those days, the whole Messiah tradition is masculine—waiting for a king, not a queen.)

The "Days of the Messiah" when goodness is complete

Some passages in the Bible don't mention the king, only the wonderful way life will go on. Micah 4 (repeated, oddly enough, in Isaiah 2, or vice versa) says:

> This is what will happen at "the end of days,"
> The mountain of the Lord's "house" will be raised up,
> It will be higher than any hill.
> Peoples will come to it in streams.
> Many nations will go around saying,
> "Come, let's go up to the mountain of the Lord,
> To the 'house' of the God of Jacob.
> He'll teach us of His ways
> And we'll walk in His paths." . . .
> They'll beat their swords into plow blades,
> They'll turn their spears into tools to prune trees.
> No nation will lift up a sword against any other nation.
> They won't even study war any more.
> But people will relax under their own vines and fig
>   trees
> And no one will make anyone afraid.

I'm not sure how great you think having a vine and a fig tree would be, but no one ever making you afraid is a wonderful dream of the future.

The Bible also talks in several places about a day of judgment coming, when the good will be rewarded and the evil punished. In one case, at least, Daniel 12:2–3 (some scholars think in other places, too), life after death is mentioned (see Part Four, Chapter 6).

I think it's important to say that the biblical hope for a

Messiah comes from belief in God, not from a belief in what people can do. In the Bible all people commit sins. They aren't perfect so they'd never make a perfect world. But God really "wants" the world to be fully good so God can be counted on eventually to get it there. The biblical symbol for this is that God is our king. But, while God's rule is real in "heaven," it still needs to be made complete on earth. Another way of talking about the Messiah, then, is to talk about establishing the "kingdom of God on earth."

The rabbis filled out the idea of the Messiah

In the statements of the Talmud we find these themes joined together. The rabbis' ideas aren't easy to sort out, but we can say they form a sequence of four stages. First, the very human King Messiah comes and human life is set right. After some time goes by there is a resurrection (see Part Four, Chapter 6, for more discussion). The dead bodies, now healed, purified and perfected, get their spirits back. They come before God to be judged. After some period of punishment, they enter the final glory, the life-of-the-world-to-come. The rabbis' term, "days of the Messiah" (yemot Hamashiach), generally refers to the early part. A term like "the world-to-come" (olam haba) usually means the latter stages of the coming of the Messiah.

Occasionally a rabbi says what he thinks the "days of the Messiah" will be like, but mostly the rabbis discourage this. It led too many people to dream up all sorts of fantastic visions. (See the latter parts of the Book of Daniel.) All some people could think about, apparently, was what an easy time they'd have when the Messiah came. I like the comment which says that in those days you'll be able to stick a faucet into one grape and have enough wine for a year. I suppose such wishes might have triggered harsh-sounding statements like that of the teacher Samuel (early 200s C.E.). He said there's no difference between the world as we know it and "the days of the Messiah" except that then Jews won't have to serve foreign kings. Most of the rabbis felt that God's Torah teaches us in detail what to do in this world so we should concentrate on that.

Bar Kochba made the Jews suspicious of all would-be messiahs

Some rabbis had a terrific disappointment in a person they thought was the Messiah, Simon Bar Kochba. (There is no clear mention of Jesus in rabbinic literature which is surprising to us who live among Christians. Apparently, the Jews of his time didn't take him very seriously when he claimed to be the Messiah. I'll talk more about this later.)

The Romans had destroyed the Temple in 70 C.E. and then treated the Jews harshly. In 132 Simon Bar Kochba led another revolution against Rome. Rabbi Akiba, a leading religious figure, announced that he believed Bar Kochba was the Messiah. (That was how human and political the rabbis' idea of the Messiah was.)

Bar Kochba was defeated, and the revolt crushed. To be beaten down again was bad enough. It was doubly painful because the Jews had expected that Bar Kochba—with God's help—would bring about "the days of the Messiah." Not for a long time—to be exact, until the time of Shabbetai Zevi, about 1665—would the Jewish people ever again get so aroused about someone who said he was the Messiah. They never gave up hope the Messiah would come. They just were skeptical about anyone who claimed to be the Messiah.

This probably explains some hard-boiled rabbinic statements about the Messiah, like this one by Rabban Yochanan ben Zakkai. (He lived during the first rebellion, about 70 C.E., but many scholars think this statement was really from the Bar Kochba times and was put in his name because he was so important.) "If you're doing some planting and someone comes along and says the Messiah has arrived, first finish your planting, then go greet him."

Jesus was surely not the Messiah the Jews expected

Jesus of Nazareth lived in the first thirty or so years of the Common Era, a century before Bar Kochba. The attitudes Jews developed to the Christian claims that Jesus was the Messiah are based on the sort of hopes they had for Bar

Kochba. The Bible says the Messiah will be a great Jewish king who sets up a perfect society and starts us to the life of the world-to-come. The Jewish attitude to Jesus is simple: he didn't do anything like that. Therefore, he's not the Messiah. A story of a much later time makes the Jewish position on the Messiah very clear. In the 1700s the Chasidic Rebbe Menachem Mendel moved from Vitebsk, Russia, to the Land of Israel. One day a man went up to the Mount of Olives and started blowing a shofar, leading people to think the Messiah had arrived. Someone came running with the news to Menachem Mendel. He went to the window, looked out at the way people were going about business as usual, and said, "The Messiah hasn't come." Then he went back to his study and prayer.

The Messiah is supposed to bring the world complete justice, peace, and love. Neither Jesus nor Bar Kochba nor anyone listed in Jewish encyclopedias under "False Messiahs" has done that. So the Messiah hasn't come. Just look out your window and see how true that is.

Christians therefore have an interesting counter-argument: the Messiah is supposed to come twice. The first time lets people know there is a Messiah; the second coming starts the final days of the world. We Jews don't see that idea in the Bible at all. And there was no such notion in rabbinic tradition. Since the prophets had already taught us that the Messiah was coming, it seems odd for the Messiah to have to appear a first time to let us know the same thing.

But, Christians say, Jesus changed the idea of the Messiah and taught the true one. Nevertheless, Jews say that the idea is a Jewish one, unique to the Jewish sense of God and the Hebrew Bible, and we ought to know what our special idea says.

We do not see the Bible predicting the coming of Jesus of Nazareth

Often that leads to an argument about Jesus' fulfilling many of the prophecies in the Bible. Surely some of the stories in the Christian biblical books—what they call the New Testament—read that way to Jewish readers. Often they were written for that purpose. Their authors were less interested in recording facts than in convincing people of what they themselves believed—that Jesus was the Messiah so their stories about Jesus got to be told in ways that made him fulfill the prophecies. Even so, Jews feel there are important differences between what the Hebrew Bible and the New Testament say. Let's take two famous cases:

The New Testament tells how Jesus was born to Mary who remained a virgin. Instead of his being conceived by Mary after sexual intercourse with Joseph, she was—by a miracle—enabled to have a child by a direct act of God. According to Christianity, this fulfills Isaiah's prophecy (Chapter 7) about the coming of the good king. The Greek translation of Isaiah, which many people knew in those days, can be read that the child would be born to a virgin. But the Hebrew says *almah,* a young woman. Today, a number of Christian translations of Isaiah no longer say "virgin" but "young woman." Here the New Testament "fulfills" a prophecy that isn't even in the Bible.

Another famous example comes from Isaiah 53. It speaks of God's servant, and scholars see it as the model for many of the things Jesus is said to have done. God's servant is described there as suffering instead of ruling. This chapter is then used to argue that Jesus introduced a new understanding of the Messiah, as suffering servant rather than king. But there are still a lot of differences between what Isaiah 53 says and what Jesus did, according to the New Testament. Verse 2 of that chapter, even if it exaggerates, says the servant was ugly: "No form of handsomeness that we would want to look at him, no beauty that we would delight in him." That's not the Jesus of the New Testament. In Verse 3, the servant is described as "acquainted with disease" and in Verse 7, twice, as not opening his mouth at his suffering, all contradicted by the New Testament stories.

Some people are so convinced Jesus is the Messiah that you can't reason with them. They won't listen. They only want to convert you. When you show them Bible texts that don't apply to Jesus, they show you a dozen others that they claim do. Whatever these people say, Jews know there can be no

92

argument about the world. It hasn't changed much since Jesus or Bar Kochba. Jews are still waiting for the Messiah to come and make things perfect . . . once and for all time.

Our modern Jewish ideas about the Messiah

When Reform Judaism started in the 1800s it taught that our understanding of the Messiah needed changing. There were three reasons for this. First, in the suspicious anti-Semitic world in which they found themselves, they felt that calling for a Messiah would spoil their chance to be full citizens. Remember, the Messiah the Jews wanted was not a rabbi or a priest but a king. He was to take the Jews back to their land and set up a proper government. The Jews, truly wanting to be a part of France or Germany, felt they needed to make clear that the Messiah was no longer a political idea but a religious one.

Second, particularly after hundreds of years of waiting and dreaming, people connected the Messiah with miracles and a sudden dramatic change in nature. One man comes along and everything is made perfect. First human life is set right, then resurrection, next judgment, and finally the life of the world-to-come. To a modern, scientific mind that seemed very hard to believe.

The Reform Jews created the idea of the Messianic Age

Third, there was a better way of looking at it. It wouldn't be a miracle if everyone helped do it. In a time when education was giving people understanding and democracy was giving them power, this fit in nicely. Instead of leaning on God and waiting for some heavenly act to change things, human beings would make things right through personal and social ethics. We would ourselves create a world of just and merciful, kind and loving, learned and cultured, creative and sensitive people. Reform Jews therefore stopped talking about the coming of the Messiah and spoke instead about our working for a Messianic Age. It is a little change in words but a big one in beliefs. Everyone is now part of "the Messiah." You can see why Reform Jews have worked so hard for all good causes and not only for Jewish ones.

When we think this way we can find the roots of this idea in our Jewish classics. So, when the Jews are at the shores of the Sea of Reeds and the Egyptian army is coming, Moses prays for help. But God says, "Why are you crying out to Me? Speak to the Children of Israel and let them go forward" (Exod. 14–15). Here the Torah seems to say action is more important than ritual—though, obviously, a miracle is coming. I like a similar sort of story told about the Chasidic Rebbe Menachem Mendel of Kosov. When he was asked why the Messiah didn't come, he quoted the biblical verse, "Why didn't David come yesterday or today?" He then said, "Because we are no different today from what we were yesterday."

Reform Jews like stories which emphasize what people should do. Of course Reform Jews say we work for the Messianic Age by changing society while the Chasidim say we must change our own inner life.

In recent years some Reform Jews have worried about the idea of the Messianic Age because it seems to say that people can bring perfection by themselves. But people don't seem that good. We can make things somewhat better but we will need some help to get us to perfection. The present-day thinkers suggest God needs to be brought back more strongly into this idea. They want to make people and God partners in bringing the Messianic Age. We do some of the work but we also expect God to do some. That has led these thinkers to suggest we return to using the term, "the Messiah," in a highly symbolic way, of course. Since the Messiah is a human "king," who works with God's help, this term expresses the sense of partnership that will bring us to perfection. Most Reform Jews, though they trust people a little less than they did some years ago and trust God somewhat more, will prefer to use the term, "The Messianic Age."

5

What Does the State of Israel Mean to Jews?

WHEN are you going to the State of Israel?

I suppose that's a strange question to be asking people who take trips mostly with their parents. It's hard enough taking a family on vacation in our own country. Getting them all to the State of Israel seems like a dream, but maybe you've thought seriously about it. And if your Jewish community is large enough there are certainly some families that have managed to do it.

Have you ever chatted with anyone who's come back from a visit there? They don't talk about the usual vacation things:

the great fishing, the gorgeous mountains, the wonderful entertainment, or the fantastic shopping. Usually the visitors are moved by the people. The Israelis are extraordinary. What they've accomplished despite what they've had to put up with, how they manage to carry on despite all their problems, the way they still dream of creating a great society are exciting.

Today, the world admires the Jews best for the Bible and the State of Israel. To organize a nation and keep it going is quite an accomplishment. Most people thought the Jews could never do such a thing. We did not have our own government for about 2,000 years. We lived away from the Land of Israel most of that time. The modern return of Jews there began about a hundred years ago but the large numbers went only immediately after World War II. Many were survivors of concentration camps, sick and frightened from their terrible experiences. They came from all over Europe and later from the Arab countries, with many different languages, customs, and life styles. To turn them into one self-governing nation was a small miracle.

The State of Israel is
our way of saying we intend to live on

Maybe it was a big miracle, for the State of Israel needs to be seen as the Jewish People's response to the Holocaust. From 1941 to 1945 Hitler killed six million Jews. He almost completely wiped out the greatest centers of Jewish learning and religion in the world. In some countries 90 per cent of the prewar Jewish population was killed. Many who survived had lived through such terror they could never live quite normal lives again. This happened in the advanced twentieth century, in one of the most civilized countries of the world, Germany. Human beings who were once leaders were forced to wear Jew-badges, were beaten on the street, lost their jobs or their businesses, could not attend public affairs, and eventually were sent to ghettos and concentration camps. Those who survived the starvation, sickness, and hard labor were killed—hundreds at a time—and their bodies burned in huge furnaces. (When you visit Jerusalem, go see the Yad Vashem exhibit about the Holocaust—and the grove of trees planted in thanks to the non-Jews who helped our people.)

Can you imagine the feelings of the rest of the Jews when they learned about the mass murders that were kept secret during the war? Can you think how empty and awful the survivors felt when they found themselves finally out of the death camps?

I think any normal group which had been through something like that would probably have said, "We quit. Life was bad enough for Jews for much of the last 2,000 years. Modern times were supposed to make things better but they've only made them worse. If that's the way the world is going to treat Jews then we'll just disappear and let people find someone else to persecute."

We answered the Holocaust
by rebuilding our lives and our people

I think that would have been a normal way to respond to such suffering. Only the Jews aren't a "normal" people. Through a long history we turned away from idols, survived away from our country, and kept making extraordinary contributions to humanity. There's something special about the Jewish passion to survive. We religious Jews say it's because of our connection with God. Although we don't understand God very well, we know our history is tied up with God. No matter what people did to us, we knew that, in time, God would help us set things right. No matter how bad things looked we did not lose hope. Something of these old Jewish dreams stayed with us though the Holocaust was worse than anything we had ever suffered in our history. The Jews didn't do the "normal" thing. We refused to quit being Jews.

Did we do this to keep Hitler from winning after all? Was it because we had the old Jewish tradition of hope? Did God now give us the help that God did not give during the Holocaust? I have thought about it for many years and I still don't know. I think a little of all three reasons must be right. What was even more astonishing, the Jews didn't want to just go on. We were determined to be better Jews than we had been before. For many of us this meant a country of our own. There had to be one place in the world where Jews could go and not be turned away. There had to be one place in the world where Jews would make the laws so that there would be no question of Jews having full rights as citizens. There had to be one place in the world where Jews would set the standards and would not have to live according to someone else's style.

The Israelis worked
one wonder after another

To almost everyone's surprise, the Jews who had been living in Palestine and those who arrived there after World War II established a Jewish state in 1948. They had to fight off the attack of eight Arab armies to survive but they did. Then they started performing small miracles. They took in and began to heal hundreds of thousands of Jewish refugees. They turned rocky and barren land into productive farms. They built cities where before there was only sand. They built a modern economy and an education system almost as good as any in the free world. They learned to defend themselves against enemies many times their size. They built a rich cultural life in every field you can think of. With no great natural resources of oil or iron or coal, with great pressure from neighbors and the international community, the State of Israel has met its problems with a decency that is rare in modern politics. The State of Israel is a true democracy— how many countries founded since World War II can you honestly say that of? The State of Israel has conducted war with uncommon humanity and treated the people in the areas it conquered with unusual consideration. The State of Israel has taught all of world Jewry what it is to be a free and self-respecting Jew. No wonder Jews everywhere take such pride in it and agree that it is, indeed, a "Jewish" state.

Don't misunderstand, please. I'm not saying the State of Israel has no faults or that every Israeli is a saint. All governments have problems and all people have their likable and unlikable members. The Israelis are human beings. Not angels. But, considering the ethics of most countries these days and what most societies are like, we Jews are full of pride at what our people has accomplished so far in the State of Israel.

We love the State of Israel
yet it's not our nation

I think the State of Israel is something of an example for all human beings. We Jews were so beaten down, it seemed as if we could never get up again—but we did. In recent years so many governments are corrupt, it seems people can't do anything decent through politics—but the Jews have. War is so prevalent and societies so unstable it seems generals often are the only ones who can control their countries—but not in the State of Israel. Something wonderfully human—and not only Jewish—is going on in the State of Israel and that, too, is why we love it.

Yet for all this feeling we have for the State of Israel it's not "our country" in the way that the United States or Canada is. Here we are citizens. There we are friendly, interested visitors. Here we have legal duties. There our hearts move us to be of help. Here we pay taxes, make decisions by voting, and serve in the armed forces to keep our country safe. For the State of Israel we give charity, work through organizations, and try to help our countries understand Israeli problems. Even our "religious" life is closely linked with the Land of Israel, with a very real city in it, Jerusalem, and with a special hill there called Zion.

It sounds as if we have two lands we love—but so do many people on the North American continent. All of us except the Indians came from someplace else. We have an ethnic home and a political one. The Irish, the Italians, the Poles, and many other groups are just like the Jews in this way. And every American who loves the Bible will know why we care about the Holy Land.

How Reform Judaism changed
its attitude to a Jewish state

When Zionism started—long before anyone ever thought there could be such a thing as a Hitler—most of the leaders of Reform Judaism were against it. They felt it was wrong to say the Jews were just a nation like any other nation and that religion wasn't the main part of being a Jew. They believed our neighbors would be deeply upset if they thought that what really interested Jews was going back to Palestine to start their own country. That was years ago. Today we still argue a bit with the Israelis as to how much a nationality the Jews really are. That's hardly as important as the practical question of recent times: how do you keep Jews and Judaism alive? Besides, Reform Jews (like everyone else) have seen how much easier it is to live a rich, Jewish life in the State of Israel than in other countries. Can you imagine not having to go to Hebrew school? (You'd grow up knowing Hebrew and you'd study Bible and Jewish history in your regular school.) You'd never have to worry about being absent from school on a Jewish holiday. (They're all closed.) And nobody (except emergency workers) works on Shabbat. No wonder Reform Jews have been encouraging those people who want to go there to settle. We've even started our own liberal religious Zionist group, ARZA, the Association of Reform Zionists of America. We've tried to help Israeli Reform congregations get started and recently we've set up the first Reform Jewish kibbutz. We've had only small success. One serious problem is not yet solved—Reform rabbis are not recognized to perform marriages or conversions in the State of Israel. Still, the Reform movement has, for many years now, been deeply involved in the State of Israel.

At the same time almost all American Jews intend to go on living in their present countries, Canada or the United States. More important, they feel quite certain that while there are some problems in trying to be a Jew where they live one can be a good Jew anywhere. The history of the past 2,000 years seems to prove this. For most of that time almost all Jews lived outside the Land of Israel and they were considered proper Jews. They created great works from the things they learned from their non-Jewish societies and what their Jewish beliefs taught them in that situation. The Talmud, the basis of Jewish life, is a product of Babylonia. (The Palestinian Talmud, created in Jerusalem in the same period, has less authority.) Medieval Jewish philosophy arose when Jews in Moslem countries came in contact with their neighbors' new intellectual ideas. Medieval Jewish poetry was written with the accent symbols of Arabic poetry adapted to Hebrew words. So in our times, the Jews reacting to their scientific, democratic, people-centered societies are creating a unique, modern Judaism. Once again, something very special may come out of the special challenges we face by trying to live as Jews in our exciting cultures.

There is a special Jewish challenge living away from the State of Israel

We American Jews can therefore feel that we have special problems and special opportunities. Because we are a minority, the peoples among whom we live are bound to influence us. We must work at staying Jewish while learning from the modern world. Our Israeli cousins live in a tiny country, one quite distant from the great international centers of science and culture. But they have the great advantage of living in a Jewish society as a proud and self-respecting Jewish people. They can help Jews elsewhere gain a sense of whether or not they are being true to themselves. And Jews of the Diaspora (a Greek word of Roman times, meaning "scattering") can help Israeli Jews to learn what world culture offers Jews today. Each Jewry can then be of great help to the other while living in its own special Jewish way.

This picture can only become reality if we American Jews live strong, Jewish lives here and know a good deal about the State of Israel. This whole book is about living a strong, Jewish life, but what does it mean "to know" about the State of Israel? I believe we can be expected to keep up with what is going on there by reading newspapers, magazines, and books. With a little effort we can stay acquainted with its music, its dance, and other aspects of its culture. Better, I think, we need to visit there, for a reasonably long time, if we can. (Our Reform movement has an exchange program by which high school students may spend a semester at the Leo Baeck School in Haifa. And most universities offer a program under which you can spend one of your college years in the State of Israel.) Most important, some of us need to know Hebrew well enough to have a feel for what the Israelis are really saying to themselves and to the world.

The hardest thing, I believe, is for us to learn how to criticize each other. Since we are all Jews we have some idea of what a "Jewish state" is and how the Jewish people everywhere ought to be living. Israelis need to have some say about how Jewish our life ought to be. We ought to have some say about the shape the Jewish state takes, though the Israelis must make the decisions. That's so complicated a matter there are bound to be disagreements, and we need to learn how to argue respectfully with each other just as a loving family does. I don't know that it will be an easy thing to do, but, if the love is real on both sides, I am sure we will find a way.

6
Why Do Jews Have to Be Different?

SUPPOSE your school principal decided that students these days need more discipline and made strict new rules for your school. No more choices. Everyone is to take the same courses, play the same sport, wear the same sort of clothing, have the same hair styles, and walk through the building in groups marching in step. That's not far-fetched. Some generations back, that's how schools were run. Even then it seemed bad. Today it would be simply terrible, even dictatorial. We're individuals. We want the chance to be ourselves.

Trying to learn who we are is the big problem in becoming mature.

But suppose your principal thought nothing was more important than individuality. You couldn't get into school unless your hair and clothes were different from everyone else's. Your teacher wouldn't accept any assignment until you had proved you did it in a way that was unlike anybody else's. That also would be terrible. Almost everyone wants to be somewhat like other people. We don't want to be considered peculiar and odd.

We really want to be two separate things at the same time—different but not too different, an individual but accepted in some group. That's not an easy balance to work out. If you're too different, people don't like you. If you only do what makes people like you, you often are untrue to yourself. How you will live with both needs is an important part of what sort of person you turn out to be.

The same is pretty much true of the Jews. In some ways, they are no different from other peoples. The Bible story says that all human beings are part of the family of Adam and Eve. A talmudic comment declares that when God made the first man out of the dirt God did so out of pieces taken from every part of the earth. That way, people couldn't come along, later, and say that they were better because they lived in the country with the best dirt. Yet the Jews are a separate group and not the same as others. And that's partly because the Jews wanted to be different. I'm going to discuss these two ideas separately because I think that will make them clearer. But in history they really worked together. The world treated the Jews as odd because the Jews wanted to stay separate. That gave the Jews more reason to keep to themselves.

Why the Jews wanted to be a separate people

To begin with, the Jews probably wanted to be different because everyone wants to be different. The nearby peoples, like the Hittites and the Ammonites, had their own languages, their own territories, and their own heroes. The Jews spoke Hebrew, lived in Canaan, and remembered their founders, Abraham and Sarah and their children. It's natural when you grow up among a certain people to like its special way of life.

Though that idea is in the Bible, its authors always talk about the Jews being different for religious reasons. Everyone else worshiped idols. Only the Jews believed in one spiritual God. If the Jews stopped being loyal to God then the whole world would be idol-worshipers. So the Jews had to be separate for God's sake. They had to stand up for God among all the other peoples.

The Torah, written and oral (see Part III, Chapter 5, for a discussion of the oral law), has many laws to keep the Jews separate. One says you mustn't marry someone who isn't Jewish. Another says you must eat only kosher food. There's something of this need to stay separate in the observance of Shabbat. The word "holy" (and its Latin cousins, "sanctuary," "sanct-ify") means, in part, making people or things different or separate for God's sake. Thus, we treat a Bible, the *Kitvei Kodesh,* "the Holy Scriptures," with respect and not like an ordinary book. So too a "holy day" may come on a normal Tuesday but we act differently from the way we do on other Tuesdays. The Torah says the Jews were supposed to be a holy people. God declares, "If you keep this agreement we are making, you will be My 'priest people,' a holy nation" (Exod. 19:5–6). Priests are people especially set aside to serve God, and a "holy nation" would similarly be one that was different from other peoples. The prophet Micah put it this way: "Let all the peoples go on in the name of their gods but we will go on in the name of the Lord our God for ever and ever" (Mic. 4:5).

That idea of staying separate for God's sake goes all through the later Jewish tradition. Listen to the words a Greek Jewish writer put into the mouth of Mattathias (the father of Judah Maccabee) when he was asked to lead the Jews in sacrificing to an idol. (The first Book of Maccabees was written some time after the Chanukah wars of about 170 B.C.E.) "If all the other peoples in the kingdom obey the king and forsake their traditional religions . . . yet I and my sons and my brothers will remain loyal to our ancient Jewish covenant. God forbid that we should forsake the Torah and our other laws. We will not at all obey the king's command to give up observing our religion." The next time you observe Chanukah, remember that the freedom of religion it celebrates is also the freedom to be different.

Jews were forced
to be different from other people

The world was also keeping Jews separate. In Roman times, before Christianity, the Egyptians were quite prejudiced against the Jews. Hatred is one way of keeping peoples separate. The Romans weren't much better. One of their writers accused us of being unbearably lazy since we wasted one-seventh of our lives (Shabbat) in not working. It's hard to say why people build such walls against other people. In part, it's because they don't know you and find your ways strange; for instance, worshiping a God you can't see. But getting to know people you're prejudiced against doesn't generally cure hate. Apparently, many people need to hate somebody. We say they need a "scapegoat" (see Lev. 16:21–22) on which they can load all the things that bother them. Some thinkers have also suggested that people hate the Jews because, subconsciously, people are angry at having to be good. Since it's not nice to be angry with their parents or their religion they take it out on others—the Jews, the people who gave the world the Bible. Whatever the reasons, when Christianity and Islam became the main influences in the Western World, they made laws that put the Jews in a second-class, inferior position. They didn't want to wipe out the Jews. Instead, they "only" encouraged people to treat the Jews as strange and dangerous outsiders. That went on for hundreds of years. Now most of that religious teaching has stopped. Yet many people still quietly feel it is all right to hate Jews. Despite the greatness of democracy, prejudice doesn't die easily.

With the modern world less hateful,
Jews wondered about staying separate

With modern times, things changed radically. Non-Jews are not idolators and the world says Jews are equals. Some of the first modern Jews were so excited by these changes they didn't see any good reason to remain Jewish anymore. Many became Christians, not because they believed in Christianity, but because they no longer wanted to be different. More recently, as Christianity has had less influence, those Jews don't convert; they simply stop doing Jewish things. After all, they say, Judaism teaches that all people are created in God's "image" and Jews aren't much different from non-Jews anyway.

That's not the whole truth. Let's face it. Jews have a selfish reason for wanting everyone to be alike. If there were no differences between people, there'd be no anti-Semitism. Often we're eager for interfaith understanding so we can be rid of the special problems that come with being a Jew. But democracy doesn't mean doing away with all differences; interfaith doesn't mean giving up your separate faith; "brotherhood" doesn't mean being untrue to yourself because you love your "neighbor." Ethnic groups and separate religions will exist for a long time to come. To give up Jewish difference in the hope that others will then give up their ethnic or religious heritage is silly. The overwhelming majority of people won't do that. Their traditions mean too much to them.

Yet the Messianic Age of full equality has not yet arrived

Sad to say, the world still wants to keep us somewhat separate. Anti-Semitism is nowhere nearly as bad as it was centuries ago. In many ways, attitudes toward the Jews are continually improving. Still, the world thinks the Jews are somewhat odd and we remain one of the great Western scapegoat groups. Hitler, or, in more recent years, the way the nations of the world have ganged up on the State of Israel should have taught us that.

Modern times also once made it seem that there no longer was a good religious reason for Jews to stay separate. Christians and Moslems worship one God and many of their human ideals come from the Jewish tradition. This led the Reform Jews to feel that many of the old laws that separated Jews from non-Jews should be relaxed. The Pittsburgh Platform of 1885, the first great American statement of Reform Judaism, said we should give up all the old rules of staying separate which didn't go with living in freedom. So Reform Jews stopped wearing hats or *kipot* at services; they didn't want to be different. Some congregations tried having their main service on Sunday morning. A few rabbis were so excited about the new liberal attitudes to religion which they saw everywhere, they expected the Messianic Age would arrive in another generation or two.

Today it is difficult to imagine that such intelligent people could think that the world's problems would be so easily settled. Wherever we look—our cities, our country, international affairs—there are difficulties and differences of opinion. We don't even have very good ideas about how to solve some simple problems our world faces. With no one knowing "the truth" it seems sensible for religious and ethnic groups to hold on to their sense of what's important while trying to learn why other people see things differently.

A different time has made staying separate more important to Reform Jews

As a result of this change of mood in the past generation, there are almost no Reform temples left which have a major Sunday service. Almost all of them have services instead at another untraditional time, late Friday evening. (Under Jewish law, the Shabbat service is held at sundown, whenever that comes.) It's not normal for Americans to go to services in the evening and certainly not on Fridays, but it's one way of being Jewish. It's not Orthodox to have Shabbat services after dinner but it enables the whole community to spend an evening together. This Reform Jewish creation, the late Friday evening service, which was probably started by Isaac M. Wise, is a good balance of staying separate yet being like other people.

Another example comes from the current arguments over intermarriage. Even when Reform Jews thought everyone was getting to be pretty much alike, they were against Jews marrying non-Jews. (Remember, converts are full Jews so they are not involved here.) Reform rabbis passed a resolution against it as early as 1904. In recent years, the percentage of Jews marrying non-Jews has gone up. Most Reform rabbis are still against any rabbi performing an intermarriage. They feel we need to show strongly that this is not the Jewish ideal. Some Reform rabbis now feel they should perform the ceremonies for such couples, and their argument is interesting. They feel that if they do the ceremony, then they have a chance to help the couple decide to build a rich Jewish family life. They, too, want the Jews to continue as a separate group. Once an intermarriage has occurred, however, all Reform rabbis will accept the couple in their congregations and try to help them create a Jewish home.

Keeping the Jews a healthy, distinct people seems very important

There are many reasons why these and other rabbis want the Jewish people to continue. Some would say it's simply natural: You are part of a group and, of course, you want it to go on. Others would point out how rewarding Jewish life is. If Jews would only know and observe more of our tradition how much richer their lives would be. Others would point to the special approach to life in our ethnic group. Our people (though not every person in it) values intelligence, spurns violence, loves justice, works hard, cares for our families, and is concerned for humanity. And still others would add that our people's extraordinary accomplishments grow directly out of our unusual religion. Though other people believe in one God, we must say, with all respect, that we think there is much they are still missing. Christianity, with its idea of God as three-in-one—the Trinity—clouds the issue of one God. By emphasizing faith in the Christ more than good deeds, it misses the Jewish sense that God "cares" mostly about what we do. Islam, by contrast, is very strict about one God. Yet it limits people's need to do good deeds out of a pious acceptance that whatever God does in the world is for the best. Other thinkers would argue that we know, from personal experience, say, at services or in some *tzedakah* project, that our people is still "dear" to God and we, therefore, ought to work to keep it serving God in its own way. Finally, some would say we should remain different because that is what our tradition tells us we ought to do.

That's quite a large bunch of reasons. Let me sum up the whole idea in some words from the diary Anne Frank kept when hiding from the Nazis in an attic in Holland. She was about thirteen when she wrote this: "Who has made us Jews different from all other people? Who has allowed us to suffer so terribly up to now? It is God that has made us as we are, but it will be God, too, who will raise us up again. If we bear all this suffering and if there are still Jews left when it is over, then Jews, instead of being doomed, will be held up as an example. Who knows, it might even be our religion from which the world and all peoples learn good, and for that reason and that reason only do we have to suffer now. We can never become just Netherlanders, or just English, or representative of any country for that matter. We will always remain Jews, but we want to, too."

7 Who Is a "Good Jew"?

I THINK nagging is a bad way to get people to do something. Of course it sometimes works. You get so upset with people complaining about you that, out of disgust, you do what they want. But the chances are, you don't like doing it and you can easily end up hating it. I prefer being encouraged, kidded, teased, rewarded, or even punished rather than nagged.

When people ask me, "Who is a good Jew?" they're really getting ready to nag me. As soon as I agree to some answer—preferably one that includes their pet idea—they start asking me why I don't live that way. "Are you satisfied to be a bad Jew?" They think they'll get me to do what they want by calling me names. Nag, nag, nag. No thanks. If we talk about this, let's do it to discover what we ought to be doing, not so we can put other people down.

Another thing. Living so soon after Hitler murdered six million Jews, I refuse to continue his project in any way. I refuse to say that Jews who disagree with me "really aren't Jews." You can call it being tolerant or loving Jews or whatever you want. I refuse to chase people out of our community these days. Instead, let's use the same rule medieval Jews had for "bad" Jews (those who had converted to Christianity and now wanted to return to the community). Most rabbis agreed that such Jews didn't need to be converted back. They based this on a statement in the Talmud (originally applied to something else), "A Jew who sins is still a Jew." After Hitler, my rule is: "A Jew who sins (by my standards) is still a Jew (and I will try to love this fellow Jew)."

We don't have to be perfect;
we only need to try to do what God "wants"

Whatever "good Jew" means, it can't mean someone who never makes a mistake. The Bible teaches us that there is no such person. "For there is nobody on earth so righteous as always to do good and never to sin" (Eccles. 7:20). That includes Moses—the finest Jew who ever lived. As the Torah tells it (Num. 20:7–13) he banged on a rock to get water instead of speaking and letting God work a miracle. That may not seem too great a sin to us but he didn't do what God told him. For that sin, he was denied permission to bring the Jews into the Holy Land. If Moses could sin and still be a "good Jew," that means the rest of us don't have to be perfect—which is quite a relief. We only have to keep trying to be as good as we can.

Neither the Bible nor the Talmud used the term "good Jew" but they were quite certain of what a Jew should do: follow the Torah. We might even say the same thing is true today. Then we'd start arguing over what we mean now by "the Torah." In modern times, Jews want to change the old ways yet keep the tradition going. Only we've never been able to all agree on what's a proper mix of the Jewish past and modern style. As you respond to all the topics in this book, in a way you'll give your own answer as to who is a "good Jew." Still, it will be useful to try an experiment to bring together many of our themes. We can do so by comparing our ideas with those of the Reform rabbis' organization.

What are Reform rabbis emphasizing in being a "good Jew" today?

In 1976, in celebration of a hundred years of organized American Reform Judaism, the Central Conference of American Rabbis passed a statement about our "spiritual state." Since it's the first time since 1937 that they have issued such a document, what they said is worth close attention.

The rabbis gave six numbered sections as the heart of their statement. These fall into two divisions. The first three sections deal with beliefs. The second three sections talk about our duties. Even a quick look at these six sections shows something. They write much more about our duties than about our beliefs. The rabbis feel that, for a "good Jew," doing is more important than believing. They even say, "Judaism emphasizes action rather than creed. . . ."(Most Christian churches are based on a creed, a statement of beliefs.) The rabbis are not saying that you don't have to believe anything and they are not saying that beliefs are unimportant. After all, they do have three sections about our beliefs. But they point out that, between what you believe as a Jew and what you do as a Jew, the doing is more important. It's like what Rabbi Elazar ben Azariah said in the Talmud (*Pirke Avot* 3:22): "People whose good deeds exceed their learning are like trees with few branches but many roots. Let the wind rage; it won't knock such a tree down."

(Should there be something more important to a Jew than doing the right? Is it true ideas, a sensitive soul, a great knowledge of our tradition, success, a wonderful personality? Or do you pretty much agree with the rabbis? Ask yourself what *you* think as I go through what *they* think.)

Our beliefs have a great effect on what we do

For all the stress on action the rabbis' statement talks first about belief. That's because what you believe influences what you do. For example, suppose you believe as many Israelis do—that the Jews are really just another nation such as the Turks or the French. Language, culture, and country are the most important treasures of a nation. Hence, in this Israeli system, you'd be a "good Jew" by knowing Hebrew, enjoying Israeli culture, and either living in the Land of Israel or supporting the country as much as possible.

Let's take another, opposite belief, that of the Yiddishist movement. Simon Dubnow was a great Jewish historian of the first half of this century. He said that it was a special blessing that Jews had lived away from their homeland for nearly 2,000 years. While other nations had to concentrate on taxes, officials, armies, and such, the Jews were free to give all their energies to their culture. By living in many countries our people gained a unique, international sense of humankind. Dubnow saw the Jews as the only "international nation." He felt it was especially important for the Jews to keep their nationality alive and that this was best done through the language that the Jewish masses knew and loved: Yiddish. Dubnow's "good Jews" weren't interested in Hebrew or the Land of Israel—they devoted themselves instead to Yiddish culture.

There are some, but few, Yiddishists in our communities today. There are more Zionist nationalists (though most American Zionists combine the "national" with the "religious" side of being a "good Jew," as we saw in Chapter 2). Yiddishists and Zionist nationalists agree that religion and belief in God have nothing to do with being a "good Jew." The Reform rabbis disagree. They not only include God as one of their three basic Jewish beliefs—the other two are the people of Israel and Torah—but they make it first on their list. That's no accident. According to Reform Judaism, the Jews are basically a religious group. The movement may call many creative (and perhaps unusual) ideas "religious." Still, the Reform rabbis believe that being "religious" is critical to being a "good Jew."

114

Let's take a quick look at each of the three beliefs they think are important to a "good Jew."

The classic Jewish beliefs: about God, the Jews, and Torah

The rabbis' statement doesn't describe what sort of God we must believe in. Instead it notes that our ideas have changed over the centuries. It leaves the readers to decide which of the modern Jewish theories about God make the most sense to them. But whichever idea about God they accept or themselves create, the rabbis say that "good Jews" will base their lives as individuals and as a community on it. Note the mixture. In part, we're sure; in part, we're open to a better understanding. We're certain enough of our belief in God to build our lives on it, but we admit we don't know exactly what God is like or just what we must think about God. This is definitely a "religious" sense of being a "good Jew." It also leaves a lot of room for people to be religious in their own, personal Jewish way.

The Jewish people is much easier for the rabbis to talk about than the subject of God. They're our group and we like it. We're somewhat odd. We're more religious than ethnic groups like the Swedes and we're more ethnic than churches like Protestantism or Catholicism. We're ethnic and religious at the same time. And the rabbis are saying you can't really separate the one side of being Jewish from the other. More, Reform Jews believe the Jews have a special role to play in helping all humanity get to the Messianic Age. So a "good Jew" would be involved with the Jewish community and would care about the Jewish people as a religious and as an ethnic group.

For centuries the Jewish people has felt close to God. Out of this has come a tradition. It teaches the Jews about God and how they ought to live as a people dedicated to God. This tradition and the way of life which is based on it, we call Torah. The creation of Torah has gone on in every age and still goes on. A "good Jew" will want to know the Torah tradition, for all of Jewish life today is based on it and continues it. Some Jews among us are creating Torah right now—adding ideas, practices, stories, and dreams to our tradition. A "good Jew" will not only study but will try to live by Torah. That is what we believe God "wants" of us personally and as a people.

The duties of a Reform Jew in our time

The rabbis' statement then moves on to discuss three important areas of our lives: our religious obligations, our community responsibilities (particularly to the State of Israel), and our duties to humanity as a whole. Perhaps it could have covered other parts of our lives. It certainly would have helped if it had given us more details. But since it was intended to be a short statement, it had to leave many topics for others to study and write about.

The Reform rabbis say that our duties begin with ethics, the need to do what is good. There are, of course, other things a "good Jew" needs to do, but they insist that a good Jewish life begins with ethics. Whatever else a "good Jew" is, a "good Jew" is a decent human being. If you don't behave well to all other people, don't call yourself a "good Jew."

Some people think that's all you need to do to be a "good Jew." Even the words tell you that isn't right. There's a difference between being a "good person" and a "good Jew." Being a Jew involves doing more. (Do you recall the talmudic mathematics we studied in Chapter 3? The rabbis figured the Jews had more commandments to follow than humanity in general.) The Reform rabbis' statement says that besides ethics we have other duties: "creating a Jewish home centered on family devotion; lifelong study; private prayer and public worship; daily religious observance; keeping the Sabbath and the holy days; celebrating the major events of life; involvement with the synagogue and community; other activities which promote the survival of the Jewish people and enhance its existence." Exactly what you should do about each of these is left to you as long as you are serious about being a Jew and know something about Jewish tradition. But a "good Jew" will be doing something in all these aspects of Jewish life.

The rabbis declare that the State of Israel ought to have a

special place in the heart of a "good Jew." Since it makes Jewish living possible in ways that no other place can, a "good Jew" should consider going to the State of Israel to live. Still, it is possible to be a "good Jew" in any country, and Jews ought to build strong Jewish communities wherever they live. These need to be made as democratic as possible and they should also show that the Jewish people tries to live up to high religious standards. "Good Jews" in the State of Israel and elsewhere should stay in close touch, helping each other to be better Jews, even if that requires loving criticism.

We have duties to humanity as well as to our people

Finally, the rabbis think that a "good Jew" will also help all humanity. Much of the time to work for what is good for the Jews—like fair employment laws—turns out to make democracy work better for everybody. Sometimes, however, it seems that what might be best for the Jews conflicts with what might be best for America or the world. For example, the growth of world population is now a serious problem. Some thinkers suggest everyone have fewer children. However, because the Jewish population decreased one-third when Hitler killed six million Jews, some Jewish leaders suggest that Jews ought to have more children so we can regain our former size. Those two suggestions are opposites. There's no easy way to solve the difficulty. But the rabbis say that a "good Jew" mustn't stop caring about both the needs of the Jews and of humanity. Caring only about the Jews is selfish; caring only about other groups is a sort of suicide. It may not be simple being a Jew today for we are devoted to the welfare of all human beings and to the well-being of the Jewish people at the same time.

Let me summarize what the Reform rabbis suggest a "good Jew" is or ought to be: someone who lives ethically, has a broad sense of Jewish religious duty, is involved in Jewish community life and particularly with the State of Israel, has a deep involvement with the concerns of all humanity—and all because of belief in God, in the people of Israel, in Torah. One thing more: A "good Jew" will live with hope that the

Messianic Age will one day come. Despite all the disappointments that come in life, despite all the terrible things people do to one another, a "good Jew" doesn't give up. With our work and God's help, justice, peace, and love of others can one day become real in human affairs.

Is that too much of an answer for you? Maybe what you really wanted to know was how little you could do and still be called a "good Jew." Sorry, anyone who wants to do only the minimum of something doesn't deserve to be called "good" at it. A "good Jew" doesn't try to get out of doing Jewish things but wants to do, as well as possible, what Jews ought to do. I've explained what the Reform rabbis think. Now it is your turn. The very first step in being a "good Jew" is figuring out—for yourself—what you believe and what you now ought to try to do to live it.

Part Three

WHAT DO THE BIBLE AND TRADITION MEAN TO US?

with
an Orthodox response by RABBI J. DAVID BLEICH
and
a Conservative response by
RABBI SEYMOUR SIEGEL

Introduction
1. Did God Give the Bible?
2. How Does God Speak to People?
3. Why Are the Prophets Especially Important to Us?
4. How True Is the Bible?
5. How Has Judaism Changed since the Bible?
6. Must We Observe All the Commandments and Traditions?
7. Why Are There Three Branches of Judaism?

Introduction

YOU will soon see that this discussion of the Bible and Jewish tradition is printed in an odd way. Instead of my taking up the whole page there are two other authors with me. Let me explain why I asked them to join me in this section.

Jews disagree somewhat about God, about the people of Israel, and about the ethics of Judaism. Yet those differences do not divide us into groups. Mostly it is ideas about the Bible and Jewish tradition which separate Orthodox, Conservative, and Reform Judaism. The latter two groups, whom I call "liberal" Jews, disagree about the way changes ought to be made in Jewish law.

Since I want to help you understand Judaism, I need to help you understand these differences within it. Besides, I think that if you know where the groups disagree you are likely to join me in supporting Reform Judaism. But not every Jew wants the privileges and the problems of the Reform movement. Therefore, I thought it would be a good idea to invite an Orthodox and a Conservative leader to give their ideas about their group's teachings on the disputed topics. This way you will read about them with all the power that someone who believes in a theory can bring to it. You won't have to take my word about what ideas they stand for.

Rabbi J. David Bleich, who wrote the Orthodox response, is Professor of Talmud at Yeshiva University. He is also a Rosh Yeshivah at the Rabbi Isaac Elchanan Theological Seminary of Yeshiva University which trains Orthodox rabbis. Because of his great knowledge, the Rabbinical Council of America, the largest Orthodox rabbis' association, has had him write the regular article in their magazine, *Tradition,* on what is going on in Orthodox Jewish law today.

Rabbi Seymour Siegel, who wrote the Conservative response, is Ralph Simon Professor of Theology and Ethics at the Jewish Theological Seminary of America which trains Conservative rabbis. Because of his great knowledge, the Rabbinical Assembly, the Conservative rabbis' association, appointed him chairman of its Commission on Law and **121**

Standards, its group for deciding questions of modern Jewish law.

Although I have given you some of the official positions these men hold they have asked me to make clear to you that they are writing here for themselves alone, not for their institutions. You will also want to pay close attention to Rabbi Bleich's opening statement. He doesn't want his being part of this book to give you the idea he thinks all theories of Judaism are equally right.

Here is how we prepared this section. I wrote my statement first. I then sent it to Rabbis Bleich and Siegel. They then each wrote a response to what I had said. By agreement, they did not respond to each other and I did not change my ideas after I saw their responses. They did not see what I wrote in other parts of this book and they are therefore not involved in them in any way.

As far as I know, this is the first time any movement in Judaism has published a book inviting this sort of open disagreement by leaders of other groups. I think that says something important about Reform Judaism's respect for your ability to think for yourself. There's also something traditional about this form of Jewish book. Older Jewish texts were frequently printed with commentaries. Sometimes they gave explanations; often the writers of the commentaries argued with the author. A serious disagreement can help us clarify our thinking. We all hope that this experiment will help you to a true belief about the Bible and Jewish tradition.

1 Did God Give the Bible?

THE ANSWER to this question is short but not simple: "yes and no." In a way God did and in a way God didn't give the Bible. This is what the Bible itself says.

The "yes" part of the answer goes back to the Bible's account of what happened on Mt. Sinai. It says, "When God had finished speaking with Moses on Mt. Sinai, God gave Moses the two tablets of the testimony, tablets of stone, written with the finger of God" (Exod. 31:18). Later it adds, "The tablets were the work of God and

An Orthodox Response

The author of the following section wishes to express his gratitude for having been given the opportunity to fulfill the biblical mandate, "And now write for yourselves this song and teach it to the children of Israel. . . ."

This endeavor should in no way be construed as anything more than an attempt to transmit the timeless truths of Torah to Jewish youth. Its inclusion in this work should not be interpreted as in any way endorsing material contained in other sections or as implying that views expressed elsewhere in this volume are viewed by this author as legitimate interpretation of Jewish teaching.

JUDAISM is a religion of both faith and practice. Jews accept a set of basic beliefs as the touchstone which serves to define what

A Conservative Response

DID God give the Bible?

The right answer to this question, as Rabbi Borowitz said, is "yes and no."

How can this be right?

The best way to understand this is by means of a parable, a story. Imagine you are a student in a classroom and a very important professor comes to give a lecture. This professor is a very impres-

the writing was the writing of God, engraved on the tablets" (Exod. 32:16). (The "tablets of the testimony" had the Ten Commandments on them, just like the ones we often see in synagogue art.) God also told Moses the laws the Jews were to follow and, apparently, the correct account of all that had happened in history up to that time. Later Moses wrote down all this plus what had happened to the Jews to the time of his death. "When Moses completely finished writing the words of this Torah in a book" he told the Levites to put it into the Ark of the Covenant (Deut. 31:24–26).

You can already see what I meant by saying "yes and no." According to the Torah, God gave Moses the two tablets, told Moses the rest, and Moses wrote it all down. Note, please, that Moses did not set down his own ideas or use his own words. The Bible says and traditional Judaism taught that the words, even the exact way they are written, came from God, not from Moses' head or hand.

Of course, we are talking here only about the Torah, the first five

An Orthodox Response

Judaism is all about. We also accept a set of distinctive practices as part and parcel of our religious obligation. Belief and practice form an indivisible unity.

These beliefs and practices are accepted by Jews on the basis of revelation and tradition. To be sure, many of these beliefs are accepted by many non-Jews as well. A thinking person might become convinced of their validity even without benefit of revelation. Similarly, many of the *mitzvot* of Judaism can be appreciated on the basis of sound, readily apparent explanations rooted in common sense. Yet, despite their logical nature, these beliefs and practices are accepted, not on the basis of reason or common sense, but because God revealed them to us.

A Conservative Response

sive person who has an important message to deliver to the students. You listen carefully to everything he says. You take notes. All the other interested students take notes, too.

Then when you go home you take your notes and you write an account of what happened. . . . The other students do this too.

The question I want to ask you is, in the finished essay that you have written, are the words yours or the professor's? The answer is both. What you have included in your essay is what you heard and your reaction to what you heard. Both are mixed in together. It is difficult, if not impossible, to specifically indicate which part of your essay is yours and which is the professor's.

WHAT DO THE
BIBLE AND
TRADITION
MEAN TO US?

books of the Bible. It is the holiest part of the Bible, for the whole Jewish tradition rests on it. In other books of the Holy Scripture (the *Kitvei Kodesh,* a more Jewish name than the Greek word "Bible" which means "book"), the writers do more on their own. Some books are named after their authors who speak in a very personal way in them. Amos is passionate about justice. Hosea speaks tenderly about love and mercy. Jeremiah often sounds sad and troubled. Ezekiel has a wild imagination. King David is mentioned as the author of many but not all the psalms. King Solomon is noted as the poet who created the Song of Songs. In some Bible books you get a very definite feeling for the sort of people who must have written them. Still, books weren't included in the Bible because they had interesting authors. Though the authors wrote in their own way, Jewish tradition said they did so under God's guidance. The rabbis of the Talmud said the Holy Spirit (*Ruach Hakodesh*) "rested" on them, what moderns might call inspiration. (When a

---

This is reflected in the very first words a child is taught. As soon as a child can speak, his education must begin. Maimonides records that the first words a child is taught are "*Torah tzivah lanu Moshe morashah kehillat Ya'akov* – Moses commanded us the Torah, an inheritance for the community of Jacob." Only after the child has mastered the first lesson, only after he can clearly repeat this first sentence, does the parent go on to the second: "Hear O Isreal, the Lord our God, the Lord is One." The first sentence really includes two lessons:

1. The Torah was taught to us in its entirety by Moses to whom it was revealed at Mt. Sinai; and

2. The Torah is the inheritance of the Jewish people, i.e., it was

---

If someone later wanted to find out what the professor said, he would take all the notes of the students, put them together, and weave them into an integrated whole. This final essay would contain the words of the professor, your reaction to the professor's words, and the ideas of the editor who put it all together.

I hope you see the lesson from this parable and how it affects the answer to the question with which we started.

God, so to speak, is the professor. He spoke to the people of Israel. (In the next part we will try to understand just what it means to say that He "spoke.") What we have in the Bible is a composite of several reactions to that experience. If we want to find out what God really

125

poet or an artist is "in-spired" they, so to speak, take in a new "spirit.") Prophets like Joel, Obadiah, and Zephaniah show how directly they depend on God when they say things like, "Thus says the Lord" or "The word of God came to me, saying . . ." or "So said God. . . ."

A modern view of the Bible: God's inspiration, people's creation

For centuries the Bible has been the most important book (or collection of books) ever written. It was the best place for finding out what God wanted of people. Most Jews today still think that is

---

An Orthodox Response

transmitted from generation to generation by means of an authentic and reliable tradition. Even the first sentence of the *Shema* is taught not as the conclusion of a philosophical argument but as part of the contents of this revealed tradition.

Of course, a child can know the contents of the *Shema* only because he is taught. His intelligence is much too undeveloped to comprehend the logic of this proposition. But the lesson is clear nonetheless: Man is bound by the Torah because it is God's command, not because his mind so dictates. Moreover, if the Torah in its entirety is the revealed word of God, we are not free to pick and choose the beliefs and *mitzvot* which appeal to us and to reject those which appear too difficult or which are not appealing to us. Certainly, we may question the reasons which underlie the *mitzvot* and examine the cogency of our beliefs. Indeed, that is part of the *mitzvah* of *talmud Torah* (Torah study), but our commitment to the teachings of the Torah is quite independent of this questioning and investigation. As Maimonides puts it, it is unthinkable that God would command us to believe the irrational but there are many things which may be perfectly comprehensible in terms of divine

---

A Conservative Response

said to the people of Israel we must read the Bible because it is a record of revelation. But we must also understand that this record was written by men and women and therefore does sometimes have mistakes and reflects the shortcomings of the people who set it down. How, then, does the Bible help us now to know what God wants of us?

The first thing to do is read the Bible seriously and with an open

WHAT DO THE
BIBLE AND
TRADITION
MEAN TO US?

true. But many Jews do not agree with the Jewish tradition that God's part in the writing of the Bible was very great and people's part in it very little. That God actually wrote the tablets, gave them to Moses, and dictated the rest of the Torah caused modern Jews special problems. They came to believe that the Bible was more people's creation than God's inspiration, though it was still both.

There were two main reasons for their feeling this way. One had to do with the right to change things in Judaism. The other had to do with fitting the Bible in with all the rest of the things modern Jews came to know.

If the Bible is God's own message to us then it can be changed only by God or in the ways that God is said to have told Moses would be the right way to interpret the Torah. We can see this system in

wisdom but not to the intelligence of man. For example, God cannot command us to believe that there are square circles in the Garden of Eden because the very idea of a geometric object which is both a square and a circle at the same time is mind-boggling and utterly incomprehensible. But He can command us not to wear clothing containing a mixture of linen and wool even if we do not understand the logical reason for this prohibition. If we search hard enough we may find a perfectly plausible explanation—and indeed many scholars did suggest reasons for this as well as for other commandments—but, basically, we follow this commandment because God commanded us to do so. We find ourselves in much the same position as the person who uses acupuncture to relieve pain. He does not fully understand the scientific processes involved in acupuncture, but he knows that it works. Similarly, we may not be able to plumb the depths of divine wisdom but we know that God's commandments are designed for our benefit.

It is acceptance of the divinity of the Torah in its entirety (which means we are not at liberty to make changes) and recognition of our obligation as Jews to feel bound by His commandments (which

heart and mind. We believe that God will somehow open our minds and hearts to Him if we study His word with a full intention. Also we know what generations of Jews have heard when they read the Bible. This information is included in the Talmud and in the tradition.

We will have more to say about this later.   ■

the Talmud and the later law books. It worked pretty well until modern times. Then Jews were let out of their ghettos or *shtetls* into the modern world. They began to live and think in new ways. They thought it would serve God better if some changes were allowed in Jewish law. But, since the Torah was God's own book and the interpretations had God's power behind them, they couldn't be changed. Thus the Torah says that we must not kindle a fire on Shabbat. Modern Jews often felt that turning on a gas stove to warm a meal would add to the joy of the Shabbat. So, too, the Torah says that a man who is supposed to be descended from the old priestly families, the *Kohanim,* may not marry a woman who has been divorced, though all other Jews may. This seemed an odd reason to stop the founding of a loving Jewish family. And there is an old puzzling rule in the Torah, a Jew may not wear a garment made of mixed fibers of linen and wool.

If God gave these and other laws of the Torah, you should follow them even if they don't seem to make much sense to you. But if they really don't seem a sensible way of doing what God wants then there is another way of looking at them. Perhaps, instead of being God's laws, they are people's ideas of how to serve God. As it turns out, very much of what Jews said years ago still sounds right to us. In fact, much of it is smarter than anything we could have thought up ourselves. They were people like us but they were truly inspired. So we study what they said with the greatest respect. But being people

An Orthodox Response

means that we cannot select and choose what appeals to us and reject what does not) which constitute the basic premises of Judaism. While there is room for, and indeed over the ages there has often been, legitimate disagreement over certain points of law, practice, or belief, these disagreements took place within a framework of acceptance of the divinity of Torah and of the binding nature of its commandments. Such disagreement is *within* the tradition, not *about* the tradition which is the very essence of Judaism. Traditional or Orthodox Judaism cannot but reject as inauthentic any form of Judaism which does not accept these basic premises. That is why Orthodox rabbis feel that they cannot do or say things which might appear to confer legitimacy upon forms of Judaism which they feel to be inauthentic. That is why I must stress that my contribution to this book should not be construed as meaning that I accept the other contributions as being expressive of alternate and acceptable Jewish points of view.

128

God *did* give the Bible—*in its entirety.* There is no significant difference between the Ten Commandments and the rest of the

they put things in terms of their day: disarmament was "swords into plow blades, spears into tools to prune trees." That still makes a lot of sense—but today some of their laws trouble us. Following them doesn't help us feel closer to God. Sometimes they even seem to get in the way of our being religious. This seemed so true, so real to modern Jews, that they changed the old Jewish idea that God gave the Torah and was responsible for the rest of the Bible. For us, then God "gave" means that people wrote the Torah and all the Bible and God was their inspiration.

The Bible as a human book fits nicely with what else we know

Reading the Bible as a human book makes it fit in with all the rest of what science has taught us about the history of religions. Everywhere in the world people have told stories of how their gods created the world, of the miracles done to help them, of their temples and holidays, of the laws they were to follow. Some of the Bible stories are like those of other people, particularly like their neighbors in the Near East, the Sumerians and Babylonians. If God gave the Torah it seems strange to see similar stories in other people's books. If people wrote them we'd expect them to be like other stories of the same time and place. What's interesting then is to see where,

---

Five Books of Moses. It was precisely to prevent such a mistake from arising that the Ten Commandments were eliminated from the daily liturgy. True, the Ten Commandments were inscribed upon stone tablets by God Himself, but the rest of the Torah was dictated by God. Moses merely transcribed what God told him to write and Moses did so in the precise language commanded by God. The Torah was given "by the mouth of God through the hand of Moses."

The same is true for each of the books of the Prophets. The Prophets were not merely "inspired." They related and recorded the contents of their prophetic messages precisely in the manner in which God commanded them. Certainly, they speak in the idiom of their day. "The Torah speaks in the language of mankind." God wants His words to be understood, so He transmits a message which will be comprehensible to all the people He wishes to address.

The text of the Bible as we have it today—that of the Torah Scroll which is read in the synagogue—is identical in every significant detail with the original Scroll of the Torah written by Moses in the

despite the similarities, the Jewish story differs. Compared to the Babylonian flood story, for instance, it's clear the authors of the Noah story had a very much better sense of God and people.

Many other things in the Bible seem odd if we believe that God wrote or said them. For example, some stories like the stories of the creation or the flood seem to be told in two different ways. So, too, a story told about Abraham is repeated about Isaac. Some commands hardly sound like what God wants. Thus, Abraham is told to kill his son Isaac and the Jews are directed to kill all the Canaanite women and children. Other things seem odd if God wrote the Bible this way. In some places, scholars think the Hebrew text clearly has spelling mistakes. And in the Torah scroll a few letters must always be

An Orthodox Response

wilderness. Even what may appear to be spelling mistakes and letters which seem to be written upside down are present in all existing copies of the Torah Scroll. These aren't mistakes at all, but textual vagaries designed for a specific purpose. They are frequently designed to teach specific laws or moral lessons. Many laws and maxims are recorded in the Talmud as being derived in this manner.

The Midrash comments, "Moses wrote thirteen Scrolls of the Torah, one for each tribe, and a thirteenth to be placed in the Ark so that the Torah would not be falsified by anyone." Every tribe needed its own Scroll of the Law for study and public reading. The thirteenth Scroll of the Torah was not the property of any single tribe but of all Israel. It was preserved in the Ark in the Tent of Meeting and later in the Temple where it was constantly guarded. It was not designed to be used for study or public reading. It had only a single purpose. Should any person dare to tamper with the sacred text of the Torah he would immediately be exposed as a falsifier of God's word. No group could initiate changes and point to a false Torah text as support for its innovations, claiming that its Torah Scroll was the proper version and the Torah Scrolls of the other tribes were false. The thirteenth Scroll was carefully preserved as the "master" copy. Any Torah which did not correspond in every detail was known to be fraudulent.

It is not at all surprising that other peoples of the ancient world had stories very similar to those of the Bible. In the earliest period of mankind the entire human race had a common history. All people shared a common tradition with regard to the creation of man. The

130

Flood was too close in time and too cataclysmic to have been forgotten. If anything, the fact that these stories are in other peoples' books as well shows simply that they are historically true. With the passage of time these stories undoubtedly became blurred and somewhat inaccurate in detail. God included them in the Torah

written hanging or upside down. If God gave the Bible one has to do all sorts of explaining about why God would want such things. If people wrote the Bible we can easily understand how errors or different versions of a tale got into the text.

All in all, it seems much more sensible to many modern Jews to say the Bible was written by people. These authors were real geniuses, geniuses at knowing God and what God wanted. However, they weren't perfect. Over the centuries, we've learned some things they didn't know so we feel we can disagree with them. For modern Jews, to say God "gave" the Bible means that God inspired its authors or was especially close to them. ■

---

which He gave to the people of Israel, not merely to correct the historical record, but also to teach moral and religious truths. The Torah teaches that the Flood was a punishment for crimes of violence. It was not simply an unfortunate calamity. God takes note of the actions of mankind. He abhors violence and immorality. He punishes as well as rewards.

The story of the *Akedah* (the binding of Isaac) teaches a great deal about faith and trust in God and that man should not presume to believe that he knows God's ultimate intention. Yet we should not lose sight of the obvious lesson, namely, that human sacrifice was not unusual in the days of Abraham and that the story of Isaac makes it abundantly clear that God rejects such sacrifice.

It goes without saying that God loves good and despises evil. We have been taught that lying is bad. And usually it is. But sometimes a falsehood is virtuous. The Talmud teaches that distorting the truth for the sake of promoting good will or avoiding bad feeling is meritorious. A harmless lie designed to make someone feel good is praiseworthy. Abraham says that Sarah is his kinswoman but doesn't admit that she is his wife because he is afraid for his life. Jacob does not tell Isaac about the sale of the birthright because that would only cause pain to his aged father. These acts were not bad, they were good.

It is wrong to think that people ascribed their own anger and hatred to God. Remember, the Bible is the word of God, not man's fantasizing about God. God's decrees may seem harsh in some given situations, but they are born of a concern for all of mankind and a concern for all of human history. The Talmud relates that, had Saul not delayed the execution of Agag, Haman would not have been born and would not have been able to torment the Jews of his day. Saul's delay gave Agag time to perform an act which only led to unspeakable misery. In seeking to prevent this and similar agony to all of mankind God is not brutal, but kind. ■

2 How Does God Speak to People?

IN MANY books of the Bible God seems to speak to people very often. In the Torah, particularly, God is regularly described as giving Moses rules for the Jews. "The Lord spoke to Moses and said, 'Speak to the Israelites and say to them. . .' ." The same sort of thing happens elsewhere in the Bible. God comes to Samson's mother to tell her she's going to have a child. God gives Isaiah speeches for the Jews.

How, exactly, God "speaks" the Bible never makes clear. I would guess that is because most religious people years ago thought it natural that God would talk to people. The Bible does give us some hints, though. God comes to Balaam, the non-Jewish prophet, and to others, in dreams. Daniel has visions. Abraham has three visitors but later in the story it is God who speaks to him. A *malach,* one who does God's work (usually translated "angel"), gives Zechariah God's message.

An Orthodox Response

I REMEMBER vividly trying to explain to my son, who was then about three years old, that God does not have a body. He said, "Okay. God doesn't have hands or feet. I understand." Then he screwed up his little nose, assumed a posture of defiance, and continued, "But he has a face, a mouth, and a neck, doesn't he?" One of the most difficult things to explain to a child—or to an adult—is how God can "speak" if he has no body.

A Conservative Response

THE BASIC idea of Jewish religion is that there is a God and that He somehow communicates with people.

If there is no God, then there can be no religion. If this God is just there and does not open Himself to people, then the assertion that there is a God does not mean very much.

The people of the Bible frequently spoke in picture-words or what

132

WHAT DO THE BIBLE AND TRADITION MEAN TO US?

Once, the Bible says, God spoke directly to the Jewish people as a whole. That was at Mt. Sinai. Then, says the Torah, God, not Moses and not any messenger, made ten statements to all the Jews assembled at the foot of the mountain. Jewish tradition normally did not call these Ten Commandments, though that is not a bad title for them. It called them *Aseret Hadibrot,* the Ten Words, better, the Ten Utterances. You can imagine how important they are if God is said to have spoken them directly. That explains too why the Jews, having heard God speak to them, agreed that they would, as a people, serve God forever. These events at Mt. Sinai—which include giving the whole Torah, not just the Ten Commandments—were seen as the basis of the whole Jewish tradition.

As people ask more questions
God's speaking becomes a problem

In the rabbinic literature, the Talmud and Midrash, written in the first five centuries of the Common Era, some individuals tried to imagine how God had spoken at Sinai or to people in the Bible. But the rabbis never came to any agreement about this. They apparently didn't think it a very important question. How God could "speak" began to bother thoughtful Jews only when they came in contact with medieval science and philosophy, in the 900s C.E. and later.

This question is hardly new. It troubled the early Sages of the Talmud and the Midrash. (Curiosity, incidentally, did *not* originate with, nor is it limited to, liberal Jews. Traditional Jewish scholars from the earliest periods of our history until this very day were, and are, motivated by intense curiosity. But instead of rejecting Jewish tradition because of questions, they thought long and hard in order to understand that tradition as fully as possible.) Only instead of putting their difficulty in question and answer form, the Sages explained these phenomena in short, cryptic statements. They

---

Rabbi Borowitz calls symbols. We use such words all the time. I have heard people say, "This painting speaks to me." "This movie really had something to say." Well, movies have sound, but they do not speak to people in the way that people speak to each other. Paintings don't have sound. What we mean when we say that the painting speaks to me or the movie has something to say is that some kind of message, some kind of impact is made upon me when

Some of them worked out an idea which, though we have to change it to meet our understanding of the world, is still appealing. Thus Maimonides (about 1080 C.E.) talked of God as the Supreme Intelligence behind the universe. God ordered the world by thinking. The prophet "heard" God because his mind was able to think thoughts great enough to approach God's level. For Maimonides God "speaks" by thinking, almost as if God were broadcasting ideas, but only some people—prophets—had radio sets (minds) sensitive enough to pick them up.

Many modern people have trouble with the idea that God speaks. On a simple level it implies that God has lungs, a voice box, and a mouth, which doesn't make much sense. It hardly seems what the Bible meant. Even trying to think of "the voice of God," without a body behind it, is difficult. Americans like to think of God's "voice" as a rich baritone, suggesting that women aren't created as much in God's image as men are. Does God's "voice" speak Hebrew as some people think? It all sounds too little for the great God of the whole universe.

An Orthodox Response

describe our ancestors' experience at Mt. Sinai as being one in which they "heard that which is seen and saw that which is heard."

Scientists have demonstrated that an electrical stimulus applied to a certain area of the brain will cause "visions" even if the eyes are closed. A stimulus applied to a different area will produce the sensation of sound even if no noise is present. The subjects of such experiments experience certain perceptions—and the perceptions are very real—but they hardly reflect the reality of the physical world which surrounds them. My analogy is, of course, very crude, but this is the explanation our Sages intended to convey. Our ancestors heard a voice, but it was not produced by sound waves. They saw a vision, but it was not caused by a visual object. That is

A Conservative Response

I look at the painting or see the movie. Somewhat the same thing is meant when we say that God speaks and that God spoke. He communicated with the people, especially the Jewish people. What did He communicate? He communicated that He was making a special kind of agreement with the Jewish people that they would

134

be His people and He would be their God. He communicated His love for human beings. He also communicated that He wants us to follow justice and to return the love with which He loves us by loving our fellow men. He also told us that He wants us to order our religious life through Law. But more about this later.

WHAT DO THE
BIBLE AND
TRADITION
MEAN TO US?

Besides there's nothing like God "speaking" in our own experience. We'd be pretty suspicious of anyone who came to us and said they had heard God speaking to them. It seems far more sensible for most modern Jews to call God's "speaking" a symbol-word. (I'll explain this more in Part IV, Chapter 2.) People use everyday language to describe things that seem greater than any words we have for them. That takes place when we try to explain how God communicates with us. Since the symbol—"speaks"—comes from our regular language, we can understand it. But "God speaks" also points to something which our words can't easily describe. It's our way of saying that people can get to know what God "wants" of them. (Note how I had to use another symbol there.) It doesn't mean that God goes around whispering Hebrew in people's ears.

Yet how can a modern person explain how this really happens? This is a question on which Jews strongly disagree.

Many traditional Jews suggest that even today it is best to follow the Bible and the rabbis and not pay too much attention to this question. What's important is that we have some idea of what God

---

why *Targum Onkelos,* the ancient Aramaic translation of the Bible, translates the terms "And God spoke," "And God said," etc., as "And God revealed Himself."

Prophecy is a topic which medieval Jewish philosophers discuss in great detail. Maimonides explains that prophecy is very much like extrasensory perception. It would be impossible for us to explain what color really is to a person who has been blind from birth. In talking to one another about color we can use only words which reflect our common experience. These words are meaningless to a person who has not had a similar experience. Prophecy is very much like a sixth sense. The only one who can really understand what it is like is a prophet. But it is an experience which

---

I think that God communicated and communicates in the ways which Rabbi Borowitz mentioned. I do not think that anyone excludes any other. There is, however, one other way in which God "speaks" to men and women. This is through events, through things that happen to us. If, for example, you recover from a very severe illness, this event "speaks" to you so that you want to make more of life and be a better person. If your mother or father stays up with you all night when you are sick or afraid, this event speaks to you about the love that your parents have for you.

The ancient Israelites believed that certain things that happened

wants of us. We should concentrate on doing the right thing, not trying to figure out just how God gets in touch with people. There are many things too great for us to understand and this is one of them. For some people questions of "how" and "why" are dangerous. They bother people so much they end up not believing in our old and great tradition simply because they can't figure it all out. People shouldn't stop loving because they can't really explain what love is or how one falls in love. Similarly, there's enough about the Torah we understand and love to make us realize how much greater and wiser than us it often is.

Most liberal Jews are somewhat more curious than that. For them, to be modern means to think for themselves as much as they can. Since they believe people are mainly responsible for the Bible they are interested in exploring what people "hear" when God "speaks." And, of course, they feel we can be a lot more certain when we talk about what people do rather than what God does.

An Orthodox Response

cannot be misinterpreted, just as a person who experiences visual perceptions of color knows exactly what it is that he is experiencing. "The Torah speaks in the language of mankind" and uses words like "spoke," "said," etc., as a simple and easily understood metaphor for the prophetic experience.

Prophecy is by no means to be equated with inspiration. It is not a matter of conscience, feeling, sensitivity, or even simple intelligence. It is a very special form of perception of God. Care should be taken not to confuse prophecy as an experience with prophetic messages recorded in the Bible. Prophecy is primarily an experience. At times God does transmit messages through the mechanism of the prophetic experience. Those messages which applied to all generations are recorded in the Bible and are the word of God.

At Mt. Sinai our ancestors all shared in a prophetic experience. Moreover, they saw (note how I slip into imprecise language) that

A Conservative Response

to them were ways in which God spoke to them. The most important event was their liberation from the land of Egypt. The fact that they were freed from Egyptian bondage in what seemed to them was a wonderful and miraculous way meant that they were a special people of God and that they too would have to dedicate themselves to the liberation of slaves and the righting of injustices.

When they came to Mt. Sinai, they spelled this obligation out and accepted the obligation to become God's people and to follow His

Some modern ways of understanding how God "speaks" to us

Here are what I think are the four main liberal explanations of God "speaks" and people "hear" God.

1. Somewhat like Maimonides taught, one view is that we learn about God through our intelligence. As human knowledge and experience have grown, so we can get to know more about God. That explains why our ideas have changed over the centuries and continue to change. In olden times new ideas may have come as such a surprise that people thought someone must have given them to the thinkers. Today we know we "get" ideas by thinking. Here "God speaks" means that God sets up the world with intelligence and "gives" us the mind by which we get to know the world and God.

2. Another idea says one part of our intelligence is particularly

---

God "spoke" to Moses and that he was the trusted messenger of God. There are different levels of prophecy. All prophecy requires spiritual and intellectual preparation. The level of prophecy to which the prophet may aspire is directly commensurate with his preparation and spiritual achievement. Moses was the greatest of all prophets. His vision was clearer and more precise than that of other prophets.

God "speaks" to man only through prophecy or the holy spirit which is a form of prophecy. Other references to God communicating with man should be understood as being a figurative or poetic use of the term. Although God "speaks" only to prophets, and even to them only at certain times when they are properly prepared to receive the prophetic spirit, man may quite literally speak to God whenever he wishes to do so. Man's talking to God is called prayer—and God is always ready to listen. ■

Law which was a way in which they could express their love of God and bring justice and compassion into their lives.

God also speaks to us through the deeds and thoughts of other people. Other people, especially great and inspired people, are vessels which God uses to "speak" to us. In our tradition, we believe that the great teachers of the Talmud and their disciples and followers were the vessels which God used to speak to us today. ■

important in understanding God and what God "wants" of us, our conscience. Everyone has this sense of good and bad, though they often get confused. Still people at their best can know what is important in the world and what they ought to do in it. When conscience is at its deepest and "speaks" to us of what we really should or shouldn't do, then God "speaks" to us.

3. The next theory includes our feelings as well as our conscience. Being religious isn't merely being ethical. It starts with that but goes beyond doing the right to something which is very much more personal. It involves feelings, our sense of the mystery of all things, our notion that as unimportant as we are we are still personally connected to the Source of all life. In such a spiritual mood, open to what the world and reality are, we get understanding and a sense of duty. From such a feeling we say God "speaks" to us.

4. The last idea says it's more complicated than that but still like an experience we all have. If there's someone you like very much, a friend, a brother or sister, your parents, you get to know what they want of you. Often they don't even have to say anything. You just know. It's not clear how you know it but when you love someone you get a special sensitivity to who they are and what they expect of you. So with God. As you get close to God you begin to know what God wants of you. (Remember, right after saying the *Shema* we repeat the Torah's words that we should "love" God.) God "speaks" now is our way of saying what often happens between all people who are close to each other.

How much is God? How much is people?

Did you notice that I put these four liberal ideas in a certain order?

The higher the number the more important a part God plays in them. Of course, God is involved in all of them. But there is a big difference between saying God is behind our minds or conscience and saying we have a mysterious feeling for God or that we learn from being close to God. Each theory will suggest a different way to read the Bible. It can be mainly a book of ideas, of ethics, of our feeling for the mystery behind reality, or the diary telling of the love between the Jews and God. Whichever of these ideas you accept, none of them suggests God "speaks" with a voice in people's ears. All of them teach that God communicates with people, in Bible times and today. ■

3 Why Are the Prophets Especially Important to Us?

IN TRADITIONAL Judaism the five biblical books which make up the Torah—Genesis, Exodus, Leviticus, Numbers, and Deuteronomy—are especially holy. We keep scrolls of the Torah at the front of the synagogue. Reading their sections in order, Shabbat after Shabbat, we go through the whole Torah at services in one year. Not so with the books of the Prophets. We don't read through all the prophetic books from beginning to end. Each Shabbat, we read only a special part, selected from them (the *haftarah*). They are, of course, holy to us but not on the same level as the Torah.

Liberal Jews consider the Prophets much more important than that in their understanding of Judaism. We find in the Prophets' teaching something of our own sense of Judaism as a changing, growing religion.

I am now going to point out some differences between the Judaism described in the Torah and in the Prophets. I believe what

An Orthodox Response

THE FIVE BOOKS of Moses have always seemed more important to Jews and have been studied more assiduously than other books of the Bible because they are the source of Jewish Law. The Torah provides not only ritual laws such as dietary laws, regulations concerning Sabbath observance, etc., but also laws governing business dealings, farming, and many, many aspects of everyday

A Conservative Response

FOR TRADITIONAL JEWS, the Prophets are not different from the rest of the Bible. The rabbis in the Talmud say that the prophets do not come to say anything new—only to call the people to repentance—that is to say to help them follow the ways of the Torah and the teachings of Judaism.

I say here is fair but because I will be brief my ideas may come out somewhat exaggerated. Please keep in mind that I don't think the Torah and the Prophets have completely different teachings. That's nonsense. Some of the things liberal Jews like best about the Prophets are certainly in the Torah. For the liberals, too, the Torah is the basis of Judaism. Remember the Torah calls Moses the greatest of all the prophets. For all the differences we liberals sense between the Torah and the Prophets they are still two parts of one great tradition.

In general, the sort of Jewish instruction one gets in the Torah is law. It tells us what to do, regularly, for all time. In general, the Prophets speak to a specific situation, criticizing the way the community is behaving and reminding the people of what they should be doing for God. I think I can point out three specific differences between the Torah and the Prophets which made many modern Jews want to stress the Prophets in their Judaism.

One difference: the Torah focuses largely on the Temple, the Prophets on decent behavior

Much of the law in the Torah deals with the Temple and the services that were to go on there. The end of the Book of Exodus gives instructions for building the traveling tent-sanctuary in the

---

An Orthodox Response

life. These have to be studied in detail in order for one to know how to conduct oneself in life. The Prophets did not have the power to add or to modify these laws. They certainly did not have the authority to annul or to revoke any laws of the Torah. As a matter of fact, the Torah itself tells us that if a prophet seeks to abrogate any of the laws of the Torah that in itself is absolute proof that he is a false prophet.

It is incorrect to say that the prophets wanted to modernize Judaism. The words of the prophets are the words of God. God is

---

A Conservative Response

That is why, though the Prophets are obviously important, traditional Jews do not speak of prophetic Judaism, for, to them, there is no special type of Judaism associated with the Prophets.

That, of course, does not mean that the Prophets are not sacred and beloved. We do read from the Prophets every Sabbath and every festival.

wilderness. Leviticus is mostly about Temple sacrifices. Sections of Numbers and Deuteronomy are occupied with the priests and Levites and their duties. These laws tell us how Jews in Bible times believed they should serve God and so are still worth our attention. They don't tell us much directly about how we should live as Jews. There hasn't been a Temple in Jerusalem in about 2,000 years, so almost none of these laws has been carried out for all that time.

The Temple was surely the center of Jewish religion in the time of the prophets. Interestingly, the prophets don't spend much of their time talking about it. (Haggai is an exception and so is the last part of Ezekiel.) Instead, the prophets are disturbed that the Jews are not serving God in everyday life and building a better society. Amos complains they abuse the poor. Isaiah says their rulers are not doing justice. Habbakuk criticizes the strong for taking advantage of the weak. These sound like things going on today, things Jews ought to care about and try to help change. Even 2,500 years after the prophets, Jews believe that God "cares" how we treat other people and that this should be one of the most important parts of our religious duty.

Some scholars say that the Prophets are especially important to modern Jews because they teach us ethics. I don't think that is quite accurate. True, they are quite concerned with people doing the right. With modern Jews living as part of the general society much of our Jewish duty now has to do with our responsibilities to

unchanging and so are His words and wishes. The prophets were charged with specific missions. Usually, their task was to point out that Jews had become lax in fulfilling God's will in certain specific ways. Often, the prophets charged the Jews with being lax in ethics and morality which led to the erroneous impression by some that the prophets were not concerned with other aspects of Judaism. Actually, they were very much concerned with all of Jewish teaching. They simply addressed themselves to those areas of Jewish life and values in which the need for correction was most pressing.

For traditional Jews, the Prophets bring forward ideas that are inherent in the rest of the Bible.

The main idea is that the rituals of Judaism, like going to the Temple when it existed, the observance of dietary laws, synagogue worship, etc., are vitally important and the heart of Judaism. However, the observance of these important commandments has to

non-Jews. Still the Prophets teach religion, not just ethics, for their ideas are founded on what God "wants." They are not just talking about being good, but on being true to God. Micah's famous quotation begins "People have been told what's good. They know what God wants, that they should do justice and love mercy." But remember how it ends, "and walk humbly before God." (Try reading some of the Prophets and see if you think they are teaching ethics or religion.)

In any case, because the Prophets made our behavior to other people central to Judaism they became particularly important to modern Jews. Until about two hundred years ago Jews had been forced to live segregated from other people. The Torah largely dealt with a Jew's duty to other Jews. When Jews came out into the society and asked what Judaism said about their duties to non-Jews they took much of their guidance from the Prophets. True, the Prophets had spoken of a Jewish society but the modern Jew saw—with great joy—that the same standards should be applied in the countries of which they were now citizens. Since so much of their lives would be lived among non-Jews they felt that these general Jewish duties were now as important in their lives as were the laws of the Torah.

An Orthodox Response

There is no difference at all between the Judaism of the Prophets and that described in the Torah. While certainly many ethical concepts are expounded by the Prophets with great beauty and eloquence, the basic concepts are all to be found in the Five Books of Moses. The Torah is, after all, more than just a book of laws. It teaches ethical values and moral sensitivity no less than do the Prophets.

Jewish law specifies that the person who reads the *Haftarah* (the prophetic selection read in the synagogue on Sabbaths and festivals) must first read at least a brief section of the Torah. Rabbi Samson Raphael Hirsch comments that this procedure is especially

A Conservative Response

go hand in hand with the practice of justice, love of fellow man, compassion, and the pursuit of peace. The prophets are particularly angry with people who use their observance of the rituals as an excuse for not doing justice, not being honest, and not pursuing peace. To such people, the prophets say, your piety and observance are worth nothing in the eyes of God—because He wants us to serve Him in everything we do and not divide our lives into two compartments, one called religion and the other called ethics.

A second difference: the Torah focuses on details, the Prophets on our goals

A second reason why liberal Jews stress the Prophets has to do with the Torah's emphasis on the details of what we should do. Suppose, for example, you own, as people did in Bible times, a Jewish "slave" (someone who has sold his services to you for no more than six years). The Torah makes clear what happens if you provide your slave with a wife and they have children; what his rights are if you injure him; what must be done if he wishes to stay with you; and much more. Considering what slavery was like in the rest of the world at that time, these laws are remarkably humane. We can still learn much from them. But the law tends to deal mainly with the details of "slavery" and very little with the Jewish sense of what it is to be a person, God's creation, on which the law is based.

The Prophets seem more concerned with the purpose behind religious duties. Isaiah and Amos both explain that bringing sacrifices while being great sinners is useless. Jonah (not primarily a story about a fish!) stresses God's willingness to forgive, in this case the non-Jewish people of Nineveh, awful sinners and hated enemies of the Jew. (That is why Jonah ran away—he didn't want God

---

designed to teach that there is no distinction between prophetic Judaism and the Judaism of the Pentateuch. The two are identical in every respect.

There is a universalism in many prophetic writings which calls forth a ready response in many who do not have a strong feeling for the particularism of Judaism. These messages are therefore perceived as compatible with a Judaism which is undemanding in terms of specific beliefs and performance of *mitzvot*. To traditional Jews this is a misreading of the Prophets. To us the Prophets are an intrinsic and integral part of the single rich tapestry of Torah.

One theme which repeats itself over and over again in the

Seen in this way, the prophets are not bringing a new religion or even a new way of looking at the old religion. They are rather stressing what was already implicit in Judaism from the very beginning.

Traditional Jews are therefore not happy when liberal Jews think that, because a person is committed to the ethical life, he does not need to observe the rituals and traditions of Judaism. Traditional Jews argue that just as the prophets were angry when people

to forgive them—and why the Bible says God sent a great fish to bring him back.)

When Jews came into the modern world many felt that some of the old Jewish practices needed to be changed. They were mostly concerned about laws which had helped Jews in days when their neighbors segregated or persecuted them. These laws did not seem to be as helpful in serving God in a free society as they had been earlier. Some details remain important. But, for example, it seemed more important to socialize with non-Jews than to worry about just how they made their cheese or who had touched the wine they offered you, both important details in traditional Jewish law. So because the Prophets helped modern Jews look at the way the law served God and not just its details, they became especially important to us.

A third difference: the Torah emphasizes the permanent, the Prophets the need to change

Finally, the Torah laws speak of what is always to be done, year after year, century after century. True, traditional Judaism has ways to help the law change as time goes by (we shall talk about that later), but the main concern of the Torah is what goes on continuously. In such matters as not holding a grudge, doing charity, having a Sabbath, worshiping God, modern Jews agree the law should remain what it was. But in some cases modern times

An Orthodox Response

Prophets is the call to repentance. The prophets were sent by God to warn that improper conduct would lead to punishment, but that God is forgiving and accepts all those who sincerely regret their misdeeds. Repentance, of course, involves dedicating oneself to *all* the teachings of the Torah and observance of all the commandments, not just some. The prophets also carried a message of consolation. They assured the people that, even though they would be banished from their land and be forced into exile, ultimately they

A Conservative Response

separated the ritual obligations from the ethical obligations and thought, if they did the former, they had no need of the latter, so it is not right to separate elements of Judaism the other way. That is, thinking that if one is ethical one has no need to observe the traditions of Judaism.

The ritual observances bring us closer to God, and serving our

have made radical changes seem necessary. Again the Prophets hinted at what a proper Jewish attitude would be.

Occasionally, the Prophets say the Jews are putting the emphasis on the wrong thing. Isaiah argues that sacrifices and festivals are not as important as "doing good, pursuing justice, defending the oppressed, helping orphans, and pleading for widows." Jeremiah warns the people that God will even let the Temple be destroyed because they think that because they have Temple services they can do whatever sins they want and God won't "mind." Liberal Jews were moved by such speeches.

The prophets had great courage; they felt they were saying what God wanted. They went against what most Jews in their days thought was right. More, they insisted that the Jewish religion they saw around them was wrong and needed to be changed. They argued against what people had made of Judaism and said that there were more important things for Jews to do then. That was just the way many "modern" Jews felt about Judaism in their time. In the prophets, they found an example of what they believed God wanted them to do, to modernize Judaism.

For them the Prophets were almost more of an inspiration than the Torah. They even liked to call their ideas "prophetic Judaism." But for all their love of the Prophets they never abandoned the Jewish tradition of reading all the Torah and only parts of the Prophets. I like to think that they always knew the two parts of Judaism cannot really be separated one from the other. ∎

---

would be redeemed and the Temple would be rebuilt.

Sometimes the same prophet performed several different functions and his messages express diverse themes. That is why the tone and style of the writing would make it appear almost as if it is different people who are speaking.

By far the most important point to be made about the writings of the prophets is that they are, in their entirety, the words of God who conveyed His message to Israel through His prophets. ∎

---

fellow man also brings us closer to God. We need both to fulfill our responsibilities as Jews.

Traditional Jews would rather speak about Judaism than about prophetic Judaism or even rabbinic Judaism. After all, both the Torah and the Prophets (and the Writings) are parts of one Bible. ∎

4 How True Is the Bible?

IF GOD "gave" the Torah and inspired the whole Bible then it ought to be as perfect as anyone could imagine. True, it has to be in words people can understand. Still, anything in it that might seem to be false or immoral or even poorly written must be the reader's mistake. God's book is not wrong. So goes the traditional understanding of the Bible, particularly the Torah.

Liberal Jews hold another view. Since we think the Bible is as much people's work as God's inspiration, we find some parts of it are not true. Here the Bible authors showed how human they were. They gave the facts or ideals of their day and we, who live many centuries later, have learned better. So, liberal Jews have a special problem when they read the Bible. We have to keep asking ourselves whether the specific part we are reading is true or not. And there is no easy way to tell this. That is a problem. Liberal Jews

An Orthodox Response

THE BIBLE is true in its entirety. Belief in the truth of Torah is but a corollary of belief in its divine origin. The Bible is not a history book and therefore doesn't always tell us everything that we might like to know. If historical events are included, they are included for a purpose. Only that information which serves the biblical purpose is included. For example, the names given in the Bible are not always the names by which those people were called by their

A Conservative Response

TO ANSWER this question, let us remember the parable or story I suggested to you at the beginning of our discussion.

We believe that the Bible is the *record* of revelation. It is the humanly written-down account of the impact of God's speaking to the people of Israel. Therefore, we should not be surprised that there are some errors of fact in the Bible. Why?

First of all, because when people are anxious to tell a story

WHAT DO THE
BIBLE AND
TRADITION
MEAN TO US?

would rather face that difficulty than the one traditionalists have: to show that God really meant something good or correct by the problem passages. When liberals think about some of these explanations they sound pretty far fetched. It seems so much more sensible to believe that people who often make mistakes are responsible for the difficulties in the Bible.

This problem in the Bible should not be exaggerated. I think many liberals find most of the Bible true. The Psalms speak for us too when they praise God for the marvels of nature or for making people God-like. The Proverbs sound modern when they tell us that wisdom enriches our lives but foolishness destroys our humanity. Ezekiel tells a lasting truth when he says God prefers forgiving people who now want to do the good rather than punishing them. Surely we agree with the laws against cursing deaf people or making blind people trip. Again and again as we read the Bible we can hear ourselves saying quietly, "That's true."

The problems modern Jews have with the Bible

The questions we have about some of the Bible are of two major kinds. One has to do with its facts. The other is about its sense of good and bad.

---

parents or known to their friends. Names were originally descriptive, as is evident from the opening sections of Genesis. They were chosen or coined as a means of commemorating an event associated with the birth of the child or as a reflection of the emotions experienced by the parents. Later the Bible assigns descriptive names to people who may during their own lifetimes never have been known by those names at all. Jethro is a good example. The Sages tell us that the Torah refers to him by this name which, in

---

sometimes they overlook details. If you remember the story about the lecture and the lecture notes, they could be dated wrong. People frequently are not sure whether it is April 13 or 14 today. However, what they are sure of is what happened to them. Also people sometimes misspell the words in a love letter. This does not mean that the sentiments they express in the love letter are altered because they write *recieve* instead of *receive*.

Second, we do not really believe that God dictated the Bible word

147

HOW TRUE
IS THE BIBLE?

Sometimes, the Bible's history books seem pretty accurate. Today when archeologists dig up something which differs from the Bible's account of the kingdoms of Israel and Judah, they would suppose that they had misread what they found in their dig. The Bible is that reliable. But we have big problems with the Bible's early history—the period before the kingdoms—and lots of little problems in various books. Of course, if God is responsible for the Bible then there shouldn't be any questions about the accuracy of the text at all.

Sometimes the Bible doesn't fit in with other historical facts we know. According to the Books of Kings, the Exodus from Egypt took place in the middle of the 1400s B.C.E. Modern students of ancient Egyptian history think the most likely date would be the mid-1200s. That difference of opinion is troublesome—but the archeologists make it even worse. The Jews are said to have wandered in the wilderness for forty years after the Exodus and then came to Canaan. The first thing they did was conquer Jericho. Only the archeology of Jericho shows the town was destroyed in the 1300s and again in the 1100s. All these historical facts just don't fit together.

Another example is the Book of Esther. Ahasuerus seems a Persian king and we know a good deal about Persian kings. There's

An Orthodox Response

Hebrew, connotes "addition." Jethro is commended for suggesting the establishment of a judicial system and, upon God's concurrence, in causing an entire section to be "added" to the Torah. The same is true of names of places. The Sages frequently comment that the name describes a historical event and is not simply a geographic place name. These comments serve to dispel many of the alleged historical discrepancies. Others were noted and discussed by the Sages of the Talmud and Midrash long before the age of Bible criticism. Evidence of the apparently rather advanced age

A Conservative Response

for word. When people "heard" God's voice and learned about Him as the Creator of the world and as the One who wants justice and truth, they remembered the old stories that they had heard before about the creation of the world. They did not abandon all of the old stories but changed them in significant ways in order to conform with their new knowledge. For example, people all over the Near East told stories about a great flood that had destroyed most of mankind. In the old pagan stories, which are in many ways similar

WHAT DO THE
BIBLE AND
TRADITION
MEAN TO US?

no Ahasuerus in any list we have of them. There were strict rules for kings in Persia. They could not marry out of the leading Persian families, say a Jewish woman like Esther. They could not appoint alien prime ministers, such as Haman the Agagite or Mordecai the Jew. Then, again, if Mordecai came with the Jewish exiles to Babylonia in 597 B.C.E., he was old indeed by the time of one of the later Persian kings whom we might identify with Ahasuerus. (The chief possibilities seem to be Artaxerxes who died in 425 B.C.E. or Artaxerxes II who died in 328 B.C.E. Besides, if he was so old how did he get as pretty and young a cousin as Esther?)

Occasionally, too, the Bible says someone wrote a book but the evidence in it makes that difficult to accept. For example, Isaiah was apparently a grown man at the time of the Assyrian invasion of 722 B.C.E. In later chapters of his book, Isaiah talks about Cyrus, the Persian conqueror of 435 B.C.E. He talks of Cyrus as if he himself (Isaiah) were actually present at the time. If this were so, Isaiah would have been over two hundred years old. You can see one reason some people question the authorship of Isaiah.

It seems more sensible to believe another prophet wrote these speeches and they were added here. (We call him Deutero-Isaiah or the Second Isaiah since we know nothing more about him.) Liberal Jews would also say that the Exodus and the fall of Jericho were so

---

of Esther, for example, was recognized by the Sages and evoked considerable comment.

The Torah also uses hyperbole or exaggeration on occasion. For example, the Sages were emphatic in stating that neither Reuben nor King David was guilty of a heinous sin. But Reuben did act in a disrespectful and presumptuous manner. King David was greedy and lacking in compassion. To us, their transgressions would be relatively minor affairs, but for someone of Reuben's or David's high moral stature it was a very serious matter indeed. And

---

to the one in the Bible, the gods stopped the flood because they needed the food that humans brought to them in sacrifices. So they stopped the flood and allowed the survivors to bring animal offerings. The Israelites, believing in a God who was above nature and did not eat, when they told the story of the flood, of course, did not include the part about the divine beings needing food.

When the Jews heard God's voice they did not abandon all of their old laws. They kept some of them but changed them to reflect their

far back in Jewish history that, in the years of telling the story, the facts probably got mixed up. By contrast, the Book of Esther doesn't seem history at all but a story made up to teach us about anti-Semitism. Even if it isn't accurate history, its lesson about the need for Jewish courage is certainly true.

Sometimes the Bible goes against what we know about nature

Some stories, particularly the early ones in Genesis, go against what science has taught. The Torah says that creation took place in seven days. It seems to mean our sort of week since it ends with a Shabbat day. But science says that evolution, from creation to people, took about two billion years. Many other stories—all people coming from one couple, the flood, the origin of different nations—don't fit in with our scientific data.

An Orthodox Response

therefore the Torah censures them in extremely harsh terms. It brands them as having committed sins which they did not commit. The Torah is equating the enormity of their misdeeds with actions which we all recognize as repugnant. For persons such as Reuben and David the actions which they did perform were equally odious. This does not mean that the description is "untrue." The description is certainly true: it is a simile and simply has to be understood in proper perspective.

The biblical story of creation may be even more difficult to understand. Many Jews do not accept the theory of evolution. Those who do accept some aspects of evolution would speak, not of

A Conservative Response

new understanding. For example, we know that Hammurabi and the Babylonians had laws similar to the ones we have in the Bible, like paying for damages that had been done. However, whereas in Hammurabi's code you paid more to a nobleman whose property you injured than you did to an ordinary person, in the legislation in the Book of Exodus there is no recognition of difference of class. Everyone paid the same fine if he did wrong.

Third, the Jewish tradition has a long history of Midrash, which means searching the true meaning of the biblical text. In the Midrash we learn that we don't have to understand the Bible literally. If it says that the world was created in six days, we do not necessarily have to understand this to mean six days of twenty-four

150

WHAT DO THE BIBLE AND TRADITION MEAN TO US?

Miracles, too, go against what we know about nature. We can understand an east wind blowing the waters of the Sea of Reeds off a sand bar. But the Bible says that the waters parted just when Moses held up his rod, that the Jews walked across on dry ground, and that when Moses held up his rod again the waters immediately came back in on the Egyptians. The Bible also says that Joshua got the sun to stand still. There may not be many miracles in the Bible, but it is hard for a modern mind to believe they happened as described.

To liberals these stories are typical of the sort all people tell. The world over people have told stories about how the world began, how people got started, how death came into the world, and so forth. Naturally, they told their stories with the facts they knew. When it comes to facts, we think our modern ones are correct. But ancient people also put into their stories what they believed about God and people. We still can learn from these teachings. Their science may be old-fashioned, but their religious ideas are often still true.

random occurrences or of survival of the fittest, but of divine creation and a divinely guided evolutionary process. But even the most literal face the difficulty of explaining the phrase, "And it was evening and it was morning," which occurs in describing phases of creation which occurred prior to the creation of the sun and the moon. Remember that heavenly bodies were not created until the third day. But then, to what does the word "day" refer when used in referring to the first two days of creation? If there is no sun and no moon, what do the words "evening" and "morning" describe? Quite obviously, the reference is not to a day measured by sunset and sunrise. The Torah is referring to stages of creation. The use of the

hours. It could mean six epochs, six millennia, or something else.

Because of these reasons, we can understand why there are things in the Bible which we now know are not factually true—though of course they are religiously and morally true.

When we read things in the Bible that offend our moral sense, we should understand that these words have to be understood in their context. When a liberated Jew of a German concentration camp says very harsh things about Nazis, we understand that he is right in the circumstances he is living through—though he would have other ideas about other people who have done wrong at another time. We must remember, and this is hard to understand, that some of the directives in the Bible are not for all time but for the specific

Some stories are less about what happened than about what we believe

Modern scholars call such symbol-stories myths. Some questions are so deep they can't have simple, straight answers. A story which carries lots of meaning is a good way of giving the answer. So all religions have their myths. But be careful: Many people use the word myth only to mean something false. "Don't be foolish," they say, "that's only a myth." But, in serious religious discussions, myth means a story that may be untrue as fact but is used to teach hard-to-explain religious truths. The story of Cain and Abel is unlikely to have happened. Yet, after several thousand years, it still teaches us religious truths.

We don't normally call miracle stories myths, perhaps because they are so obviously created by people. When something wonderful happens to you it's natural that each time you repeat it the story

--- **An Orthodox Response** ---

term "day," at least in this early period, is metaphorical. A metaphor is not a myth. It is not a "story" used to teach a moral but a word or a phrase which has a meaning quite apart from its usual literal meaning.

Miracles are indeed events which defy natural law—that is why they are miraculous. But miracles must also be understood in proper perspective. We take regularity for granted. The sun always rises in the east and always sets in the west. We take cause and effect relationships for granted. One puts a flame to a piece of paper and it always burns.

But these phenomena are dependent upon the will of God. It is He who ordained that the world shall obey what we call the laws of nature. Indeed, the orderly nature of the universe and the regulari-

--- **A Conservative Response** ---

time that they were said. When, for example, a person is sick we tell him that he must stay in bed for some time. When he gets well, if he stays in bed all the time, we think he is sick and not well. The commands of God are sometimes applicable to all times, and sometimes applicable to a specific time with its specific problem. As a general rule, we must say that those commands which are offensive to our moral feelings were meant to meet a specific need at the time and not meant to be applied for all times. An example, the Bible does say that we can have slaves. This was because in

grows a bit. The Bible miracle stories are a way of praising God for helping the Jews or some pious person. Think for a minute about what crossing the Sea of Reeds says about God: sometimes when Jews were in terrible trouble they were saved—and they have been grateful to God for it. Again, though we may reject some of the facts, we agree with the belief. Even today, when something exceptional happens to us, we should thank God. So when a baby is born or a dangerous operation succeeds we too say, "It's a miracle." We mean that God was very good to us.

Sometimes the Bible seems to confuse good and bad

I think the hardest parts of the Bible to accept as God's truth are the few cases where our great heroes do evil things or God commands people to perform horrible acts. If they were not our patriarchs we

---

ty of causal phenomena are themselves nothing less than miraculous. God can just as easily will that on a given occasion the opposite take place. The Talmud tells us a story about a very great but poor scholar. One Friday afternoon his wife came to tell him that she had no oil for the Sabbath lamp. The scholar told his wife to fill the lamp with vinegar. When the wife protested that it would be purposeless, he explained that: "Let He who told oil to burn come and command the vinegar to burn." And, lo and behold, the vinegar did burn and there was light in the house for Shabbat. The moral of this story is very simple: There is no intrinsic reason why oil must burn and vinegar must not. It is no more difficult for God to perform a "miracle" than it is for Him to cause events to occur in accordance with the so-called laws of nature.   ■

---

those times everyone had slaves and the writers of the Bible wanted to humanize the institution. They did not mean that it should remain in force for all time.

A short word about miracles. The Hebrew word for "miracle" is *nes*. This word also means a flag, an emblem, a standard. A miracle is any event in which we recognize the presence of God, His flag, so to speak. Of course, we see this *nes* in extraordinary happenings. But if we are really religious we can see the *nes* even in ordinary, everyday happenings.   ■

153

would quickly say that Abraham and Isaac tell lies. Jacob takes advantage of Esau. Jephthah kills his daughter, apparently to fulfill a vow to God. Saul is removed as king because he did not kill an Agagite king and all the cattle he had captured. There are occasional laws and prophecies and psalms which call for the complete extermination of certain groups, including women and children. They go against almost everything else the Bible teaches, that God loves life and is full of mercy. Rather such passages sound very much like people of ancient times putting their hatred into God's mouth. Perhaps centuries back, when life was very much more brutal, that seemed like the truth. It isn't today, thanks to what Judaism has taught us. To be more truly Jewish, liberal Jews feel they must say these passages came from people—not God—and we know better than that today.

Having said all this, let me repeat what I said above. The parts of the Bible which seem untrue as fact or as religious teaching are very few compared to the ones that still inspire us. Particularly when we see the Bible as a human book written thousands of years ago, we are continually astonished at how great its human authors were. They really were geniuses. We can appreciate them best when we read their work remembering that God still "speaks" to us as God spoke to them. So we need to open our minds, our consciences, our religious sense, our feeling for relationship with God as we read their words. If we "listen" God often still "speaks" to us out of their writings. ■

5 How Has Judaism Changed since the Bible?

CHRISTIANS who know the Bible are often quite surprised when they participate in a religious observance in a Jewish home or come to a synagogue. The way we do things is often not what is called for in the Bible. That's because Judaism did not stop growing when the last Bible book was finished. (A popular scholarly opinion is that the last book was the Book of Daniel, at the time of Judah Maccabee, about 170 B.C.E.) Judaism has kept developing down to our own time. Many of our Jewish ideas and practices come from the rabbis of the talmudic period (the first five hundred years of the Common Era). To understand how their teachings got to be as important as the Bible you need to know their idea of the Oral Torah.

The rabbis of the Talmud take it for granted that God gave Moses more than the five books of the Torah. If you won't take me too seriously, I'll say they believed God gave Moses two Torahs. One

An Orthodox Response

IT IS NECESSARY to stress that the Oral Law possesses precisely the same status as the Written Law. The former is no less authoritative and no less binding than the latter. The Rabbis of the Talmud recorded the traditions handed down to them and made use of the canons of interpretation included in the Oral Law to set down previously unrecorded laws. Those pronouncements are every bit as much the word of God as are the Ten Commandments.

A Conservative Response

A GREAT TEACHER, Abraham Joshua Heschel, once said that Judaism consists of a minimum of revelation and a maximum of interpretation. We have the Bible. That is precious to us. But also we have the history of interpretation of the Bible which is basically in the Talmud but continues also until our own day. Getting back to

was written down and that is the Torah we have in our Torah scrolls. But God also gave Moses many instructions that were not written down. Like much of the teaching in a time when books were scarce, it was oral. The teacher said the lesson and the student memorized it. This teaching which God said and Moses memorized, the rabbis called the Oral Torah (*Torah shebeal peh*, literally, "the Torah which is in one's mouth"). It is normally called the Oral Law and I will use that term but I don't like it. The Oral Law contains a lot more than law. All that the rabbis have to say about what they believed or felt or did is part of the Oral Law. Even more important, the rules for interpreting the Written Torah are part of the Oral Torah. It is true that much of the Oral Torah is law—some of it is interpretation of the Written Torah and some of it is independent tradition. Yet even though we call it the Oral Law, it has stories, religious teachings, ethical ideas, short sermons, and a lot more than just rules.

An Orthodox Response

The Sages of the Talmudic period also enacted new laws and ceremonies. But there was a clear distinction between what was transmitted as God's Oral Law and rabbinic legislation. Some of our most beautiful ceremonies are entirely the product of rabbinic legislation. The observance of Chanukah, including the kindling of Chanukah lights, is a good example. The Sabbath candles and *Kiddush* over a cup of wine are others.

The Rabbis were never given the power to *change* the laws of the Torah. They were given the power to proclaim the New Moon. Remember, Judaism follows a calendar based upon the moon. The lunar month is a bit more than twenty-nine and a half days in length. That means that some months must be twenty-nine days in length and others thirty. The Torah teaches that in order to sanctify the New Moon a pronouncement to that effect must be made by the *Beth Din*. The *Beth Din*'s power in this area is absolute. It had to be absolute or else we could never be certain on which day the festivals really occurred. This is reflected in the respective Sabbath and Holy

A Conservative Response

the parable which we told at the beginning of our discussion, people, who were not present when the great professor spoke, read the record of the lecture and find how the message of the professor affects their own lives. They start doing new things, continue doing old things with some changes, and think new thoughts. In somewhat the same way, the tradition of Judaism is a tradition of

It's oral but it got written; it's law but it kept growing

You need to know two more things about the Oral Law. Despite its name, much of it got written down, probably because the rabbis felt there was an emergency. The Mishnah and the Talmud are the two main written parts of the Oral Law. The Mishnah was set down about 200 C.E.; the Talmud was probably put into writing about 500 C.E. But—and this is the second thing—while these are the most important collections of the Oral Law, there are lots more. Some were written down after the Mishnah and the Talmud; some were just passed on from teacher to student. It's best to think of the Oral Law, not as a book or group of books, but as a way of studying and thinking which has gone on until today. For example, it's part of the Oral Law when rabbis today try to figure out when it's right for hospital patients to be hooked up to life-preserving machines.

Day prayers. The Sabbath prayer reads, "Blessed are you O God who sanctifies the Sabbath." The Holy Day prayer reads, "Blessed are you O God who sanctifies Israel and the seasons." The reason is simple. Shabbat occurs automatically on the seventh day of the week. *Yom Tov* occurs only because the *Beth Din* has proclaimed the New Moon. Unless Israel were granted this power there would be no Jewish calendar and hence no festivals. Hence the formula, "who sanctifies Israel"—first Israel must be sanctified and given the *mitzvah* of sanctifying the New Moon and only then can the festivals be sanctified.

The *Pruzbal* is often cited as an example of rabbinic power to change the law. But that is simply not the case. Hillel did not change the law. In order to facilitate commerce and in order to assume that the needy would be able to secure loans, he employed and institutionalized provisions which were already inherent in the law. The *Pruzbal* involves turning a debt over to the *Beth Din*. Only private debts are canceled by *shmittah*, the seventh year. Debts

rereading the Bible and trying to find out what it means for us. It is turning the written book into a book of life.

That is why the Oral Tradition, as it is called, is so important for us. And that is why, as Rabbi Borowitz points out, it was thought that the history of interpretation is of equal importance to the written word itself.

Modern people often think of the Written Law as the unchanging, permanent part of the Torah. One can then think of the Oral Law as the changing, growing part of the Torah. That's helpful because the rabbis really didn't believe there were two different Torahs, only Written and Oral parts of one great system of Torah. Note then that the word "Torah" can be used in two ways. In the narrow sense, it means the five books with which the Bible starts. In the broader sense, it means all of God's guidance for the Jews, written and oral, old and modern.

Our Judaism was largely shaped by the Oral Law

The Oral Law is the source of much of what we practice in Judaism today. Shabbat candles and wine (*Kiddush*) are not mentioned in the Bible. Neither are synagogues nor the kind of prayer services we have. We learn about these from the rabbis. Because they were experts in the Oral Law the rabbis were allowed to make certain

---

An Orthodox Response

owed to the court can be collected afterward as well. Once the debt is turned over to the courts the money is no longer owed to a private individual and may be collected even after the seventh year. The Rabbis also had the power of *Hephker Beth Din*, roughly equivalent to the power of eminent domain which is recognized in Western society, i.e., the power of the state to seize private property in order to advance some overriding public good. Some authorities maintain that the *Pruzbal* was based upon the authority of *Hephker Beth Din*.

The Sages also had the power to decree passive nonperformance of *mitzvot* if they felt some compelling reason for doing so. It is for this reason that the *shofar* is not sounded when Rosh Hashanah occurs on *Shabbat* and the *mitzvah* of *lulab* and *ethrog* is not performed on *Shabbat*. The Sages were afraid that as a result of

---

A Conservative Response

In the process of interpretation, it was necessary to change some of the old laws, as Rabbi Borowitz points out, and to create new ones. Even if the individual laws change, the idea of ordering our religious life by means of laws and observances does not change. This is something like the way we look at the Constitution of the United States. It is a document that has been interpreted by thousands of judges in the past two hundred years. These interpretations have brought about many changes in the way we live. But

rules for the Jews. What they then said was Torah, God's instructions for us.

Their power to set the law could go very far. One of my favorite imaginative stories in the Talmud is of the time the angels came to ask God what day Rosh Hashanah would be. God said that was up to the rabbis' court to decide (based on observations of the moon). So God said they'd all have to go down to earth to find out what the court had ruled!

The rabbis sometimes made drastic changes in the law. Hillel, then apparently head of the rabbinic court, saw that people weren't making loans in the year or so before the sabbatical year. People knew all loans would be canceled when the seventh year arrived so they didn't want to lend their money out and not get it back. Hillel then introduced a system of registering the loans with the court (called a *Prozbul*), and this allowed them to remain in effect despite the sabbatical year. This certainly helped many Jews—but the Written Law had nothing like this in its commandment that the sabbatical year cancels all loans.

great zeal in seeking to fulfill the *mitzvah* people might inadvertently carry the *shofar* or the *lulab* and *ethrog* through a public thoroughfare and desecrate the Sabbath in the process. So they decreed that these *mitzvot* not be performed on *Shabbat*.

The powers given to the Rabbis are carefully spelled out in the Oral Law. They were always careful not to exceed their power. They simply had no authority to make sweeping changes, no matter how advisable those changes might appear to be in light of changing social or economic conditions. The teachings of the Torah may be readily applied in all societies and in all ages. Historically, Jews lived in many different lands over the course of centuries, without abandoning their commitment. The Sages speak of Torah as existing prior to the creation of the world. God didn't create a world and then compose a Torah suitable to the needs of the human

the idea of the Constitution and the idea of law do not change.

Conservative Jews agree that we must change some of the old laws. What we do not agree to is the abolishment of the idea of law itself. If we did this, we would encourage each person to act Jewishly the way he prefers to do so. Of course, in a free society, everyone has a right and privilege to follow his own conscience. We are not speaking of what people do but what they ought to do. ■

Modern times raised new questions and opened new opportunities

This system of rabbis teaching and sometimes changing the law seemed to work pretty well until modern times. Then, rather quickly, Jews started living most of their lives among non-Jews. But Jewish law was largely adjusted to Jews living cut off from other people, setting their own styles and changing things rather slowly. Happy to be part of general society, the Jews now had many problems. Some were only matters of custom: Should Jews give up Yiddish for German or English or get a general education? Some were matters of law: To what extent could Jews eat in restaurants that weren't kosher or use musical instruments at Shabbat services? Some had to do with a new sense of human rights: Shouldn't women be equal to men in the rights and privileges of the practice of Judaism?

Modern life also brought with it new opportunities and challenges, for example, the use of electricity. Under the rules of the Oral Law, traditional rabbis had ruled that electricity was to be treated as a form of fire. (When most switches are thrown, there is a spark.) Since the Torah says you must not make a fire on Shabbat the rabbis ruled that Jews could not use electric switches on Shabbat. With so much that we think important hinging on electricity this became a major problem to many modern Jews. The automobile was also

---

An Orthodox Response

society which He created. He did precisely the opposite. "He scrutinized the Torah and created the world." The Torah is the archetype or blueprint. The world was molded to fit the Torah, not vice versa. The world was created so that the teachings of Torah could be implemented. This means that we can and should mold our lives to meet the demands of the Torah.

The modern era was by no means Judaism's first confrontation with the non-Jewish world. Jews succeeded in leading a full life in many diverse cultures while retaining an uncompromising allegiance to their own traditions. The difficulty or ease of their life was never the yardstick of observance. Actually, modern technology has made observance of many *mitzvot* much easier than in past generations. But sometimes the observant Jew is grateful that Torah law in its wisdom insulates him from the encroachments of technology. *Shabbat* rest would not be the same on a crowded highway behind the wheel of an automobile. Nor can it be fully savored when accompanied by the insistent intrusion of a ringing telephone. Twenty-four hours minus radio and television are need-

160

WHAT DO THE
BIBLE AND
TRADITION
MEAN TO US?

forbidden on Shabbat. When Jews lived in small villages or compact city neighborhoods, not driving on Shabbat was no great sacrifice. But Jews soon became widely scattered and not to be able to drive to the synagogue or visit one's family on Shabbat seemed to prevent our doing important Jewish acts.

The Reform movement arose to show that one could be modern and Jewish

Reform Judaism was started in Germany out of this feeling that Judaism needed to change sharply to meet the challenges of modern times. A key issue in the 1820s—when Reform got started—was modernizing the synagogue service. The Reformers wanted to use German as well as Hebrew, have up-to-date music, shorter services, sermons, and men and women sitting together. They felt such changes would show that Judaism could adopt some of the good things of the modern world. Besides, they felt they weren't changing what was at the heart of the Jewish religion, only some of the forms in which it was expressed. Hence their name— they wanted to re-form Judaism.

The traditional authorities in those days seemed to feel that almost any changes would be bad for the Jews. Despite the new freedom they thought Jews should do pretty much what their

ed for recharging spiritual batteries.

In an effort to adapt to modern life Reform Jews instituted many fundamental changes in ritual and prayer. However, with the passage of time many have come to recognize that in changing the form they also lost much of the heart. Hebrew as a language of prayer, *talit, tefilin, mezuzah, sukah, lulab,* and *ethrog*—what sort of Judaism does one have without them?

One final point: Judaism survives because of a commitment to the Oral Law. The Oral Law is more than a list of rules and regulations. It is precisely what the term indicates—a tradition passed on from teacher to student. It remains so even though it is now committed to writing. What is transmitted is not only a method of study but also a manner of living. No one ever became proficient in Talmud or in living as a Jew by reading without the benefit of a teacher. The Oral Law is an experience into which one must be initiated. Pursuing it is also a pleasure which has no peer. The only way you can hope to appreciate it is by finding a *rebbe* (teacher). By all means, do so! ■

parents had done. The Reform Jews felt that Judaism needed to change to stay alive. In fact, the more they studied the history of Judaism the more they saw that there always had been change—sometimes great change. So to create a modern Judaism seemed to them to be the true way to be a Jew. When the traditional leaders refused to allow any changes, the Reform Jews made them themselves. They were saying that they would not always follow the Oral Law and its leaders. They would try to learn from it but, if they felt things had to be done differently today, they would go ahead and do it. That was a radical change indeed.

The story of the creation of a new style of being Jewish and the arguments over it is an interesting one. How much to change, how much to stick to older ways of doing things, remains a major human problem, not just for Jews but for most human groups. Now, about a hundred and fifty years later, Reform Jews are proud that many of the things they fought for have been accepted by many other Jews. Conservative Jews have learned a lot from the Reform Jewish experiments. Orthodox Jews have accepted far less, but even modern Orthodoxy is strongly influenced by the Reform pioneering in how to blend Judaism and modern culture. Yet the three groups differ on the very important question of just how closely we should follow the Oral Law and when and how we can change it. ■

6 Must We Observe All the Commandments and Traditions?

LET'S BEGIN with a simple rule: If God "speaks" to us, we ought to do what God "says" (or "wants" or "cares about"). We can argue about how we know that or what it includes—and that's what most of this chapter is about. But if God "asked" us to do something, we ought to do it. The Jewish sense of duty starts with this idea. Note, please, that we won't talk here about whether a person will really do it or not. (You might want to go back to Part One, Chapter 1, to see what Judaism says about that.) Now we're only discussing what we *should* do.

From the Written Law and the Oral Law, from the great sages of our time and through their own study and conscience, traditional Jews can know, in most situations, what God wants them to do. So in waking up, getting dressed, eating, operating one's business,

An Orthodox Response

YES, we must observe all the commandments—or at least all of those that God wants us to observe. He certainly doesn't want an Israelite to perform the *mitzvot* given specifically to *Kohanim* (priests). Similarly, if God sent us into exile he doesn't expect us to perform the sacrificial rituals which can be performed only at the site of the Temple. In fact, part of the punishment is the accompa-

A Conservative Response

WE have said that the Jewish tradition is a tradition of attempting to find out what God wants us to do. We also believe that God's care and concern are reflected in what has happened in the tradition. That is to say, God speaks through the tradition. This means that the traditions we have inherited have a claim upon us. Yet sometimes we find it difficult to observe all the traditions. In general, we would say that the traditions are binding upon us unless:

caring for one's family, helping in the community, Jewish law and tradition can guide one's life. That doesn't mean there's a rule for everything. A lot is left to the individual, like just how much and for how long parents ought to help their children. New questions keep coming up, for example, your responsibility to your parents when you live far away from them.

Yet even Jews who are quite careful about their observance of the Torah can't really keep "all the commandments and traditions." Some can't be done at all: since there's no Temple in Jerusalem, no one can offer sacrifices. Some few commandments don't operate because the rabbis weren't certain of what we should do: The Torah calls for a blue thread in the tassel Jews were supposed to put on the four corners of the outer garments they wore in olden times. But, when the exact color of the dye became doubtful, the law was suspended for fear of doing it improperly. The cup of wine for Elijah at the Seder table is another example: it's not for Elijah to drink but, tradition says, for him to decide about. The rabbis couldn't agree whether we should drink a fifth cup of wine (we drink four) at the Seder. There is a tradition that when Elijah appears to an-

An Orthodox Response

nying denial of the opportunity to perform many of the *mitzvot*. We are no longer able to identify the *chilazon*, the worm (or fish) which provided the blue dye used in making the *tzitzit*. There is no reason for us to have guilt feelings about not having *techelet* or for not being able to perform the Temple rituals. Certainly, in these matters, we are not at fault. But we do pray for the day when we will be able to perform *all mitzvot*. Only then will our service of God be complete.

Minhagim, or customs (I do not like the word "tradition"—that is a term I would prefer to reserve for something received from God by Moses and passed on from generation to generation), are somewhat different. They are not God-given. *Minhagim* grew up among Jews

A Conservative Response

1. They are based on scientific facts we know are different than what our ancestors thought. An example, the definition of the moment of death. In the past the main test was breathing and heartbeat. Now that we have knowledge of the workings of the brain unavailable to our ancestors we should use the test of brain functioning.

2. If they have results that are against our sense of ethics. The best examples are those dealing with women in the synagogue.

3. They are based on ideas we do not accept, like the custom of

WHAT DO THE
BIBLE AND
TRADITION
MEAN TO US?

nounce the coming of the Messiah he'll answer all our questions. So at the Seder we open the door to look for Elijah and the answer—but we don't drink the fifth cup. Some laws apply only in the Land of Israel, like not harvesting the corners of your field but leaving them for the poor. And some practices are only traditions, customs, and thus may be recommended but not required. European Jews once very widely ate cheese dishes on Shavuot but fewer Jews think this is important today. Having a ceremony and celebration for *bar mitzvah* has been a custom for about seven hundred years. *Bat mitzvah* was started only about fifty years ago.

A good Jew will try to know what laws still hold and do them

Being a serious, practicing Jew doesn't mean doing everything that was ever written down or followed anywhere. It means to most Orthodox Jews doing the laws and respecting the traditions which the Torah and the great sages of our time say apply today. There is a

either as a "fence" around the law to prevent transgressing the actual law or as expressions of religious sentiment—but were never formally promulgated by the rabbis. They may vary from country to country and from locale to locale. To be sure, they should not be dismissed lightly. Some customs have the binding force of law. In fact, one has to be somewhat of a scholar in order to be able to determine which practices have the status of rabbinic law and which are simply a matter of custom. Even *minhagim* which do not have the status of law have been hallowed by generations of Jewish practice and contribute significantly to a feeling of Jewish identity. But then, not everything that Jews do has the status of a *minhag*. Eating gefilte fish on Friday evening is an example of a common

kaparot which are rituals followed before the Day of Atonement in which fowl or money is used to take away our sins.

This means that most of our tradition is binding upon us. We should not magnify the number of rituals that have to be changed.

In the Conservative community, groups of rabbis assisted by the laymen in the congregations try to decide which rituals should be changed or even abolished.

There is still a large part of life, as Rabbi Borowitz observes, that is left to our own sense of right and wrong. No law can cover all

difference between "commandments" (*mitzvot;* or law, *halachah*) and "traditions" (customs, *minhagim*). In theory, traditions are easier to change than commandments—I guess you could make a whole wheat *matzah* if you wanted to. Still some traditions become so precious that they get the status of a law, like having your head covered when you pray. But you can't make a leavened *matzah;* that's against the law. Sometimes the law changes—as with Hillel's rule on the loans or in the case of the blue thread. More often, it is customs that change. Still, though there is some flexibility and growth, Orthodox Judaism emphasizes continuing the laws and traditions of our people.

But now I must make sure you don't misunderstand me. I know as you do that most Jews don't pay much attention to what is taught in their synagogues. Whether they call themselves Orthodox, Conservative, or Reform, they do pretty much as they please. Such people aren't serious about Judaism and so they only give us a bad idea of what Jews *ought* to be doing. I'm not going to talk about their kind of sloppy Judaism. I want to talk about proper Jewish ideals.

An Orthodox Response

practice which does *not* have the status of a *minhag.* Eating dairy dishes as part of the meal on Shavuot morning does (and, incidentally, it is as widely practiced among observant Jews in America as it was in Europe). The difference is that a *minhag* is based upon a reason (see if you can find someone to tell you the reason for eating dairy dishes on Shavuot), whereas practices designed for convenience or pleasure are not *minhagim.*

Maimonides describes the person who is spiritually perfect as the person who examines every act to see if it somehow furthers the service of God. Of course, very few people can ever reach such a state of worship—but, like every goal, it is something to which man aspires and which he tries to approximate to the best of his ability.

A Conservative Response

situations. Here we have to rely on our good sense and character.

The important thing is that Judaism is a religion which at the minimum is based on law, that is a series of obligations which are not created by yourself and which require us to do things on a regular basis, even when we do not feel like doing them at the time. From our own experience we know how important this sense of discipline and fixed obligations is for our own development. We go to school according to a schedule. Many of us have lists of duties we have to perform at home. We try to have regular mealtimes and

WHAT DO THE
BIBLE AND
TRADITION
MEAN TO US?

Liberal Judaism says
you must decide for yourself

Liberal Jews believe people have had as much a role in making the Oral Law as God did, maybe more. To us, the Talmud isn't as holy as is the Bible. Much of what the rabbis said seems less what God wants us to do today than what the scholars thought God wanted of Jews in another age. It isn't always easy to know whether the rules or teachings of the Oral Law apply to us or not. You will have to make up your own mind depending on how you think God "speaks" to us today and what you "hear" God "saying" to you in the Oral Law. (Remember our discussion in Chapter 2?)

This is the hard part of being a liberal Jew. You have the responsibility for deciding which "commandments and traditions" you think are what God wants. Of course there's lots to read and your rabbi and community will be glad to help you. Still, what makes people liberal Jews is that after all the searching they want to make up their own minds about what they'll do. This is also the advantage of being a liberal Jew. No one can tell you what you must

---

But certainly, insofar as actual *mitzvot* are concerned, one should fulfill as many as physically possible. And if a person cannot bring himself to fulfill all God's commandments, he certainly should feel guilty and try to improve himself bit by bit. But he should never allow his guilt to overwhelm him so that he feels unworthy or that he can never improve. A good way to start is a little bit at a time. A popular translation of a verse in Psalms reads, "Taste and you shall see that the Lord is good." Jewish living is a source of joy, not a burden. In order to be appreciated, *mitzvot* must be experienced. Although it may not appear so at first, with practice, observance is no longer experienced as a difficulty. In fact, it becomes a wonderfully satisfying and uplifting experience. *Mitzvot* import a sense of

---

even times when we have to clean our rooms. This helps us do the right thing. Many people are lazy some of the time. They have a great way of creating excuses for not doing things they ought to do. The genius of Judaism is that our religious obligations are regulated. We are told what to eat (or rather what not to eat); we are given fixed times for prayer, and when to have holidays and festivals. This gives us a sense of God's presence at regular intervals. It is also a way of disciplining and training ourselves. It is also a way in which we unite with other Jews. All of this is important. ■

do. As you grow and become more mature you can change your ideas of what you ought to be doing as a Jew, something that's probably already happened in your life. Serious liberal Jews feel honest about their Judaism for they have played the main role in shaping it.

It needs to be said that many liberal Jews have used the right to make up their own minds as an excuse to do very little. That's certainly not what Reform or Conservative Judaism stands for. People who care about God and the long association of the Jewish people with God would surely feel they ought to be doing things for God as part of the Jewish people. And I think many liberal Jews are becoming more observant of Jewish law and tradition today.

Liberal Judaism's teachings about what Jews must do

How do liberal Jews figure out which commandments and traditions to follow? They see what God "says" to them and what they feel their duties are as part of the Jewish people.

The early Reform Jews thought God "spoke" through our intelligence and conscience. They figured out a general rule from this: Ethics came from God but rituals were created by people to gain a feeling for Jewish ethics and for other Jews. I think that old idea still has a lot of truth to it. Whatever else Jews ought to do they ought to be decent human beings, caring about other people and improving our society.

Though many Reform Jews think ethics is all God wants of us many others feel our sense of duty is greater than that. If you have a sense of God's reality or a close relationship with God (the last two ideas about God "speaking" are discussed in Chapter 2), you'd have to do more than be good to people. Praying is a good example. It's not part of ethics but if you have a feeling of God's nearness, you certainly ought to spend some time regularly "talking" to God. You would do that not as some idea you just thought up but because God was very real to you. In that sense you would say that God "wants" you to pray. So too with many other things which aren't ethics—for example, study and rituals and holy days.

An Orthodox Response

WHAT DO THE
BIBLE AND
TRADITION
MEAN TO US?

seriousness and purpose. It is through observance of *mitzvot* that the life of the Jew becomes suffused with meaning. To Jews the question is not, "Must we observe all the *mitzvot*?" which seems to echo a sense of onus or burden. Jews have always asked, "How can

We have a people we care for as well as a God

But now we can no longer leave out the Jewish people. When we talk about Judaism we're not just talking about you alone, as if there were no other Jews in the world. True, you must decide what you want to do. But you're not the first person in the world to get to know God and try to figure out what God wanted you to do. Mostly we get our ideas about people and duty and God from our tradition—unconsciously from parents and relatives, consciously from religious school. Two things are at work in us. We seem very different from other people and want to be individuals; we're also deeply Jewish and part of the Jewish people. Their centuries of experience have come down to us; their stubbornness in not giving up will carry on Jewish ideals long after us. So now, as loyal members of the Jewish people, we ask not only what we should do for God but for the Jews as well.

Many Jews like the Jewish people simply because they are an interesting, exciting, richly human group. So they want to do things Jews do: read Jewish books, celebrate Jewish events, and work for Jewish causes. Some are excited by the State of Israel; they want to help it and enjoy its culture. They visit the State of Israel, learn about its writers and artists, and study the Hebrew language. Some people realize that Judaism is a community religion. Jews serve God not just as individuals but as part of a people with a long, complicated, and very deep relationship with God. So you should not be satisfied to be a Jew privately, all by yourself. You should connect your life to that of other Jews, linking yourself to our people by following its customs and joining in its community activities.

Liberal Jews obviously haven't arrived at the one best way of figuring out what our Jewish duties should be. But we want to do many things Jews have always done and create new ones (for instance, Confirmation) that will help us serve God as Jews, today. Any religion which makes no demands on us and which does not get us to care what God "wants" us to do is, by Jewish standards, hardly worth calling a religion. And any movement within Judaism which does not get us to want to serve God and to do so because we are part of the Jewish people—who respect the Jewish tradition and want to add to it—is hardly worth calling Judaism.   ■

---

we best observe the *mitzvot*?" a question which gives expression to a sense of love and eagerness and to the feeling, "How goodly is our lot, how beautiful our heritage."   ■

7 Why Are There Three Branches of Judaism?

THE JEWISH community has Orthodox, Conservative, and Reform groups. Yet, to be accurate, it has more than these three groups. The Orthodox community has the greatest variety, probably because its groups still carry over some differences which began in Europe. So Chasidic Jews, who are themselves split into several argumentative factions, dress and carry themselves as if they still lived in Eastern Europe. Other Orthodox communities differ on just how American one's life style should be. Should Jews get college degrees? Have arranged marriages? Allow boys and girls to go to the same school? These questions divide Orthodox Jews, but mostly the divisions have no widely accepted names.

Things are somewhat simpler among Conservative and Reform Jews. There's more of Jewish tradition in the Conservative move-

An Orthodox Response

IT IS CORRECT to speak of different groups among Orthodox Jews only in a sociological sense. All Orthodox Jews subscribe to the same basic set of beliefs and practices. To the extent that they differ in practice they recognize that the positions of all groups are legitimate expressions of authentic Jewish teaching. The differences insofar as religious practice is concerned are relatively minor.

A Conservative Response

RABBI BOROWITZ has given you a good summary of the differences between the various groups of Jews. Naturally, because I belong to the Conservative group, I believe that our way of holding on to the idea of law but being willing to change it when it is found necessary to do so, of advocating freedom of expression and thought within Judaism, of stressing the importance of study—is better than the other suggestions about Judaism. (Of course, Reform and

WHAT DO THE
BIBLE AND
TRADITION
MEAN TO US?

ment and more openness to change in the Reform group. Still each has people who are more traditional and people who are more interested in modern Judaism. The traditional Conservative Jews are more like Orthodox Jews than they are like the traditionally inclined Reform Jews. And the Reform modernists are very much more radical than the Conservative modernists. Still, many Reform and Conservative families live very much the same way. On an everyday level, the groups have become fairly similar, and many Jews feel quite easy about shifting from a Conservative to a Reform synagogue or vice versa.

One interesting group that has come out of the Conservative movement is called the Reconstructionists. They take an in-between stand. They want to be more creative than Conservative Jews seem to be. Yet they also have a greater sense of loyalty to the Jewish people and its customs than they think Reform Jews find comfortable. And there are other small but interesting movements in our community.

What divides our three largest movements?

Yet the three, well-established groups in our community—Orthodox, Conservative, and Reform Judaism—deserve special

---

Certainly some Jews dress in distinctive clothing. But only the most naive would argue that God decreed that we are to wear long black caftans and beaver hats. This does not mean that people who do so do not have valid reasons for dressing as they do. They seek to follow the customs of their ancestors. For many it is not only a matter of distinctive garb. They wish to preserve their way of life, their standards of morality and religious observance and to be

---

Orthodox Jews believe in the importance of study and certainly Reform Jews believe in freedom of thought.)

I believe that this way is the best way to be loyal to the traditions of Judaism and to face the future.

What makes us different from Reform Jews is the emphasis on law.

What makes us different from Orthodox Jews is our emphasis on the possibility of changing the law.

attention. There are two major causes for their differences from one another: their beliefs and their backgrounds.

The big problem of belief has to do with how we shall decide what should remain and what should change in Judaism. Must we largely follow the decisions given by Jewish sages in previous centuries? Should we accept the answers given by the Orthodox authorities of our time? Shall we think about these questions the way Jews have done over the ages?

Orthodox Jews say an emphatic "yes" to these questions. God gave the Oral Law. To change it is to defy God and to break with the genuine Jewish way of making religious rulings. Moreover, all the radical changes others have made have not improved Jewish life but hurt it. Whether their leaders like to hear it or not, Conservative and Reform Judaism are an excuse for doing little and not caring very much. Once you start changing things people don't know when to stop. Only a return to the slow and thoughtful traditional way of letting Jewish practice evolve can save our people and be faithful to God. So argue the Orthodox.

An Orthodox Response

assured that their children will not become assimilated through intermarriage. By living in their own communities, speaking their own language, dressing differently from their neighbors, and, in general, keeping to themselves as much as possible, they seek to preserve themselves from much that they find threatening in a secular culture. Other Jews feel that they can cope successfully with the threats of the dominant culture. The differences are really about matters of custom or about questions of policy, about what is best and wisest, rather than of religious observance.

All these groups share a common acceptance of the Torah in its entirety as the word of God. All of them recognize an obligation to

A Conservative Response

Even so, I believe it is important to understand that:

1. What unites all loyal Jews is much more important than the differences between them. We should not think that until modern times Jews all thought and acted the same way. There were differences between philosophers and mystics, rationalists and nonrationalists. There were differences of custom and practices between Sephardic Jews and Ashkenazic Jews, Russian and Hungarian Jews, disciples of one rabbi and another rabbi. Sometimes these differences were minor. Other times they were very important. Nevertheless, we remained one community, big enough to include everyone who was a part of the Jewish people. Even though

172

Where liberal Jews agree
and disagree with one another

Reform and Conservative Jews are pretty well united in rejecting this Orthodox position. The Reform Jews believe that the Torah is as much the product of people as of God. Hence Jewish law can and should be changed when Jews begin to live in a different situation. Girls need as much education as boys; women should have a right to be rabbis.

Conservative Jews have not taken a stand on where Torah comes from. Whatever that stand might be, they feel the Oral Law has many ways for making new rules that Orthodox authorities aren't using. Now that Jews live in a modern way as part of general society, Jewish law needs a fresh reworking. Eating fish in a non-kosher restaurant should be "kosher"; birth control should be openly accepted.

Reform and Conservative Jews favor change but disagree about who should make the changes, how fast, and in what way. Conser-

---

fulfill all of God's commandments, and all of them share a commitment to obey Halakhah (Jewish Law) as recorded in the Oral Law. These shared commitments unite Orthodox Jews and distinguish them from others.

To be sure, there are liberal Jews who find it difficult to fully accept these principles. But that is not the only reason which prompted the establishment of the Reform movement. It was very, very hard to live as a traditional Jew in Europe a hundred or a hundred and fifty years ago. There was a feeling in many circles that if Jews would only be more like their non-Jewish neighbors they would find greater acceptance. The desire to avoid anti-Semitic

---

we are proud of the group within Judaism we belong to, we should not deny the possibility that other groups may be right also.

2. It is a good thing that American Judaism offers the Jew a variety of ways of being a Jew. People are different; their experiences are different; their understanding of things is different. It would not be good if there was only one standard brand of Judaism to which everyone had to adhere. The Jewish community is too rich and too varied for that. What we seek and we hope we will find is a unity which will bring together all Jews who want to be participants in the adventure of Judaism. ■

vative Jews object that Reform Jews seem to have given up the whole Oral Law. They feel that's wrong, for the Oral Law has been central to Judaism for nearly two thousand years. While Conservative Jews want more change than the Orthodox, they want it to come by using the methods of the Oral Law. The decisions therefore need to be made by scholars who know the law and are devoted to its continuation. Therefore, the Conservative movement has a special Commission on Law and Standards which studies and rules on questions of modern Jewish law. This commission recently permitted congregations who wished to do so to count women in the *minyan* needed for a full Jewish prayer service.

Reform Judaism bases itself on respect for the individual

Reform Jews have felt that, all things considered, it is best to let people make up their own minds about what they should do. There's a lot they should keep in mind: what God wants, what Jewish tradition says, and what other Jews are doing. Many people will need help from their rabbis and communities in making a mature decision. Obviously this is a big responsibility for individuals and a break with having to follow the Oral Law. But it doesn't make much sense to Reform Jews to decide about our use of electricity on the Shabbat in terms of its being "fire" in the Oral Law. Often the Oral Law can teach us a lot even when we feel it is outdated. But sometimes our sense of right and wrong demands that we simply reject an old law. For example, according to Oral Law, a child born to a mother who committed adultery is, for no sin of its own, not

---

An Orthodox Response

---

discrimination and to be treated with decency and respect was undoubtedly very strong. The result was a conscious effort to imitate Christians not only in speech and dress but in prayer as well. The organ, for example, was borrowed directly from the Church as were the clerical robes worn in the pulpit by Reform clergymen. Traditional Jews bemoan not only the rejection of Jewish practices but also the dejudaization of Judaism which occurred. Fortunately, with the passage of time, many liberal Jews have experienced a longing for their Jewish "roots" and a slow

174

return to distinctive Jewish ritual and practice has begun—but is far from complete. (I would like to think that even the invitation

extended to me to write these lines for you is part of that journey.)

Obviously, Conservative Judaism has preserved more elements of Jewish tradition and law than Reform. Nevertheless, Orthodox

allowed to marry other Jews. Reform Jews know that's wrong and say it must not be a law of Judaism today. Or, to take a more important example, Reform Jews think women should be given equality in Judaism, in services, as rabbis, as witnesses, and in Jewish divorce proceedings. (Part of the reason the Reform movement abandoned the old tradition of having Jewish divorces was that women were not equals in the process.) We see no reason for delay in such matters. Here the difference with the Conservative Jews appears. Though the Conservatives are willing to make some changes, they prefer to do so only after much discussion, and then they try to follow the procedures of the Oral Law. To Reform Jews it often seems that other Jews wait until we have taken the risks of trying new things and have discovered which will work. So we have counted women in our *minyans* for a long time and have ordained women as rabbis, something which the Conservative movement will, I am sure, one day get around to approving.

Trusting people so much creates difficulties for Reform Judaism

Letting people make up their own minds does cause Reform Jews some special problems. Some people do nothing—but I do not see that they believe in Reform Judaism. Caring Reform Jews do many different sorts of things, some emphasizing ethics, others Shabbat and holy days, or the State of Israel, or everyday prayer and piety. There's some but not much sense of what *everyone* ought to do. That can be pretty annoying, as in the argument about rabbis officiating at intermarriages. And Reform Jews have hardly educat-

Jews view Conservatism as an attempt to water down Jewish law, to equivocate on matters of fundamental belief, and to give people the type of religious observance they wish to have rather than the type of observance which God wants from them. But Judaism is not a "religion of convenience." Judaism is, in addition to being a religion, a system of law. The Conservative movement has modified this system of law significantly. Examples of such modification include permitting the driving of an automobile to the synagogue on Shabbat, elimination of the second day of the festivals, drinking wine prepared by a non-Jew, and eating fish in a non-kosher restaurant. Orthodox scholars find it impossible to agree that any valid interpretation of the law could lead to these conclusions. We dare not begin with predetermined conclusions. We must start with God's word and accept whatever conclusion we must reach on the

ed their people, whether as children or as adults, to make such important Jewish decisions. Despite these difficulties, most Reform Jews feel that modern Judaism has to start with trusting individuals and count on their wise use of their heads and their hearts.

Note how this book is written. I didn't plan it to give you only the Reform view. We want you to know other Jewish ideas so you can make an intelligent decision. That's the Reform idea. And while it sounds a little odd, even if you decide to accept a Conservative or Orthodox attitude to the law, I'd consider it "Reform" as long as you knew you were doing so because it was your personal choice to do so.

People live less by what they believe than by who their friends are

But for all this study of beliefs, I must confess that I find that they don't mean much to most Jews. Most people care more about how they grew up and whom they are associating with today. The Conservative movement was as much a matter of geography and culture as it was of beliefs. American Reform Jews were once mostly Germans who had become Americanized before the East-European, Polish and Russian Jews came here. The two groups hadn't liked each other in Europe and they brought many of their old disagreements with them to America. Since East-European Jews who wanted to modernize didn't feel comfortable with Reform Jews, they created Conservative Judaism.

That was long ago. About 90 per cent of today's North American Jews were born here. Almost all Jews have been Americanized for a

---

An Orthodox Response

basis of the teachings of the Torah.

There is one other point which gravely concerns all Jews. That is the preservation of the Jewish people. History has taught us one lesson. Whatever the motivation of liberal Jews, we have seen that abandonment of Jewish practices and observances has resulted in a tremendously high dropout rate. The numbers of second, third, and fourth generation Reform Jews who intermarry and/or do not identify themselves as Jews increase radically with each succeeding generation. Beginning with Ibn Ezra and continuing down to the dominant personality of the Enlightenment, Moses Mendelssohn, Jewish thinkers have long recognized that observance of *mitzvot* (quite apart from everything started earlier) produces one very beneficial dividend—it enhances Jewish awareness and helps us preserve our ethnic identity. Preservation of the Jewish people is

176

generation or two. The smaller the city or suburb Jews live in, the less the difference between the ways Reform and Conservative Jews live. Today's Reform Jews are more conscious of Jewish tradition and more concerned with the Jewish people than their German founders were one hundred years ago. Conservative Jews have increasingly modernized, for instance, in suggesting the possibility of celebrating only one day of each Jewish festival (something Reform Jews have done for some time). It's not surprising then that in some small towns Reform and Conservative groups have merged to form one synagogue. I think more of that will go on but the two groups are unlikely to become just one. Many people simply like their own institutions. Some people are quite serious about the individual's rights as against a scholarly body telling them about modern Jewish law and vice versa. But compared to the big problems of Jewish life—making Judaism live and keeping Jews alive—the differences between Reform and Conservative Jews are not very great.

The differences between the liberal Jews and Orthodoxy are much larger. There can't be just one Judaism in our time as long as we differ so strongly on how to interpret Jewish law. Still, all Jews share a lot. We are devoted to the same God. We are part of the same Jewish people and its relationship with God. And we all believe that our Judaism comes from the Torah, even though we disagree about how it is to be understood today. Since Reform Jews believe in people's right to decide for themselves what sort of Jewish life they want to lead, they should show respect for those who choose another form of being Jewish. Yet they will also insist on their Jewish right to develop modern Jewish life in ways that they feel God wants them to do as part of the Jewish people.   ■

one goal to which all Jews subscribe. History has shown that the best way to preserve the Jewish people is through the observance of *mitzvot*. The more intense our observance, the greater our success in self-preservation.

Traditional Jews are particularly pained that entire generations of Jews grow up without ever being exposed to authentic Jewish teachings and practices. A Jew loves every fellow Jew and wishes to share everything with his neighbor. Certainly, he wishes to share his most precious possession—the Torah. The desire to teach Torah and the service of God to others is born of this love. Traditional Jews pray fervently for the day when the schism which divides us will be breached and we will all be united in the service of God. Only then will the Kingdom of God be complete and only then will God be "King over all the Earth."   ■

Part Four
ON BELIEVING
IN GOD

1. Has God Changed
   since Bible Times?
2. How Can We Talk about God?
3. How Do We Know God Is Real?
4. What Do We Think God Is Like?
5. Why Does God Let Bad
   Things Happen?
6. What Happens after You Die?
7. Why Do We Have
   Different Religions?

1
Has God Changed since Bible Times?

How do you feel when someone older says to you:

> My, how you've changed. When you were little, you always seemed silly. Laughing at everything, fooling around all the time. I wondered if you'd ever grow up. Now, look at you. Quiet, thoughtful, and so serious about your responsibilities. I hardly recognize you. In fact, when someone told me your name, for a moment I didn't believe it was you.

180

We could change that comment a number of ways but it would still be the same story. Once you were sloppy, but now you're careful about your things and those of others. You always had your nose in books, but today you're mostly interested in people. You used to be skinny, but now you're nicely rounded out.

When you see some people after a few years, it can be quite a shock. You see such great changes in them it's hard to believe it's the same person—but it is. We would be disturbed if they hadn't changed at all. We believe people have to change in order to be healthy.

Life means growth and therefore change. This is true of ideas as well as of people, although many people find it difficult to believe that ideas also change. Ideas in science have given us the biggest shocks. In ancient times people thought the sun was a god and a living thing. As science developed most people came to believe it was only a great star which went across the earth every day. Then Galileo argued that what our eyes see is wrong: the sun really stands still and it is the earth that moves. Today astronomers tell us that nothing stays in one spot, that the sun and its system of planets are all moving together in space.

That's how we understand the universe now, but if the newspapers announced a surprising new theory tomorrow—one which seems to better explain the facts we now have—we'd be ready to accept the change. That's happened often in modern times—Darwin explaining how human beings evolved, Freud teaching us about the subconscious, Einstein showing that time and space are relative. Since none of our theories is ever perfect we'd really like to create better ones.

The same thing is true in Judaism and in all religions. Modern Jews believe that Jewish ideas have changed over the years. That's what kept our religion alive. This was one of the revolutionary beliefs Reform Jews brought into Judaism. It explained why they felt it was right to make Judaism modern. Let me give an example. Traditional Jewish schools started children off learning the Book of Leviticus mostly by heart. Why nursery-age tots should study the sacrifices in the Torah was explained by saying, "The pure should begin with laws about purity." Reform Jews pioneered the idea that youngsters should study what they could understand. As a result, your first year in religious school probably began with Bible stories and holiday celebrations. What teenagers would enjoy studying is something neither we, the educators, nor you, teenagers, have been able to settle yet. Out of this question, we are offering you this book.

Once Jews began studying our history with modern methods, it became clear that even something as important as our understanding of God had changed in the past. The Bible gives many examples. Sometimes God is spoken of as almost a physical being. The second creation story talks about God taking a walk in the Garden of Eden when the day began to cool down (Gen. 3:8). An even stranger notion appears when Moses asks God to show him God's full glory. God replies:

> You can't see My face because no human being could stand that. . . . But there's a place near Me where you can stand on a rocky cliff. When My glory goes by there, I'll put you in a small cave which I'll cover with My hand until I've gone by. Then I'll take away My hand and you can see My back but no human can see My face (Ex. 33:20–23).

(We'll discuss God's "face" and "back" in the next chapter.)

The Bible and Talmud do not have just one idea about God

What the Bible most stresses about God is that no idol of any sort, shape, or description is permitted in Judaism. The second of the Ten Commandments includes everything:

> Don't have any gods beside Me and that means no piece of sculpture or any other figure of anything that's in the sky, on the earth, or in the waters below the earth (Exod. 20:3–4).

That seems to rule out God really being like a human being. Deutero-Isaiah—the part of the book which begins in Chapter 40—says again and again that there is no one and nothing with which we can compare God. God is greater than anything we can imagine. So too we are told that King Solomon said this in his prayer when he dedicated the Temple he built:

> Will God really live in a house on earth? Heaven, even the heaven above all other heavens can't contain God, how much less can this house which I have built (I Kings 8:27).

Shifting notions of God are also found in the Talmud. The rabbis had their own ways of talking about God. They could call God "The Place" and say "God is the place of the world but the world is not God's place." That seems to make God very spiritual. Yet the rabbis could also talk about God in very human ways. Some said that God, like every good Jew, prayed and studied or cried and loved. Sometimes they carefully noted it was "as if" God did these things, or it was all "in a manner of speaking." But sometimes they just said very human things about God.

The philosophers and mystics developed new notions about God

The Jews who learned Greek philosophy spoke of God in still other ways. Philo, a Jewish thinker of the first century of the Common Era, taught that God was one, in the sense of "the only one." God was utterly different from all the creatures. Philo therefore suggested that reason (in Greek *logos*, as in "logic," the right way to think) was God's first creation. For Philo the mind makes contact between people and God possible. That idea was important to later religious philosophers of the Western world. More than a thousand years after Philo, Maimonides proposed the daring idea that God was Pure Thought.

The Jewish mystics thought of God in yet other ways. Their earlier teachings were not written but were handed down orally by masters to their wisest students, generation after generation. Eventually in 1275 c.e., the great book of Jewish mysticism, *Zohar*, was put together. In it are two ways of talking about the one God. On the one hand, God is called *Ein Sof*, "Without Limits"—so pure and exalted that nothing at all can properly be said about God. On the other hand, God is called *Sefirot*, ten centers of power that may then be talked about in everyday terms. Sometimes these ten *sefirot* are described as a tree, or a garden, or even as God's body. Together these two ideas are the one God.

Mysticism is difficult to understand. But it is important for you to hear about it because it is part of Judaism as well as other religions.

As they became modern,
Jews created new ideas of God

When Jews came into the modern world and discovered its science and philosophy, our understanding of God changed again. Much of this book deals with this changed understanding. What we need to discuss here is our suspicion that if our ideas about God have changed then maybe our God has changed. Are we still following the Jewish religion? Do our ideas today need more change?

These questions all focus on the difference between God as God really is and what we human beings can get to understand about God. Jews don't think anybody is smart enough to understand God fully. That is true even of Moses who, the Torah says, got closer to God than anybody ever did. To understand God fully would mean to be as great as God. Though Jews think human beings are wonderful creatures, we don't think they are anywhere near as smart as God. That's what we think is meant by this statement in the Torah: "No human being can see God's face and live."

Though people can't understand God fully they can still know a good deal about God—and that applies to all people, not just Jews. There is always a gap then between what we can say about God and what we sense God's true greatness to be. That's one reason we use music and poetry and ritual—and silence too—in religion. Our understanding only goes so far. Then you have to open your spirit to reach even further to God. You may come up with a better way of expressing your understanding of God than terms like The Almighty, The Place, Pure Thought, Without Limits. Perhaps you will come up with an even better idea of God than we have at present. Judaism has been unusually free in letting its thinkers try to work out new ways of understanding God. Like science, it knows its theories could be better.

Yet with all these changes in our tradition, Jews have regularly felt that, over the ages, they were talking about the same God, only in different ways. There's no way to prove that. After all we have nothing like a pope to rule on who is right and who is wrong. Remember we all agree that the human mind isn't smart enough to know the whole truth.

We leave the questions of what is a genuine Jewish idea up

to history. Our thinkers create new ways of talking about God. Then the Jewish people, if it finds them worthwhile, tries to live by them. An idea that survives some generations or centuries will become a part of our tradition. Having been tested, it is taught to future generations. But an idea may also die quickly or be outgrown. It is then that we seek better ways of saying what we came to believe.

You are part of that process. With all your Jewish education and now this book, we're sharing with you our best Jewish ways of understanding God. With our combined efforts, maybe you will then go on to help us find an even better way of understanding our great God.

2 How Can We Talk about God?

IF SOMEONE said, "I love you with all my heart," we'd be very pleased. We'd know that person was trying to tell us that they loved us with nothing held back.

Yet it makes no sense to love someone with your "heart." We know the heart is essentially a bunch of muscles which pump blood. What's pushing blood with fantastic regularity through the body's plumbing got to do with loving somebody? If I said, "I love you with all my heart-muscles," you'd think that was a stupid thing to say. Why isn't loving someone with all your heart equally foolish?

In ancient times people thought the heart was the organ by which you made up your mind. In those days, loving someone with all your heart meant that you truly had chosen that person to love. Today we think brains, not hearts, are connected with our decisions. But if someone said to you, "I love you with all my brain," it wouldn't please you very much at all. We still want to hear that people love us with all their hearts.

How can a statement that makes no sense mean more to us than one that does?

Symbols:
a key to understanding much of what we say

To understand why we talk this way you need to understand modern thinkers' notion of a symbol. We have trouble when we try to speak of something exalted and lofty. We then find it useful to use something simple and near-at-hand to stand for it. I want to tell you my love for you is just about the deepest, most important feeling I have—a complicated string of words. It's much easier to say, "I love you with all my heart."

Symbols are wonderful because with everyday objects we can suggest great things, particularly those we care about. Let's first talk about using things as symbols. A flag is only pieces of cloth sewn together a certain way—but it stands for our country. A Torah scroll is a bunch of leather sheets sewed together to make a long roll on which someone writes—but it represents Jewish tradition as almost nothing else can. We often use things as symbols—a bunch of flowers, a trophy, a diploma. Words, too, stand for something and thus all words are really symbols. The letters (or sounds) h - e - a - r - t are marks on a page (or sounds from the throat) but they stand for our blood-pumping muscles. Use certain words in certain situations and they suddenly have special power as symbols. "My heart aches for you." I will call words which have unusually rich meanings "symbol-words."

Symbols need to be popular in order to work, particularly if they are to carry great meaning. Loving people with your brain isn't acceptable. But you can call somebody "a brain" and we will know you mean that person is quite intelligent. Why some symbols catch on and last a long time—for example, justice as a blindfolded woman with scales in her hand—isn't clear. And we also don't quite know why some die out—for example, Columbia, the woman atop the United States Capitol. Still, creating and using symbols makes human beings different from all other creatures.

Symbols are
an important part of religion

Symbols work in religion the way they do in the rest of human life. If you understand that, you can begin to understand the way religion talks about God. We use symbol-words when speaking about God. We have to: God is greater than anything we know or can even imagine. If you take the symbols too seriously—for example, to come under God's wings—you can get confused. Is God a giant bird? If, then, you want to understand a religion you have to learn to recognize and understand its symbols.

The Bible and prayer book contain many different symbol-words for God. Here's one of my favorites: God is a rock. Put it that way and it's hard to believe. How could Jews ever say such a thing? Yet they did, and often. You probably know Psalm 19, Verse 15, from the prayer book: "May the words of my mouth and the meditations of my heart be acceptable to You, O Lord, my Rock and my Redeemer." Other psalms often call on God "to be a rock" or they praise God for having been a "rock." God is called, "The Rock of Israel" (II Sam. 23:3), and the question can also be asked, "Who is a rock besides our God?" (II Sam. 22:32). In the poem of Moses at the end of the Torah, God is simply called, "The Rock" (Deut. 32:4).

Somebody who didn't know our religion would think we had a peculiar sense of divinity. Some stones are pretty and some are extremely hard. Surely that doesn't make it right to call them God. An outsider would be even more confused to discover that Jews are absolutely opposed to idols—that nothing in any size, shape, or form can be an image of God. How can you call God a "rock" and then refuse to use a rock to stand for God?

The explanation is simple. God isn't a rock—but "rock" is one of our great symbol-words for God. We use the word "rock" to stand for something we want to say about God. God is like a rock—or simply, God is a rock.

We need to learn to think of what the symbol stands for

Once you know a word is being used symbolically you know that it's suggesting something much greater than its simple meaning. What might "rock" as a symbol-word for God mean to Jews?

We can get some help by looking at words the Bible uses with the word "rock" to talk about God. "A rock of strength and refuge," "a rock of habitation," "an everlasting rock," "my rock and my fortress," and "the rock of my salvation." The Bible authors lived close to nature. There were some things about rocks—especially big ones, as in the Negev—which sort of reminded them of God. Rocks last a long time. You can depend on them. Things built on them won't sink as they will if built on sand. You can hide behind them or, if they are huge and craggy, you might even hide in them. You could safely shoot arrows at your enemies from behind them or build a fort on top of them beyond the reach of your enemies. What else? Use your imagination—the way to understand symbols. You'll come up with more ideas.

It's quite difficult to talk about God. But everyone knows what a rock is and has some idea of why it might be useful. If we can talk about rocks, then everyone could get some idea of God; better, in one simple word, "rock," they could get many ideas. When a symbol carries many meanings to many people, we call it a "rich" symbol.

Some other symbol-words Jews use for God

I'd guess that one reason the Bible uses many other symbol-words for God is to keep people from thinking God "is" a rock.

To understand Judaism you need to get to know its main symbols and something of what they are saying about God. "King," "master," "lord," or "owner" are symbols that tell us God is more powerful than we are, that God "sets the rules" for us. "Father," "husband," "lover," "friend" remind us that God "cares" for us and "loves" us.

You will notice that I had to explain the symbol-words with other symbol-words. To show I didn't mean them exactly, I used quotation marks—"cares," "loves." It would help if we always used the quotation marks to signal when a symbol is being used—O Lord, my "rock" and my "redeemer." That's too big a nuisance. (Many people do use quotation marks when they find a symbol-word somewhat awkward: The people of Israel is the "apple of God's eye.") I use them often in this book to remind you how much of our language about God is symbolic.

Many of our best symbol-words come from words about people

No set of religious symbol-words has bothered people more than the ones which refer to God as if God had a human form. They are called "anthropomorphisms" from the Greek root "anthropo"—meaning human being—and "morph[ism]"—meaning form or shape. They are words which say God has a human shape: God's hand, arm, eyes, ears, nose, mouth, face, and even, in one place, God's hair. We are also told God has all sorts of feelings: love, hate, anger, sadness, forgiveness, rage, and such. (Technically, these are called "anthropopathisms.") God does all sorts of things people do—listening, watching, talking, walking, sitting, even laughing.

There's something very good and something very troublesome about these symbol-words. They have lasted for so many centuries because they start with something we know well—us, people. We have no trouble understanding them. When we remember they are used symbolically, we can easily understand their meaning. We are in God's "hands" means that God rules the world and our plans have to fit in with what God "wants." To hope God's "face" will "shine" on us means that we hope God will be "pleased" with us and "do" great good to us.

Obviously some symbol-words for God say things we find difficult to accept. Anthropomorphisms can make God seem too much like us. God's greatness gives God the right to command us. If God wasn't much different from people, why should we do what God "says"? To Jews the human way Zeus and the other Greek gods behaved on Mt. Olympus showed they didn't have much right going around telling human beings how to live. Anthropomorphisms can make God so tiny that God isn't worth paying attention to. Most people today don't make idols or say they think God is just like people—but they still find ways not to care about God and what God "wants."

Clearing up the meaning of some of the old symbol-words

In the Middle Ages, more than anyone else, Maimonides fought a major battle against anthropomorphisms. By the time it was over, most people admitted that talking about God in a human way was dangerous. People would think God has a body, and no physical thing could have the greatness God has. Yet, having that idea, people continued using the anthropomorphisms. For all their danger, symbols made some things about God so clear people wouldn't give them up. Now, every once in a while, somebody comes along who doesn't understand that we know these are symbol-words. They then taunt us for having a childish sense of God. A favorite charge is to point to the anthropomorphisms as proof that, instead of God creating us in God's image, we have created God in our image. It's true people create the symbol-words for God. But that's not the same as creating God. People invented religious language. Though we made the words for God, our words can still talk about the one God.

Some traditional Jewish symbols for God have less power in our modern world. Few of us know any shepherds and we think kings are characters in fairy tales. Still it won't yet do to say, "The Lord is my gardener" or "Blessed are You, O Lord, our God, president of the universe." Though a symbol may come from another time and place—shepherd, king, and such—it still says a great deal to us.

Some symbols "die,"
others are still full of "life"

Some symbol-words seem to have lost most of their appeal—
for example, Daniel's term for God, the Very Old Man. All the
masculine words for God are a problem. They seem to say that
being a man is somehow more perfect than being a woman,
though liberal Jewish ethics teaches that all people are equal.
Changing terms like King to Queen and Father to Mother
would only give us the same problem in reverse. Just how far
we should go in giving up our masculine symbols for God isn't
clear to most liberal Jews. Of course, since we've changed
before, we feel free to change again. That is one reason we
are liberal Jews.

One symbol-word has been central to Jewish belief for over
two thousand years: one. To say that God is one seems simple.
Yet it is an incredibly rich symbol. In how many ways can
you, in everyday situations, use the word "one"? Apply them
to God as you do so. One means not nothing but something,
not a fraction but complete, not many but single, not divided
but united, having an identity, unique—the only one, the
beginning of things, the number that goes into all other
numbers but that no number goes into. You can think of
others. You'll be surprised by how many valuable notions
about God are in the ordinary word "one." The *Shema* is
especially important to us because in one sentence, almost in
one word, it says much of what we believe. A rich symbol has
that power.

I hope modern Jews create new symbol-words for God. I am
also happy that Judaism has stored up for me much of the
wisdom of its long history in its traditional symbol-words for
God.

3
How Do We Know God Is Real?

PEOPLE are funny. One day they know which friends they really like, what sports are their favorites, and what they want to be when they get older. The next day they're not sure. Somebody didn't say hello in the cafeteria so they don't know if they like that person anymore. Badminton wasn't much fun in gym today and, as for becoming an accountant, all of a sudden working with numbers doesn't seem exciting. Funny. Funnier still, tomorrow they'll tell you not to pay attention to what they said yesterday. They were in a sad mood because their dog died, but this morning their folks promised them a French racing bike and they feel better about things.

We make up and change our minds in different ways. Sometimes we have reasons that make a lot of sense to us and to the people we discuss them with. Generally that's the best way to make a decision. But you can't always give reasons or explain important choices, for instance, why you trust somebody very much. Little things often have a big effect on us. When you were younger and visited a firehouse, you decided you really wanted to work with machines. When you smelled the preservative in the laboratory, you realized you really didn't want to be a doctor. Just because you have many good reasons for a decision doesn't mean you will stick with it; having few reasons for a decision doesn't indicate you'll soon change your mind. We don't really know how people come to believe something and hold on to it all their lives.

Believing in God is like that. I think it's important to know the different ways modern Jews have taken to belief in God. Maybe one will put into words something you've felt then you'll find its explanation convincing. Mostly, though, such a decision is so deep inside us I doubt that we can know our real reasons for it. Still, believing in God is so important for our lives that we ought to be as thoughtful and as sensitive as we can about it.

Some things that faith in God doesn't give you

To a Jew, believing in God does not mean you'll never have any more questions about God. Take a look at the Book of Psalms. The biblical authors have lots of doubts.

> Pity me, O Lord, for I faint; heal me, O Lord, for my bones melt and my spirit dissolves in me. And You, O Lord, how long will You wait to help me (6:3–4).

> Why do You stand far off, O Lord, and hide Yourself when we need You? (10:1).

> How long, O Lord, will You continue to forget about me? How long will You continue to be absent when I need You? (13:1).

There are many more such examples. I find many of these questions to God in the Psalms very much like the ones you and I have. Abraham and Job worry that God isn't as just as God ought to be. Jonah gets angry that God is so forgiving.

Jeremiah complains that God makes him criticize the Jews when he doesn't want to.

By having faith in God Jews don't mean going through an emotional, overwhelming experience. Evangelical Protestants emphasize this and connect it with what they call "seeing the light."

They generally claim that this religious experience will change your whole life. From being miserable, dejected, and lonely you will become happy, positive, and strong. Jews agree in part. People who have faith can face life, good and bad, with a special power—but we don't normally expect believing in God will solve everything. If anything, faith creates new problems, and often good ones, such as: Why don't we try harder to be good?

Jewish believing seems rather quiet, deep, and steady. It is more something you grow up with and explore than something you don't have and suddenly you need to get. Technically, people aren't born Christians, they have to become Christians. Many Protestant groups don't accept you for baptism—the official admission ceremony—until you're an adult and make a "decision for Christ." Most Jews don't have to "get" something or decide something to become Jewish. We're born Jewish. (On our not being a church but a religious ethnic group, see Part Two, Chapter 2.) As we Jews grow up we learn about and try to do what the Torah tradition teaches. We have had some mystics who had great personal experiences of God. Most Jews have gone about believing without ever having had tingles or visions or a sense of being lifted up to heaven. Modern Jews, particularly, distrust the emotional approach to believing because they feel it's easy for a clever person to take advantage of people's feelings.

How did our ancestors talk about faith in God?

The Bible writers don't say much directly about why they believe in God. Mostly, God's reality was so obvious to them that they didn't talk about it. But they do mention three things very often. One, where did this wonderful good world of ours come from? It was created by God. Two, we were slaves in Egypt, one of the mightiest countries in the world, and we escaped. On our own, we never would have made it. God helped us get out of Egypt. Three, God keeps on helping us.

That doesn't mean God does so all the time and not in every way we ask. Nonetheless, God's help is here often and in important things. God keeps our people alive and we outlast our enemies; God is close to and does good for individuals as well.

Jews have repeated some or all of those reasons whenever they have talked about God since Bible times. In the Middle Ages when Jews were challenged by Moslem science and philosophy, they developed intellectual arguments for believing. Their favorite was one adapted from Aristotle's ideas about cause and effect. Nothing happens (an "effect") unless something causes it. So there'd be no universe if something hadn't caused it. The philosophers called this the First Cause. To the Moslems and Jews that meant God. When people got to know Aristotle better, they were shocked to discover he thought there never was a creation. Aristotle said all matter was somehow eternal. Maimonides met that challenge by showing that Aristotle's reasons weren't very convincing. But they were troublesome enough that Maimonides thought we should no longer argue for believing in God because God was the Creator. Maimonides then explored other ways of showing why we should believe in God. This started a new path in medieval philosophy, and Christian thinkers like Thomas Aquinas gave credit to Maimonides for suggesting it.

The special problem with modern belief: we question everything

I hope some day you will study medieval Jewish philosophy. But its intricate, elegant arguments don't directly help us with our problems. Modern thinkers are too skeptical—we ask questions about everything. Our heroes are people who refused to believe what everyone else did and then taught us something new as a result. Galileo challenged the old science; Darwin the old sense of how life developed; Marx our old sense of money and power; Freud our old belief that our conscious mind rules our lives; Einstein that space and time are absolute; the Impressionists did this in painting, Schönberg and the twelve-tone composers in music.

To be modern often seems to mean to disbelieve and to go around asking "Why?" That's good because it lets you think for yourself. But it also creates a problem. You can't go on asking "Why?" forever. At some point there's nothing more you can be told. Have you ever had a little child pester you with "Why?" "Why?" until you thought you'd go crazy? Finally you had to say, "That's just the way it is." Or, "But everyone knows that." Or, "That's what I believe."

At some point people have to stop asking questions and agree on what they accept. If people don't believe something together they can't talk together, and certainly not on any important matters.

Thinking as a way to God

According to modern Jewish thinkers, there are two different ways of explaining belief in God. One comes from our thinking, the other from our feelings. We need to spend some time talking about each way.

The people who argue from our ideas think the three so-called classic proofs of God still make sense. One I've already mentioned that some cause had to bring the world into being, so it must have been God. A second says that in the world things work for a purpose. But purposes aren't accidents. They must have been put there. So God must have put them there. The third is trickier; it comes from the very definition of God. If God is the greatest thing that could possibly be, God must exist. Why? Because, if God didn't exist, there could be something greater than God, a God-who-existed.

Most modern thinkers find other arguments more convincing. One suggestion is based on the unity which seems to underlie all science. Things don't look alike yet science shows they're all energy. Many things don't act alike yet science shows they follow similar laws. There seems to be a unity underlying all things, what religion calls God.

Another approach argues that if our ethical sense is as real as is our sense of science we have a great intellectual problem. In the scientific world there's no freedom—hydrogen and oxygen can't choose to make ketchup instead of water. But in the ethical world you're free: you can choose to tell the truth (despite the consequences). However, we live in one world, not two. If we are to understand our world we need some idea greater than science and ethics—which will tie them together. Our idea of God is not scientific and not ethical. It's an idea which is unique, that is, it is the only one of its kind. For it is the basis of the order of science and the standards of ethics, yet it is an idea greater than either science or ethics.

Another proposal is that we work from what science is saying about human nature. Science indicates that religion everywhere helps people live up to the best that is in them and in their groups. Religion does this by teaching people that nature itself will help them grow. Religions call this helpfulness in the universe God or gods. People then come to trust the world and build their lives on the help we can expect from it. So these thinkers suggest we should use the word God today to mean all those forces in the universe which help us grow properly.

Feeling as a way to God

A different group of thinkers believes our minds are just one part, though an important one, of what it means to be a person. We need to go beyond our thinking to our total sense of the world to get to God. We need to rely more on our feelings.

Many people have a deep sense that we and all things around us are not very strong and lasting. Everything passes away. Yet we also know that we are worthwhile and that life's importance can't be measured by its years. We get this rich sense of our value from something far greater and more important than ourselves, God.

Yet another group looks at how we know that people are "real." Mostly what we know about people is the way they look or sound, or what we call their personalities. But sometimes we come away from somebody and say, "Now that's what I call a 'real' person." We know they're "for real" not because we see or hear them in any different way but because, through being with them, we've gotten to know them, as we say, on a "deeper level." You can't get to know God "for real" by looking and examining—God is no idol. You meet God when you are open to the reality in what happens to us all the time.

Some people say we are being too timid. We have been so brainwashed by science that we don't see the glory in the world around us. We take snowflakes and sunrises, the taste of salt and the colors around us as if they were nothing special. They are fantastic gifts. Instead of asking questions about God we need to get excited that we were given this ability to inquire. Instead of taking wonders for granted, we need to seek their source. Thankfulness will then overwhelm us and we will live appreciating how much our great and glorious God is doing for us.

Our few modern Jewish mystics go one step further. They have personally felt the infinite unity which underlies all the odds and ends that make up life. They have come to know God with such closeness that the possibility of asking God questions or of doubting God's reality has simply disappeared. They are the Jews who are most sure of their belief. But they help the rest of us only slightly because their experience is so different from what we know even when we feel God is near.

I want to discuss later the problem of why a good God permits evil (Chapter 5). Now I only want to add a comment and tell a story.

Is it becoming easier for people to believe in God?

Our times seem to be changing. While most people still can't be called believers, some people have begun to find it almost easy to believe in God. Many of the things we believed in instead of God have worked out badly. Science, education, money, culture, for all their good, have disappointed us. They are no substitute for God—as believing in God is no substitute for doing our part. We're beginning to realize that most of us, down deep, believe much more than we were willing to admit—which brings me to a story.

Menachem Mendel, the Chasidic Rebbe of Kotzk, once asked a group of scholars, "Do you know where God lives?" They laughed at the silly question and quickly quoted the biblical verse, "The whole earth is full of His Glory." That, the Rebbe reminded them, every child knows. Then he gave his own answer, "God lives wherever man lets Him in."

4 What Do We Think God Is Like?

PEOPLE who say they can tell you what God is really like almost always say it involves some kind of secret. Their master had a great vision, taught a special technique, or left a marvelous book which will, if you join their group and follow their teachings, give you the whole truth. That's very appealing. How nice it would be to get rid of all the doubts we have when we try to figure out what we believe. And why shouldn't we know the truth about God? We've only got one life to live on this earth so why should we have to wait for some afterlife—if there is one—to really know about God?

Maybe, then, if I said that I will now tell you what your family, your rabbi, and your religious school have refused to tell you—what God is really like—you would get very interested in this chapter. I hope not. I'd much rather you got very suspicious and waited to see what I was trying to pull on you. How would I know what God was really like? I'm only human, aren't I? How did I suddenly get so smart that I know the full truth about All Reality? If I'm a thinker, is my brain really that good? If I claim to be a prophet or to have visions, are my teachings likely to be any better than those of the hundreds of other leaders of new religions? How quickly these new visions come and go. Some occasionally have some new and interesting ideas. But if they claim to have and teach the whole truth about God Judaism suggests you ask a lot of questions. The more we've learned about God in 4,000 years, the more we've realized that much is still hidden from us. And if God is as great as we have thought, that only seems right.

I'm saying that Judaism teaches Jews certain kinds of disbelief. Our sort of faith makes some things unbelievable. When someone tells you he has an idol that's God, don't believe it. Our God is too great to be an idol. When someone says there is a power greater than our God, don't believe it. Our God is the greatest thing that could possibly be. When someone promises to teach you what God is really like, don't believe it. Our God is one, the only one, unique, therefore in some ways unlike us and beyond our understanding.

Judaism stresses right living
more than clear thinking

The Chasidic master Abraham, so pious a mystic he was called "The Angel," made this comment to his disciples: he said that the higher his mystical practices took him the more he realized how little he knew and how important it was simply to try to serve God. That's the Jewish way. What we know mostly about God is what God "wants" us to do. Judaism is mostly about living—and for good reason. Think too much about what God is really like and you forget about this world and what you should be doing to make it better.

Think of our great religious book, the Bible. It is about people, how they lived, and how they ought to have lived. It's mostly history, laws, prophecies, proverbs, poems, and stories. It says very little about what God is like. According to some scholars this religious attitude can be seen in its language, biblical Hebrew. And this Hebrew is mainly a language of verbs—words of action—not one which is rich in abstract terms like the modern words we might use for God, "being," "infinite," or "energy."

Some older ideas
of what God might be like

Josephus, writing for non-Jews about the year 80 c.e., gives a brief idea of Moses' teachings about God. Obviously drawing on Greek ideas he says: God is one, not brought into being by anything else, but self-caused, unchanging for all time, more beautiful than anything human beings can think of, and, though we know God by seeing the effect of God's rule all around us, we do not know what God is truly like.

Do you recall that passage in Exod. 33:18–23 where Moses wanted to see God's glory but was told he could only see God's back? Going past the cave God proclaims (Exod. 34:6–7): Adonai, Adonai, God, merciful and gracious, long-suffering, abounding in goodness and truth, giving mercy to a thousandth generation of those that are loyal to God, forgiving all kinds of sin, yet giving some punishment to the guilty and punishing guilty families to the third and fourth generation. The rabbis of the Talmud noted that we don't hear much about what God is but rather what God does. They then taught: As God is called merciful and gracious, so you should be merciful and generous. Give freely of yourself to all people—provide clothes for the poor, visit the sick, bury the dead, comfort the mourner. We "know" God best when we see how God "cares" for people and do the same as best we can.

In the Middle Ages, when Jews began to study and to write philosophy this question of what God was like often came up. As so often was the case, Maimonides thought this through in a way that strongly affected most later Jewish thinkers. Maimonides argued that we can't say anything at all about what God is "like" because God truly isn't "like" anything, even any other so-called god. God is one. That surely means that God is the only one. Other things are not God and so there is nothing really like God. What God truly is must be different from what we are and from even the grandest ideas we can think up. Maimonides also taught that we can know something about what God does because we see its effects—God creates, rules, reveals. And we do know what commands God gave us—that is what we should work at.

Now that it's clear that Judaism doesn't think we know very much about what God is like, I am ready to try to explain what some modern Jewish thinkers think God is like. There are good reasons for doing it now. First, you're properly warned and your Jewish suspicions are aroused. Second, you're modern. We want to know as much as we can about things, not simply take them as tradition. We also have greater confidence in what human beings can understand than did people of an earlier age. Third, despite the rabbis and Maimonides, some Jews still want to know what God is like. Finally, by this time you've learned that there are four major modern ways of talking about God. We mentioned them when we talked about what God "says" (Part Three, Chapter 2) and how we know God is real (Part Four, Chapter 3). Now we can use them to help us get some answers to a most difficult question, "What do we think God is like?"

God as the idea behind everything

Philosophers argue that we should think of God as our greatest and most significant idea. They believe that thinking is what makes us different from all other animals, particularly when ethics, decisions about good and bad, is made an important part of thinking. The best thinking tries to understand the world as a whole. Our ideas try to reach out and take in more and more, leaving nothing out. When our ideas are true ideas, we are as close as we can ever get to reality. Our idea of God is our greatest idea, the one that takes in all the reality we can think of. For philosophers, being such an all-embracing idea makes God as real and important as possible.

God as the positive power in nature

A second theory wants to see God in nature. No scientific-minded person can have God outside of nature, say in heaven. Such a God then interferes in the world by sending rain, talking to people, or, worst of all, performing miracles.

We can't believe that. We have to work with nature in a scientific way. There's a lot in nature on which we rely—that the sun will come up tomorrow, that vitamins will help us be healthy, that most people whom we treat kindly will respond in kindness. We really build our whole lives on such processes in nature. All of us trust in them as we make our plans and work for the future. To us the word "God" can mean all those things in nature which help people mature to the fullest. That will end all the problems of believing or not believing in God, for the world and this God-part of it are surely real.

According to these two suggestions, our notions of what God is like ought to be ones that can be thought out and clearly expressed. That is their strength. If you can't follow them here, it only means that either I need to explain them better or you need to develop your mind so that you can understand them. But while the ideas are difficult, they're not mysterious. Anyone who thinks well can eventually understand them and can see why people would want to believe in them.

We talk about God differently if we start from our experience

The next two suggestions about what God is like start from what we sense and experience. It's not that these philosophers don't want us to think. Too many people wind up doing crazy things or living in an odd way because they've stopped thinking. But, it is suggested, we shouldn't limit our sense of reality to what our minds can grasp and put clearly into words. A person is more than a mind; human beings are more than thinking machines. The strength of these views is that if you share these feelings then belief in God touches you personally. However, as we shall see, it is sometimes difficult to know just what sort of feelings these thinkers are talking about. And perhaps you do not think they lead you to understand God better. That's why modern Jews have different ways of thinking about what God is like. It's something like that comment in the Midrash which compares the many different ways people have had of talking about God with a giant statue. A thousand people looking at the statue from different places think it's looking back at them—and describe it from where they stand.

God is the "most real person" we could get to know

One view points to the difference between thinking about somebody and being friends. A friend is someone you feel especially close to, who has some idea of what you are going through even if you don't say anything about it. It's hard to talk about such a friend because what you feel is very personal. What your friends really are to you is not just obvious things like eye color or smile or way of speaking. It's what makes them "them." It's what you feel when you spend some time with them or think back to your times together. The best you can say is that you have a certain inner sense that makes you know you're friends.

From this point of view, God is everybody's special, close, personal friend. Every once in a while we have a sense that God is with us. We feel close to God and sense God's closeness to us. If that happens to us several times we develop a "friendship," a relationship with God. Then, because we've felt so close, even if we don't sense God sometimes, we still know God is real. We aren't surprised, then, when the old feeling comes back. That doesn't say much about what God is like. Yet we can sense that God is greater and more important than anything else we know. Unlike all others with whom we are friendly, this friend never becomes simply a thing, a physical object, a body to us. That would make God an idol. So to speak, God is our Always Friend.

God is so truly great we should try to appreciate, not understand, God

Another view thinks we must go much further with our feelings. We are too calm about the world. We should be amazed at how wonderful it is. Instead of starting with our thoughts or our feelings, we ought to be shocked that we can have any impressions of the world at all. We're too conceited. Instead of trying to get an idea of God from our experiences, we should be overwhelmed with the idea that God made them possible.

God doesn't follow from anything—God is the beginning and source of everything. God is the grand and glorious Creator and Ruler of us and everything that is. Whatever beauty, intelligence, joy, or harmony we see in nature is but a tiny hint of God's greatness. Every second we should sing the ancient song: "Who is like You O Lord among the things that people call God?" And we should cry out: "Nothing. No one. God is one and unique. God is beyond our words and ideas. God is our Lord." Here God is not just in our ideas or in the helpful part of nature. God is greater than anything. God is so great we can't say what God is "like," for God is greater than anything.

We keep trying to find
better symbol-words for God

There are other modern ways of talking about God, none of them very simple. Some prefer to talk about God as the intelligence which runs through the whole universe. Others like to link God with whatever power makes evolution the pattern by which life moves on. Still others talk about the underlying reality from which all things emerge and to which they return. One recent suggestion seems to have grown up by itself in our community. Many people once believed science and culture would answer all our problems. They once took the place God once had in our lives. But today, for all their worth, science and culture cause us as many problems as they solve. If they cannot tell us what is good and what we should live for, if they can no longer give us much hope and courage, we must be getting these standards from somewhere else. So we realize these "come" from God, the measure of our goodness and the model of our maturity.

There are other such ideas as well. Yet I think we can sum up best by reading a statement by the modern thinker Martin Buber. He said that he saw the soul of Judaism turning around two centers, as in an ellipse. "One center of the Jewish soul is the deep, deep experience that God is wholly raised above man, that God is beyond the grasp of man. The other center of our belief is that God 'faces' us, that God is present in a direct relationship with people, even though human beings aren't at all God's equal. To know both these

things at the same time so that they cannot be separated, that God is far and God is near, this constitutes the living core of every believing Jewish soul."

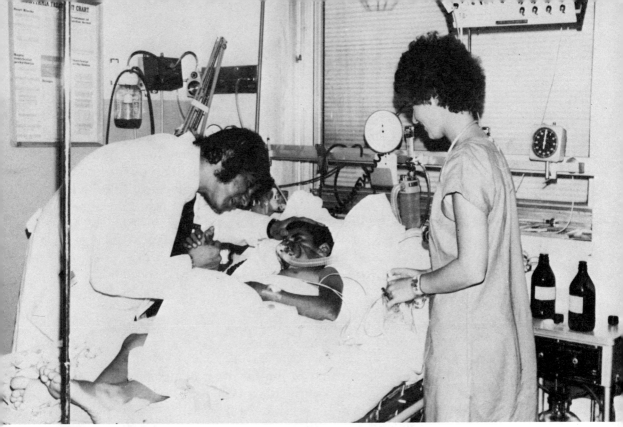

5 Why Does God Let Bad Things Happen?

RABBI YANNAI said: "We can't really explain why evildoers have good lives and why good people suffer so." He lived somewhere about the year 250 C.E. but what he said hasn't changed much. We have a number of answers to the problem of evil and some of them are helpful in facing life. But if you want it all explained clearly and in a way that leaves you completely satisfied that's more than Judaism—or any other religion—can give you.

The Bible teaches three things which are very important to Jews—only they contradict one another. God is good; God has all possible power; there is real evil in the world. Let us consider each idea for a moment.

If God was neutral and not positively good (as in some Asian religions) or even evil (as in the Gnostic faiths of

Roman times), evil would be no problem. Our world would reflect its uncaring or nasty God. Again, if a good God was weak (as in Zoroastrianism where the God of good fights but can't yet defeat the God of evil), there'd have to be some evil. Finally, maybe there really isn't any evil. It's your mistaken way of looking at things—which is something like what Hinduism and Christian Science say. Then, surely, there's really no problem except that you see things improperly. But Jews have felt all three of their beliefs were right. God is good and powerful and there is real evil in the world. Can we explain how all these beliefs can be held at once?

Jews have not dodged
the problem of evil in the world

When we have a serious problem, most of us are tempted to run away from it, to deny there is a problem. The biblical authors and rabbis don't do that. Many of the Psalms ask why righteous people aren't helped by God. The prophet Jeremiah is sick at heart because he can't understand why God must punish the people of Israel so severely. The whole Book of Job—a beautiful but difficult set of poems—charges that God isn't doing justice. None of these authors is an atheist. If they didn't believe in a good God they wouldn't worry about the evil. They dare to bring their problems straight to God. They can't understand why God doesn't clear up the evil. They complain that they are exhausted from waiting for God to act. But facing evil didn't keep them from being religious Jews. Indeed, we consider their grumblings holy and have them in our Bible.

They occasionally go a step further and argue that God ought to "behave" better. Abraham can't understand how a good God could think of destroying the few just people along with all the wicked ones in Sodom and Gomorrah (Gen. 18:20–33). Most of Job's speeches about injustice in the world call on God to appear and argue this out with him. You might think it was improper for a believer to be so impertinent to God. Not so in Judaism. If God is good then God can be challenged when God doesn't seem to be doing good. Not many Jews have had the courage for such challenges, but from time to time we hear of such figures. Levi Yitzchak, the Chasidic Rebbe of Berditchev, threatened to take God before a Jewish court for not living up to God's promises to the Jewish people. I like the Yiddish folk saying which is so modern a mixture of belief in an exasperation with God: "If God lived in our shtetl, people would throw stones through His windows."

We blame God for silly things

Some Jews have tried to meet this problem by pointing out that many things for which people get angry at God aren't really evil. "Why did God make me so short?" (Or tall.) "Why did God make me so fat?" (Or skinny.) "Why did God give me such a bad complexion?" (Or freckles, or red hair, or, or, or.) Sorry. Those may be big nuisances because they're not in fashion but you can't say that they are evil. A short or tall, fat or skinny, pimply or freckled or red-headed person can still be a fine human being. Don't fight with God about evil when all you're talking about is some social style that may change next year or you may soon outgrow. When you have a proper sense of what's really good, a lot of what you take to be evil disappears.

But not all evil comes from our having bad standards. If life is so "important" to God that Jews are supposed to do almost anything to keep people alive, then why does God take it away from young people? If God is so much in favor of goodness why don't evil deeds just self-destruct? Or, to consider the great problem of our time, how could God allow the Holocaust? These evils don't come from our having the wrong standards. They're not something we just imagine is bad. They're real—and they are evil.

We did evil and deserve to be punished

A second approach is to try to understand God's goodness better. Judaism teaches that much of what we call evil is only punishment. We deserve it because of some evil we did. It is God's justice, which is a part of God's goodness, for who would want an unjust God? Mostly God uses punishment as a means of teaching us not to do what is bad but what is good.

This idea, that evil comes as a result of God's justice, is very strong in the Bible and the Talmud. Still it wasn't expected to operate automatically, like electricity. Plug your lamp into a socket and it will light; stick a finger in the socket and you'll get a shock. True, in the Bible, ideas are often stated that way: Follow commandments and you'll get rain; sin and God will bring a drought. Yet it is meant only in a rough sort of way. Otherwise we'd lose our freedom.

Suppose you immediately bit your tongue every time you forgot to say a blessing before you ate. Suppose you felt your muscles strengthen every time you said a wake-up prayer. You'd perform these deeds—but not like a person, out of choice. You'd soon be like a rat in a laboratory, running around a maze without ever thinking, just to get some cheese. God "wants" us to follow the commandments because we choose to and not like robots. So God has to allow us some mistakes, that we can try to learn on our own what we really want to do. Isn't that how it works in your home when your parents don't punish you as you deserve? They forgive you in the hope that you'll learn to do better on your own. This explains why the Bible and the Talmud talk so much about God's mercy, for God is not a justice machine but the greatest "teaching-parent."

Could it be good for us not to have any choices?

Would it be better for us not to be free, if like horses we had to follow our instincts or if God trained us like guinea pigs, with strict justice? Judaism doesn't think so. Our freedom is a special sign of God's goodness to us. But truly free people are able to do tremendous evil. And we do. We drive too fast and smash into safe drivers and innocent pedestrians. We claim to be peoples' friends and then "cut them apart" behind their backs. Some people even became Nazis and used their freedom to create a Holocaust. The fault is ours, not God's. We were, in goodness, made free. We used our freedom to do evil.

Surely it is true that instead of complaining about God we should admit how badly we behave. There is food in the world but we let people starve. There is medical help in our country but people still die from inattention. The failures of democracy and the greater sins of fascism and communism, the unbelievable brutality of nazism are all the result of human action. The problem of evil is a problem of humanity, not of God.

Yet Judaism knows justice doesn't explain all the evil

With all that, there are evils we don't have much to do with: earthquakes which kill so many—good and bad alike; diseases which torture and kill people who might yet have led fruitful lives. Those aren't our doing. And can a good God really let us be free to do anything? Couldn't God at least "show up" later and help us understand what a mess we've made? If God is so powerful, can't God figure out a way to keep us free yet make us less damaging?

We should confess that much of what happens to us as a result of using our freedom is simple justice. Drink too much and you'll get sick. Never study and you'll get poor grades. Cheat on your practicing and you won't play very well. Don't blame God for giving you what you deserve. And it would help to be thankful for what God does give you day by day—strength, intelligence, sensitivity, life itself. There is a rough justice—and mercy—in God's world.

Only for a God who has all power the justice-mercy we see in the world is much too "rough." Often evil people seem to get along very well while good people seem to suffer badly. The suffering of children who do nothing to deserve such punishment is utterly inexcusable. And we have seen the Holocaust. Nothing European Jews did could be so horrible to deserve killing six million of them as punishment (one million of them estimated to be children).

All that is true and terrifyingly real. Judaism is a mature religion; it does not ask us to deny how brutal history can be. Still, what I said earlier is also true. Much of the evil that **211** happens to us is just; we bring it on ourselves. Job was a saintly person who didn't at all deserve his suffering. That is not the normal case. And most of us aren't Job. Yet even one

Job, as the Bible teaches us, is a problem for a powerful and good God. And there are many Jobs in history and the Holocaust in our own time.

Suffering can be a great teacher

Sometimes you can say that an evil can be "good" because it taught us a great lesson. Haven't most of the important things you've learned in your life come as a result of your troubles? Maybe it was a physical problem you had to learn to deal with or a major problem you ran into at home or school. Such things stay with us in ways that the good times we've had or the prizes we've won don't. Or so it is for most of us.

Sickness may teach us to appreciate health, death may show us how valuable is life, but not every evil has good benefits. Some people suffer and are broken by it, and those around them are hurt in ways that never heal. Death sometimes takes a life from us in such a way as to leave us unable to help ourselves or anyone else. A powerful God surely could find less harmful ways of teaching us. We cannot explain the Holocaust in this way. Whatever God wanted us to learn about people's capacity to do evil surely could have been made clear at a lesser price.

Perhaps all our troubles will be made up to us

Another way of defending God's goodness is to say that God, though sending the trial, makes it up to us with some great good. In modern times people have said that God rewarded us for suffering the Holocaust by giving us the State of Israel, the greatest good we have had in two thousand years. Yet does one make up for the other? Suppose someone said to us, "You may have a Jewish state but its price will be the massacre of six million Jews." I do not think we would have accepted such an inhuman offer. To say God acted that way is even more disgusting if God has all power. Why should God need a Holocaust to create a state for us? And can the State of Israel, for all that it means to us, really wipe out the viciousness of the Holocaust?

Traditionally it was held that the sufferings of this world

will be made up to us after death in the life of the world-to-come. In many cases I think that answer would satisfy us as it did most Jews until recent times. Though they couldn't understand the way the good God was running our world, they trusted God now because they believed God would make it up to them in the next world. If we believed in life-after-death then I think we would not have as great a problem as we have with evil in this world. But many modern people find life-after-death difficult, if not impossible, to believe. Worse, there are some instances (most notably the Holocaust) where the suffering was so miserable that no good God should have permitted it—even if the greatest possible eternal bliss awaited people later.

A modern suggestion:
God isn't powerful enough to end all evil

This leaves one other approach. If some evil is real and can't be considered an act of God's goodness, then we should rethink the belief that God can do anything. The simplest way is to remember that we can't ask God to do what's illogical. Example: If people are to be free then God must allow them to do what they want even if it's terrible evil. So God doesn't have all the power. We have some real power—it's simple logic.

Another argument was used by Saadyah Gaon, the first great Jewish philosopher, about 920 C.E. He said that if there's to be a world it must be made out of matter. But matter is stuff that lasts only a while—sooner or later it decays and dies. So if God is going to have a world it must have decay and death in it no matter how powerful God is—that too is simple logic.

I think those arguments about freedom and matter are correct—but I don't find them at all satisfying. I know I shouldn't ask God to be illogical. Still, if God has all power God should be able to do something about our freedom and the world's matter without there being so much evil.

Some modern thinkers have made a bolder suggestion. They suggest that we admit that God's power isn't complete. God may be the greatest power but God doesn't have *all* power—at least not yet. (That's what the Messianic Age is,

WHY DOES GOD LET BAD THINGS HAPPEN?

when God's "kingship" is finally established on the earth.)
There is evil because God hasn't gotten everything under
control yet. One nice way of talking about this is to say that
God, like so much else in the world, is still growing. What's
more, God needs human help to finish becoming God. We are
truly God's partners. When we fight all forms of evil we add
our power to God's. That will one day bring an end to all
injustice and suffering.

I believe that is the only intellectually satisfying answer
that can be given to the Holocaust. God "allowed" it because
God didn't yet have the power to stop it. God couldn't—and we
didn't—prevent it. The same thing applies to any other evil.
God is doing all the good God now can. It's not God's fault that
God isn't yet fully powerful enough to stop all the evil in the
world.

My problem with this clear and logical answer

Yet I find I cannot live with that answer. I keep wondering
who is in control of the evils that God hasn't power over. Is
there, perhaps, another God? I also worry about how much to
trust a somewhat weak God. Will that God one day grow
strong enough for the Messianic Age to come? Watching the
news on television, God often seems to be losing and I do not
trust human goodness enough to say that we will make up
what God lacks. A weak God plus weak people hardly adds up
to my Jewish belief that God's "kingdom" will one day be real
on earth.

I am left where we began: with a good, powerful God who
yet allows evil in the world. That makes no sense logically.
Traditionally, what most Jews have done, despite their questions, is to believe in God's goodness and power though they
know it's not logical. How could Jews, so proud of their
thinking and intellect, do such a thing? I'd guess they did it
out of simple piety. By that I mean that they trusted God even
if they didn't understand God. They built their trust in God by
trying to be aware of all that God did for them, hour by hour
and day by day. Each portion of food, each unusual sight,
each important happening was a reason to say a blessing of
thanks to God. Add up all these blessings and prayers, look at
all of our lives, and it seems clear that God is overwhelmingly

good and generous to almost all people. In most cases the evils we face are few and small compared to the gifts we have been given. Then we are often able to say with Job, "Shall we take all the good God gives and not accept some evil?" (Job 2:10). Therefore, though one doesn't understand, one still trusts God.

Can we still do that after the Holocaust? Many people do. Mostly it was not simple believers who lost faith in God as a result of the Holocaust, but people who had relied on modern notions of God and humankind. As difficult as such piety may be for some modern Jews to accept, others face the problem of evil with this old Jewish attitude of trust.

How shall we end an unfinished discussion? With a quotation which is now part of our tradition. After the Holocaust, it was reported that people searching a cellar in Cologne, Germany, where some Jews had hidden from the Nazis, found the following written on the wall: "I believe in the sun even when it is not shining. I believe in love even when I do not feel it. I believe in God even when He is silent."

6 What Happens after You Die?

"Being dead" is scary but "life-after-death" sounds fairly good. There's quite a difference between them so let's take a look at each idea in turn.

Teenagers often have strong feelings about death. Everyone does, but these emotions are especially powerful when we are growing up. Then our sensitivity to everything increases. Life becomes much more exciting. There are many wonderful things yet to do so the possibility of not being allowed to experience them is particularly disturbing. Then, too, many teenagers never learned when they were younger about facing death. Their families thought it was better for them to be protected from it. When someone in the family died it was made a great secret. No one discussed death in front of the children and whenever the topic came up it was quickly changed. Death thus became mysterious and dangerous. It was not something which, for all that it troubles us, is a natural part of the life cycle.

There is a way to clear up one part of people's fears about death. Don't try to imagine what it's like being dead. (I'm not yet talking about life-after-death.) In the first place, whatever you come up with has to be awful. Death being the opposite of life, as far as we can tell, all you can imagine is different kinds of nothingness. The point is, however, you won't "be" dead. Think about it: When you're dead that means "you" are dead and you won't "be" or "feel" anything, not even bad. The words "being dead" make no sense together. If you have "being," you're not "dead." Either there is some sort of life-after-death and "being dead" means what you're doing in that existence or else you're dead, in which case "you" won't know it. So you can stop trying to figure out what it's like to be nothing.

Thinking means life: how then shall we deal with death?

This discussion already illustrates the problem with this topic: how do you talk about something you've had no experience with? As difficult as it is to discuss God we can say that through our minds or in our lives we've had some personal sense that God is real. How can we think about death? All we know is life. The closest thing to death in life is sleep—only we are very much alive when asleep though not very conscious of it. How can we figure from life its opposite? Death is a real mystery, one none of us can avoid, and that makes it frightening.

Some people get so upset by the idea of death that they can't stand talking about it. Maybe it opens up old sorrows. Maybe they're afraid someone will make them feel even worse about death than they now do. Such people, old or young, should have a talk with the rabbi about their fears. Judaism doesn't make death a big part of our lives but it knows that anyone who can't come to terms with death, as difficult as that is, never really matures.

Surprisingly, it's recently been suggested that maybe we can have some idea of what it's like to go on living after death. Recent medical advances make it possible on occasion to revive someone who, technically, has just died. Such cases are still rare and can only happen under special circumstances. Research on what such people report shows that many say the same thing. They knew themselves to be "out" of their bodies and had some idea of what was happening. They had no "feeling" of panic or pain but, if anything, "felt" rather peaceful. Most report choosing to return to life rather than move on to what seemed an area of great goodness signaled by a great light.

I'm not sure what to make of this data. There's only a little of it so far and there are many questions to be raised about it. Mostly, modern Jews have been suspicious of efforts to prove life-after-death from messages from "the other side." Mediums and spiritualists have generally been fakes. This new research seems to be of a different sort and may stand up under the searching criticism it should get. One impressive piece of data deserves careful checking. These people have often been able to report accurately, and in detail, what went on around them when their doctors say that, from a medical point of view, they were dead. I don't think we should make too much of these studies now, but they can remind us not to close our minds by saying life-after-death is unbelievable.

Judaism's ideas about life-after-death

There are a number of different approaches to life-after-death in the Jewish tradition. The Bible says rather little about it, concentrating instead on what people ought to do while alive. Jews feel strongly about that. In the Bible what God mostly "tells" us (see Part Two, Chapter 2) is how to live in "this world," not what's going to happen to us after we die. Some people find it strange that one could have a religion which pays little attention to life-after-death. I think it all depends on how much you trust God. A few centuries ago the Baal Shem Tov, the founder of Chasidism, who believed in life-after-death, could say, "If I love God here and now, why do I need to worry about the life of the world-to-come?" Whatever the reason, some statements in the Bible, like this one from the Book of Job, seem to rule out life-after-death: "As a cloud fades away and disappears, so a person that goes down to the grave will not come up from it" (7:9).

However there is also a strong sense in the Bible that part of us survives our death. There is much talk of our souls going to Sheol. There they live on but not in what we would consider pleasant conditions. Although we never get a clear description, Sheol seems to be a sort of pit under the earth, a place of darkness, one where you don't pray and don't praise God. Yet, the one time we hear of somebody getting out of Sheol (by the magic of the witch of Endor), it is the old prophet Samuel whose only complaint is that Saul has bothered to bring him back to earth (I Sam. 28:15).

A quite different idea is found in the Book of Daniel (some say in one or two other places as well). There it says that when the people of Israel is finally saved from all its troubles "many of those who 'sleep' in the dust of the earth shall awaken, some to everlasting life and some to criticism and everlasting rejection. Those who were wise will shine on as bright as the sky. Those who led other people to righteousness will be like stars for ever and ever" (Dan. 12:2–3). Note the themes: an end to things as we know them, people rise from their graves, a reward for the good, and a punishment of the bad. We'd love to know just how far back those ideas go, but the Bible doesn't give us enough data to draw any firm conclusions.

The rabbis' idea:
God will restore us to a new, perfected body

By rabbinic times, however, there is a firm commitment to Daniel's ideas—except for one religious group, the Sadducees. Their point of view pretty well died out after the destruction of the Temple in 70 C.E. Later the beliefs of the Pharisees became widely accepted among Jews. They taught what is called "resurrection." Some time after the Messiah came, the graves would open and the bodies, made perfect and pure, would rise, get their souls back from the "treasury" in heaven where God had been storing them, and come before

God for judgment. The righteous would go straight into the life of the world-to-come; the wicked would be punished until they were purified, but, the rabbis also taught, "All Jews have a share in the life of the world-to-come." This idea, that your soul is kept by God until the resurrection takes place and the world-to-come begins, remains the traditional Jewish belief (with many variations in the description).

Incidentally, you can now see why Easter is so important for Christians. Jesus' resurrection proves to Christians that Jesus was the Messiah and one of the "Three Persons" who make up the one God. But there is nothing in our Bible about the Messiah being resurrected in place of bringing justice and peace.

While I think I've given a fair description of life-after-death in rabbinic thinking, I want to emphasize how much difference of opinion there was among the rabbis. In the early 200s C.E., Rav, one of the great founders of the Babylonian study style which resulted in the Talmud, taught this: "The world-to-come is not like this world of ours. In the world-to-come there is no eating or drinking, no begetting of children, no business, no envy, no hatred, and no competition. Rather the righteous will sit with crowns on their heads and 'drink in' the splendor of God's presence." At the same time, Rabbi Yochanan, one of the great teachers in the Land of Israel, said: "All that our prophets told us about the future concerned only the days of the Messiah. But, what will happen when [after the resurrection] we go on to the world-to-come, we don't know. As Isaiah said, 'No eye beside Yours has seen, O God, what You will do for the person who had hope in You' (Isa. 64:3)." Keeping such different views in our tradition suggests that, though people are permitted to think about what will finally happen to us, we all ought to admit we don't really know and simply trust God.

Some other Jewish ideas about living on after death

Two other ideas never became an influence in Jewish law yet were held by some people in our community. Greek-speaking Jews in the Roman period had their own notions about religion. The rabbis mostly did not like their ideas so the Greek books never became part of official Jewish teaching.

(We have them today in two collections called the *Apocrypha* and the *Pseudepigrapha*.) Here you will find an emphasis on the survival of just the soul, an idea called "immortality." In the Wisdom of Solomon it is explained this way: "God created people to live forever and made them to be just like God is. . . . The souls of the righteous are cared for by God and no trouble shall come to them. . . . Fools think people die, that when they pass from this life it will hurt them and that their dying has brought them to ruin. But they are at peace. Though people think they've been punished by dying, they have every right to hope for life after death." The idea of just the soul living on may have come from Greek thought according to which the body was the source of most of our problems.

An even more astonishing idea developed among the Jewish mystics of the Middle Ages. They taught that there are a limited number of souls. God keeps recycling them from body to body in different generations. This idea is called reincarnation ("going back into bodies") and, since their traditions come from the mystics, is still believed by many Chasidic Jews.

The challenge of modern thinking
to belief in life-after-death

In the modern period, science challenged all these beliefs. Biology and chemistry seemed to make the idea of a soul quite unnecessary. The thought that a body, after decaying in its grave, could come back to life seemed too big a miracle for most modern people to accept. The early Reform Jews took the idea of resurrection out of their prayer books. They talked instead about our "spirit" living on after us. This modern version of immortality came from our belief that people are more than complicated bunches of proteins. They are conscious; they choose; they have goals; they even have a sense of the infinite. And each of them is quite individual. So modern Jewish thinkers used the word "spirit" to describe what makes us so humanly ourselves. (When they did use the word "soul" they meant it in this modern way.) They then argued that our spirit, since it is what we have that is most like God, is what lives on. No one tried to describe what such immortality might be like. It was connected to "being with" God and it rarely had any sort of judgment or punishment. Even so traditional a believer as the Chasidic Rebbe of Ger could say years ago that the punishment that awaits us after death will be to discover all our sins and be properly ashamed for them.

Many Jews have decided that they simply no longer believe in life-after-death. Some feel that way because of science, some because they want to make sure we do what we can in this world. They are comforted because we "live on" in peoples' memories and in what we worked for while alive. But we, personally, do not survive. Such Jews feel their attitude is something like the one view in the Bible. Since, with only this life, it has led many people to work harder at being good Jews, other Jews have respected this attitude.

Why today's Jews are more open to believing in life-after-death

Some years ago, when people's respect for science was at its height, I think many modern Jews had given up believing even in the immortality of the soul. I find a somewhat different mood today. We do not think science knows everything. Certainly science does not know what human beings really are or ought to be. Although we know a great deal and we do wonderful things, we're more humble today. We now recognize that God's wisdom operates in the world in ways we have not always appreciated. What is most real in the world is not chemicals or energy, but God. Human beings are God-like creatures. We are able to work along with God. Apparently we share something of God's power. This leads us to believe that we share in the fact that God does not die. Though we must die a bodily death, God keeps alive that part of us which is most like God. That is another way of affirming immortality. Some few thinkers, recognizing that a person is as much a body as a soul, are asking what resurrection might mean to us today.

It all comes down to how much we feel we can trust God. Having seen all the benefits which God has given us as we live, shouldn't we expect the same goodness when we die?

God is the Creator of death as of life. If life serves God's good purposes, will not death do the same?

A strong positive answer to those questions is heard in the words our tradition teaches us to recite when we feel ourselves dying: "Adonai rules all things now as Adonai has ruled until now. And Adonai will rule over them for ever and ever. Blessed be God's name; the glory of God's rule goes on forever. Adonai is the only God. Hear, O Israel, Adonai is our God. Adonai is one." One—the same good God in our death as in our life.

7

Why Do We Have Different Religions?

Isn't it obvious that it would be best if there were only one religion? Then people would stop killing each other for "religious" reasons, for example, the Catholics and Protestants in Northern Ireland or the Hindus of India and Moslems of Pakistan who have often had religious clashes. Then there would be less hatred in the world, including less anti-Semitism. People don't seem that different wherever they are, but if we are to have one humanity we need one set of beliefs to unite us. Surely if there is only one God then there really ought to be only one religion. Isn't it humanly bad and spiritually wrong for many religions to exist in the world?

I agree with much of the case for having only one religion. The vision of what ties all humankind together is inspiring and important. Since it's easy to become selfish and think only of our own group, I think we need to keep the dream of one humanity constantly in front of us. Yet I also think we shouldn't confuse what we could be at our best with, being the sort of people we really are, what we can accomplish. If human beings always lived up to their ideals, perhaps we could have one religion. Real people are imperfect—which makes it important for them to live by the vision of a united humankind. In Jewish tradition we look forward to the Messianic Age when "God will be one and God's name [what we know about God] will be one."

The wrong sorts of hopes
can be dangerous and disappointing

Two sorts of human experience have shown how harmful it can be to think that you have actually reached messianic perfection. One is that such a belief has led to terrible persecution. If you believe you have the one full truth, then you must also believe that everyone ought to follow it— anyone who doesn't is a dangerous threat. Time and again people who claimed to have the whole truth became vicious to those who disagreed with them. In modern times political parties, teaching that they have the whole truth, have done most of the persecuting, probably because they are the only dominant groups who have power.

Another difficulty has come from the hurt and disappointment a false hope brings. People have been crushed to discover that what they thought was the climax of all human history turned out to be only another event which time passed by. About three hundred years ago many Jews became convinced that a man named Shabbetai Zevi was the Messiah. They got ready for him to take them all to the Land of Israel, establish the Messianic Kingdom, and bring all humanity to peace and harmony. The sultan of Turkey, not interested in having new kings in his empire, offered Shabbetai Zevi a choice between death and becoming a Moslem. He converted. Jews all over the world were stunned. Many lost hope that God would ever save them. Writers of that period said they suffered from "dark despair." Hoping for too much, people become frustrated and often lose the desire to help themselves.

We have good reasons
for going separate religious ways

Until the Messianic Age comes, we can't expect things to change radically. There are many differences among people: climates, cultures, languages, interests, politics—and even they change from period to period. History is very much the result of the clash of these differences. Can we really hope to overcome them now? Forget about the great disputes of the world or your city, what are the chances of getting all your classmates to agree on one belief and way of life? It's not easy even in a family where people love one another. Such a question makes the stubbornness of human difference clear. Multiply it by the billions of people on earth and you have some idea of the scope of our messianic hope.

There are two good reasons for our keeping our separate religions until the Messianic Age comes. One is that such variety is natural to human beings and can be a means of enriching our lives. The other is that we really do have important disagreements about what reality is or how we should face it.

Simply, most people like doing things their way or the way it's done in their community. Many Christians who are no longer sure that they believe in Jesus' resurrection still want to do something about Easter. They try to get together with family or otherwise make Easter a special day. Likewise, the holidays *you* grow up with get to mean a great deal to you. To give them up so that everyone is alike would make your life much poorer. Rather, your group's celebrating, its carnivals, its singing, feasting, parading, its studying make our civilization that much more exciting.

226

Some Jews have a special problem with this in modern times. Take Christmas. Even though they don't believe it is the day the Messiah was born, these Jews want to have a tree, exchange presents, and celebrate. They give lots of reasons: that it's only a folk custom or that it's beautiful or ethical or such. I think the truth is that these Jews don't want to feel like outsiders by not taking part in what is going on around them. Isn't that also what's behind much of our interest in one religion? Jews often feel bad because we're a minority and we'd like to give up the pain of being different. If that sounds harsh, please note that such Jews who are eager for religious unity almost always expect us to follow other peoples' customs. They rarely call for other people to observe some Jewish practices. Overcoming differences shouldn't be a sort of honorable way to escape being Jewish. That's hardly respecting peoples' right to be true to themselves, including the Jews.

Symbols aren't easily exchanged for they carry the wisdom of centuries

The human talent for variety has a special aspect we must consider. Each group develops its own symbols. The cross, the star, the crescent, the Torah scroll get much of their power from having been in use by many people for many centuries. To those who have grown up with them, they say far more than can be expressed in words. That is why we create symbols and why it is far harder for us to give them up than to change our ideas. They seem so simple, yet they are incredibly precious. A scroll of the Torah is only an old-fashioned sort of book. There are thousands of them around the world. Yet if somebody threw one on the floor we would be shocked, angry, and hurt. If a person tore one up or splattered filth on it, as the Nazis did, we would be outraged. When a synagogue is on fire people will do all sorts of brave things to save the Torah scrolls (though Jewish law says they should not risk their lives to do so). Someone watching might say, "It's only a book." That's right—but it's our symbol and we will risk a lot for it.

One major reason that different religions continue is that people don't want to give up their symbols. That's not just because they love them but also because of what the symbols stand for. A statue of the Buddha says something quite different from the Tablets of the Ten Commandments. And that brings me to my other theme: that religions have different ways of looking at the world.

Religions often see reality quite differently

Remember that Judaism teaches that we need to keep working for a united humanity. That's an important ideal in modern Judaism and we mustn't forget it as we explore where religions disagree. Creating harmony among us is a noble dream just because our differences are real. Our ideal is to create unity despite our diversity. That is what loving your neighbor is all about.

I am not going to try to show why Judaism has important differences with other religions. I think that could never be convincing. No matter what I said you would probably think, "What did you expect from him? He's a rabbi. He had to say that." Instead, I will stick strictly to our question about why there are different religions. I will answer it by discussing only non-Jewish religions.

The world's great faiths don't agree on what is truly real. Moslems take the world and what happens to them in it very seriously. They believe God created it and controls it. They therefore think that everything that happens is for the best. The most important thing is to have faith in God's wise rule. So their religion is called Islam which means "Pious acceptance." Hindus think the opposite is true. The world and history are not real. One can easily see that everything around us and we ourselves are changing. They will soon be gone and something else will come along. One needs to think of life and all its activities as an illusion, a sort of strange dream we are involved in which we need to stop taking so seriously. Hindus suggest that we need to find our way to the true reality which is beyond space and time, beyond all happening, beyond even our being individuals, to The One, Infinity, Absolute Reality.

I do not see how both these views can be right at the same time. I don't see how you can say they really mean the same thing; or that one idea really contains the other; or that there's an honest compromise between them. They are different and so we get two different religions.

Christianity and Buddhism differ on the major theme of life

One can find similar differences about how we ought to face life. One of the great symbols of Christianity is Jesus' crucifixion. Christians believe that for the love of humanity and for the love of God, Jesus suffered on the cross. All Christians can learn from this for God sends each person great suffering in life. They think that people need to see this as their special way of serving God and showing their love for God. In their suffering they are like the Christ and thus as close to God as a human being can be. Buddhism considers suffering the great problem of human existence. The Buddha's great moment of enlightenment came when he discovered the source of suffering, that people want things. Stop desire and you stop suffering. Buddhism's great promise to its followers is that it can teach them how to stop suffering. They may therefore reach the joyous realm where one is beyond all wanting and getting—Nirvana. Its great symbol is the calm, contented, seated Buddha.

According to Christianity, suffering is a special way of drawing near to God and that the greatest man who ever lived suffered specially. According to Buddhism, we ought to spend our lives learning to escape suffering and the greatest man who ever lived achieved just such serenity. I don't see how you can put those together. I think you must decide between them.

Do you know enough now to begin to study?

Judaism has its own special way of looking at the world and what our responsibilities are, but I don't propose to begin to compare it now to the views of other religions. The topic needs long and serious study, not just a few pages or so at the end of a chapter. Are you ready for such an investigation?

This book should have helped you understand Judaism more deeply. Along the way, I tried to indicate some of the differences I see between Judaism and other religions. But you will need to know a good deal more about Judaism if you are to study the similarities and differences between it and other religions. For the moment, it seems that we do not have enough similarities to let us all have just one religion. But we must not let our differences shake our age-old Jewish faith that the Messianic Age of human unity will one day arrive.

In Parting:
Do You Now Understand Judaism?

You'll be doing some wonderful things within the next few years. High school, driving a car, perhaps travel or some sort of job, then college or going to work. Each year will bring some new experience to help you become the adult you can begin to see in yourself.

Had you lived a couple of hundred years ago or were you growing up in an underdeveloped country today, your education would now be over—if you were lucky enough to get this much. For the rest of your life you would probably have to work at the same job in the same place. You'd learn some things at the synagogue and at the market. Mostly you'd have only your childhood ideas to work with all your adult life. When you think of all the things that you're going to learn during the next few years, having to make do with the things you know now would be a shame.

Some people never learn more about Judaism than what they were taught at twelve or thirteen years of age. They grow up in every other way but their understanding of our religion remains on a teenage level. Your teachers and I hope we've helped you get far beyond what children in religious school know about Judaism. We hope it will be helpful to you now and in future years. You've seen how deep Judaism is, so it won't surprise you when I say, "This is only a beginning." There's a lot more to our religion than could be said in this book or this year in class.

Have you ever wondered why so many artists have made pictures of old Jews—often with a book? I think they were saying something about our tradition. The truth is: Judaism is a religion mainly for adults. You fully understand Judaism only when you've lived a long time. Then, out of your life's experience, you can ask the very deepest questions of our religion and receive its fullest wisdom. This year's study has been your start to such a mature understanding of Judaism. **231**

I've tried to give serious answers to your serious questions. But each year, as your mind develops and your experience deepens, you'll be able to ask more searching questions and understand more complicated answers. So if you're to continue growing as a Jew you'll need to spend some of your time, all during your life, studying Judaism. For now that means continuing to study in religious school—and on your own. Later it might be coming to services, thinking about what the prayers mean, what the Torah teaches, and what the sermon says. Or you could learn much reading Jewish newspapers, magazines, or books, visiting the State of Israel, helping out in some Jewish agency. Maybe you'll be able to take a course in Jewish studies at your university or join a study group at your synagogue. Perhaps you'll invent your own special way of growing as a Jew while you grow as a person.

I hope so, for we need every thoughtful Jewish teenager we can get. But with Judaism, as deep and demanding as you have seen it to be, it is clear that we need learned Jewish adults even more. Now that our study together is over, I guess that's what these chapters were about: helping you get a good start as a thoughtful teenager on the lifelong task of becoming another wise old Jew.

About the Photographs

Cover and title page

Menorah (detail, stained-glass window). Temple Sinai, Los Angeles. Sidney Eisenshtat, architect.

Part one

1 Purim festival. Brooklyn, New York, 1978.

2 Times Square. New York City, 1974.

3 The March to Montgomery, Alabama, 1965. Among the marchers are Abraham Joshua Heschel, Martin Luther King, Jr., and Ralph David Abernathy.

4 Staten Island, New York, 1976.

5 A *siyyum*. The chavurah school, New York City, 1977.
   The members of the school—children, parents, and teachers—read the last chapter of Genesis together and are now celebrating completing their study of the first book of the Torah. The silk top hat and leopard skin *talit* add gaiety to the festivities.

6 Sukot morning service. The chavurah, New York, 1977.

7 *Shavuot*. The chavurah, 1977.

8 Abandoned synagogue. Lower East Side, New York City, 1978.

Part two

1 Torah scribe (*sofer*). Lower East Side, New York City, 1975.
   Torah scribes in the United States cannot compete economically with the Israelis because labor and materials are costly. American scribes, therefore, only repair damaged scrolls.

2 Rally protesting the visit of Yasir Arafat, PLO (Palestine Liberation Organization) leader, to the United Nations. UN Plaza, November 1974.

3 Indian Jews, dancers from Kibbutz Dimona. The Dalia Dance Festival, 1968.

4 Soviet Jews arriving in Israel.
   The new immigrant is laughing with joy; her brother, an Israeli citizen, is crying with joy.

234 5 Demonstration in support of Soviet Jewry. Battery Park, New York City, May Day 1977.

6 Condemned Jews awaiting deportation. The Holocaust (*source unknown*).

7 Demonstration in support of Soviet Jewry. Fifth Avenue, New York City, *Simchat Torah* 1976.

Part four

1 Ushabtis and other figurines from Egyptian tombs, 1570–610 B.C.E.
Ushabtis, placed in the tomb with the mummy, represent the servants who are to do the agricultural chores expected of the deceased in the land of the dead. Ushabti figurines are small; tie head in the center is 8 inches high.
The figurines are from the collection of the Skirball Museum, Hebrew Union College-Jewish Institute of Religion, Los Angeles (*anonymous gift*).

2 Sinai mountains.

3 *Bat Mitzvah,* 1976.

4 The Torah van. New York City, *Sukot* 1976.
Members of this Lubavitch synagogue travel through the city in a van, teaching Orthodox principles and rituals. On this day, they are inviting men to step inside to recite the *Sukot* blessings with the *lulav* and *etrog.*

5 Hadassah Hospital. Jerusalem, 1977.

6 The cemetery of the Reform Jewish community. Havana, Cuba, 1978.

7 The Mandelbaum Gate.
Catholic nuns are leaving Jerusalem to celebrate Christmas in Bethlehem.

Picture editor: Gerry Gould
All the photographs are
by Bill Aron
except for those on the following pages:

20 Matt Herron for Black Star; 79 State of Israel Government Press Office; 86 Israel Press and Photo Agency; 186 Israel Government Tourist Office; 207 and 224 Consulate General of Israel.

The photograph on the cover and title page is through the courtesy of the UAHC Synagogue Art and Architectural Library.

235

Commission on Jewish Education

of the Union of American Hebrew Congregations
and the Central Conference of American Rabbis

as of 1978

Martin S. Rozenberg, *Chairman*
Solomon B. Freehof, *Honorary Chairman*

Dorothy G. Axelroth	Ronald Kronish
Morton A. Bauman	Janet Lerner
Herbert M. Baumgard	Louis Lister
Alan D. Bennett	Audrey Friedman Marcus
Morrison D. Bial	Stanley Meisels
Howard Bogot	Jonathan Plaut
Eric Feldheim	Cecil B. Rudnick
Harvey J. Fields	Lenore Sandel
Roland B. Gittelsohn	Frederick C. Schwartz
David S. Hachen	Sylvan D. Schwartzman
Judith Hertz	Leivy Smolar
Jack Horowitz	L. William Spear
Samuel E. Karff	Martin Weiner
	Joel Wittstein

Ex Officio

Moshe Avital	Fred W. Marcus
Lewis Bogage	Earl Morse
William Cutter	Ely E. Pilchik
Leon Fram	Matthew Ross
Stuart Gertman	Jacob P. Rudin
Joseph B. Glaser	Alexander M. Schindler
Manuel Gold	Paul Steinberg
Philip Jaffe	Ira Youdovin
	Bernard Zlotowitz

Union Education Series
Edited by

Daniel B. Syme, *Director of Education*
Steven M. Reuben, *Associate Director*
Ralph Davis, *Director of Publications*
Edith Samuel, *Adult Study Programs*

ST. JOHN'S SEMINARY
COLLEGE LIBRARY
CAMARILLO CALIF